Praise for

"This brave and unflinching second-generation family memoir is a daughter's coming of terms with her parents' tragic past and with her own demons. Stone wrests a redemptive victory for the survivors and their descendants."
—Elaine Kalman Naves, author of *Journey to Vaja* and
Shoshanna's Story

"Remembering can be painful, and eliciting and sharing painful memories takes courage. Stone and her family prove they are more than courageous. *Resilience* will hurt your heart but may also help heal some of our deepest wounds."
—Amy Friedman, author of *Desperado's Wife*

"How many of us have said of aging parents and grandparents, 'I wish I had asked more questions'? Judy Stone did just that. This book is well researched and well written and fills in gaps that have previously been left for many of us in our attempts to understand the Holocaust."
—Jack Paskoff, Rabbi, Congregation Shaarai Shomayim,
Lancaster, Pennsylvania

"A beautiful and important read, Judy Stone's memoir is a daughter's quest to memorialize not only the pain and sorrow her immigrant mother and family faced but also how they transcended the unimaginable. She draws readers into the vulnerable space of her family life, and we emerge more fully human."
—Sunita Puri, MD, author of *That Good Night*

"In these times, the memories of Stone's family members are not just a blessing—they are a stern warning of horrors that must never be forgotten lest they be repeated."
—Steve Silberman, author of *NeuroTribes*

"Judy's indefatigable research and remarkable ear for detail give us an honest, near-firsthand account of Jewish family life in the small towns of Eastern Hungary before the Holocaust. *Resilience* bears witness to the Holocaust from the standpoint of one family but holds lessons for all who embrace 'Never Again.'"
—Alfred Munzer, MD, Holocaust child survivor, retired physician, and volunteer, US Holocaust Memorial Museum

"Stone's story is full of sharp observations and insights. Her portrait of the chaos following the war and the toll it inflicted is especially riveting. By sheer persistence and determination, Stone's family members survived seemingly insurmountable difficulties with their essential humanity and decency intact. This book lovingly recounts their strengths and weaknesses while portraying their experiences and offers lessons to us all."
—Judith Graham, journalist

"Stone brings her family's stories to life and underscores their message: to go on being kind and brave in such a savage place is what it means to be human."
—Miriam Shuchman, MD, physician-journalist and author of *The Drug Trial*

"Judy Stone's book not only preserves for us the unique story of her family but also shows what horrible destruction is brought to the world by racism, chauvinism, and antisemitism."
—Victoria Khiterer, PhD, Associate Professor of History, Millersville University

"Stone, in her amazing analysis of the Holocaust…stands up courageously in protecting future generations of survivors and rescuers who know that for documenting and analyzing the Holocaust, we never can claim 'enough.'"
—Hillel Levine, PhD, Professor Emeritus, Sociology, Religion, and Judaic Studies, Boston University, and President, International Center for Conciliation

RESILIENCE

JUDY STONE, MD

MOUNTAINSIDE MD PRESS

Mountainside MD Press
24501 Alicia Parkway, #L512
Laguna Hills, CA 92653
www.mountainsidemdpress.com

Framed portrait of Kati "Kitty" Williams in Holocaust Survivors' Gallery used with permission by David Radler.

Judy Stone, MD, gratefully acknowledges the USC Shoah Foundation for allowing us to use transcripts of the following testimonies: Magda Stone (February 11, 1996), Elisabeth Kasik (August 18, 1995), and Katherine Williams (June 19, 1996).

The photo on page 229 is used with permission of the *Denver Post*.

A note on the cover image: Dr. Stone has long been drawn to images of resilience—flowers growing from cracks in rocks or, in this case, a tree emerging from a lifeless form in the water. To her, this tree represents the Tree of Life. The Museum of Jewish Heritage in New York City has a Holocaust memorial called the Garden of Stones. Each boulder has a tree growing from it, symbolizing the tenacity and fragility of life, as well as death and renewal. Other Holocaust memorials share similar imagery. Budapest's Raoul Wallenberg Memorial Park has a metal sculpture of a weeping willow in a barren courtyard of gravel and stone. Each leaf is inscribed with a Hungarian victim's name. Dr. Stone's family had leaves made for a number of their family members. The photo that appears behind the tree is that of the author's aunt's wedding and has an especially poignant history, told in chapter 16.

Ordering Information
Orders by U.S. trade bookstores and wholesalers. Please contact Cardinal Publishers Group: Tel: (800) 296-0481; Fax: (317) 879-0872, www.cardinalpub.com.

Cataloging-in-Publication Data
Names: Stone, Judy Ann, author.
Title: Resilience : one family's story of hope and triumph over evil / Judy Stone, MD.
Description: Includes bibliographical references and index. | Laguna Hills, CA: Mountainside MD Press, 2019.
Identifiers: LCCN 2019901525 | ISBN 978-0-9749178-2-5
Subjects: LCSH Stone, Judy Ann—Family. | Holocaust survivors—Family relationships. | Children of Holocaust survivors—United States. | Holocaust, Jewish (1939–1945)—Hungary. | BISAC BIOGRAPHY & AUTOBIOGRAPHY / Personal Memoirs
Classification: LCC D804.195 .S76 2019 | DDC 940.53/18/0922—dc23

Printed in the United States of America

First Edition

25 24 23 22 21 20   10 9 8 7 6 5 4 3 2 1

Interior design and composition: Graffolio
Editing: PeopleSpeak

Dr. Stone will donate the net profits from this book to organizations that promote Holocaust education.

*For Anyu and Sanyi, who instilled in me
the importance of family and history;
Kati for her boundless energy for Holocaust education;
and all those targeted by hatred*

Magdus (Anyu) (60), 1972,
Los Angeles

Sanyi (about 82), circa 1998,
Cumberland

Kati (90), 2014, Omaha

Contents

CONTENTS

Foreword

EVERYBODY WORKING IN THE FIELD of Holocaust studies knows that all too soon, the last survivor will be no longer. Seventy-four years have passed since liberation, and if the average survivor was between the ages of eighteen and forty, the reader can do the math. The last survivors will be child survivors, those often too young to have clear memories of what happened.

Holocaust survivors cheated death many times, but time brings its own mortality, which has placed a unique burden on those who have lived in the presence of survivors. Institutions such as Holocaust museums have attempted to fill the vast shoes of survivors to fulfill the role as the keepers of memory.

Judy Stone's *Resilience* shows us the role that children of survivors can play in preserving and transmitting the memories and the legacy of survivors. Rather than choosing merely to retell the story of her mother, she has taken upon herself the much more difficult task of recounting and retelling the story of her family, piecing together extended interviews with those who would speak with her along with the testimony they gave some two decades ago to the Survivors of the Shoah Visual History Foundation (now the USC Shoah Foundation). She writes with candor and without sanitizing either the past or the present. Stone often writes without reserve, preferring to tell the unvarnished truth as best she can ascertain it.

And what a story she has to tell.

The Holocaust started late in Hungary. As an ally of Germany, Hungary was expected to impose the Final Solution on its own Jews, but it dallied. Hungary turned over foreign Jews for execution in 1941 and persecuted its own Jews—drafting Jewish men into labor battalions—but did not transport them to be murdered.

Then in March 1944, fearing that Admiral Horthy would sign a separate peace agreement with the West, Germany invaded Hungary. Ghettoization soon followed, and within a span of eight weeks, some 437,402 Jews were transported on 147 trains primarily to Birkenau (Auschwitz II); eight of ten were murdered upon arrival. Only the young, the able bodied, and the lucky survived. The only Jews left in Hungary were the Jews of Budapest.

Stone's family was no exception. The young and the lucky survived—some by hiding, some by sheer endurance, and some by happenstance—the old and the very young did not. Stone tells their stories in great detail. She reminds us that everyone's experience was different, and each has a story to tell.

Her family's roots are in rural Hungary, where in small towns and villages, Jews knew their non-Jewish neighbors and non-Jews knew the Jews of their village. There were friendships and rivalries, animus but also fondness. As in many small towns, Jews were not abstractions but people one was acquainted with. For some, this facilitated hiding and rescue; for others, betrayal and punishment.

Stone entitles her work *Resilience* but also writes of fragility and fear. Her aunt in Iowa marries a non-Jewish man for security and the possibility of escape but pays a steep price, being asked to hide her identity as a Jew and a Holocaust survivor. Only much later does she find the strength to be honest and open, to become a witness and teacher. And Stone herself, living as a successful physician in Cumberland, Maryland, chooses not to have her son circumcised, not quite secure enough even in the United States to trust that Jewish fate will not repeat itself.

Still, the resilience of survivors is apparent: after all they experienced, they had the capacity to rebuild their lives, bring children into the world, and in some way bear witness to their experience.

Stone is truthful, sometimes painfully so. Writing after her mother's death and while some of her mother's generation are still alive and while their children and grandchildren are still part of the extended family, she reveals what she must of their past without romanticizing it. She writes of topics that more sanitized memoirs would simply avoid. She is to be congratulated for her courage.

I was particularly moved by her indefatigability. Like a dogged reporter, she went back to her subjects time and again, accessing what they would willingly share at first and then returning, inviting them, coaxing them, inquiring of them to elaborate on parts of their story that she didn't quite get right until she actually got it right. We are often there with her in the kitchen of the survivor or at the dining room table as she asks her questions, rooting for her to get the answers she seeks, the clarity she needs.

And the reader is blessed by the multiplicity of stories of her surviving family members—some who retained their faith and some who lost it, some who developed a zest for life and some who went through the motions of living in the aftermath. In truth, what they all have in common is not only the family connection but the reality that even in healing, scars remain and each survivor lives in the shadows of the ashes, which takes considerable resilience. Survival both during the Holocaust and perhaps equally so, if not more so, in its aftermath is about resilience. Over the past several decades we have seen survivors less as victims and more as exemplars of resilience—and most importantly as witnesses.

Permit me a personal word of pride in that I was privileged to lead the Shoah Foundation as it took these testimonies and recorded the memories of survivors for future generations to discover. Stone is one of many who accessed these recordings taken when survivors were but a half century from liberation and could look back and share with the world what they experienced. Stone has done a herculean job in recovering all these stories and has vindicated the vision we had when we gathered them.

Michael Berenbaum
American Jewish University
Los Angeles, California

Glattstein Family Tree

(Read from left to right)

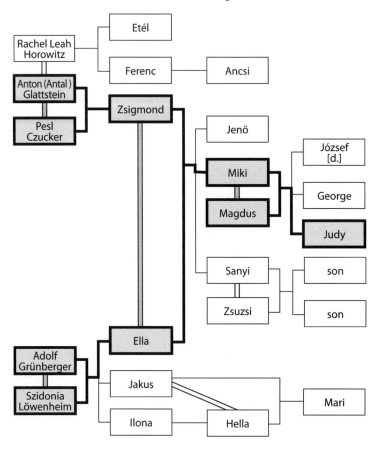

Ehrenfeld Family Tree

(Read from left to right)

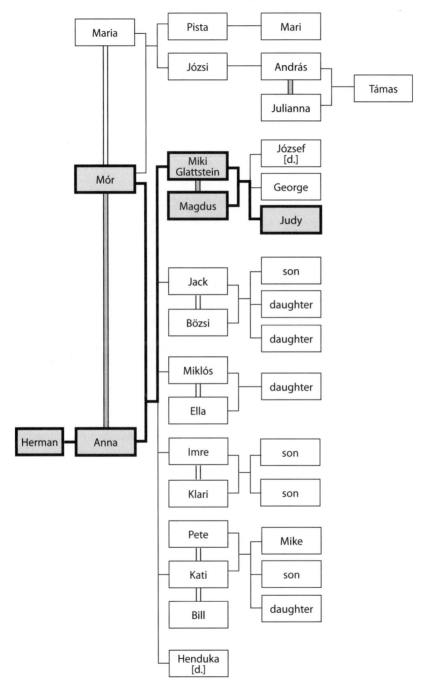

Author's Note

All incidents and dialogue in this book are described to the best of my and my family members' recollection, although none of our recalls are perfect. The experiences I share are real.

The following names are fictional: András, Tamás, and Julianna. Any similarities between these fictional names and real people is strictly coincidental.

Visit www.drjudystone.com for a cast of characters, family portraits, Hungarian pronunciation guide, maps, and additional resources.

The Promise

I CAN SEE MY MOTHER in her hospital bed, frail, tethered to her oxygen tubing, yet pulling herself up to direct me, a reproachful tone in her voice: "Get your computer out and start writing. I know you won't remember this." And so she began recounting bits of family stories that were important to her, something she had avoided doing until I was an adult and my children were studying the Holocaust in school.

Her eyes were piercing, not the milky soft cow-like eyes I had liked when she was healthier and in a gentler mood. Her face was wrinkled, with lines impressed by the tubing, and framed by thin, snow-white hair wisping out around her headband. All of her sisters (and her brother Miklós) had strikingly beautiful, snow-white hair. Me? A thinning, mousy gray. Short-changed again.

As Ma recounted family lore, I dutifully recorded dates and people and places so I could try to piece them together later. I chided myself for not having a better memory—after all, she and Uncle Sanyi, both in their nineties, even now reveled in reciting poetry to each other from their school days.

As an infectious disease physician, I grew more intrigued by my mother's stories and how hard growing up in the pre-antibiotic era was—and how many lives were lost. My family was deeply affected by a variety of infections, including my mother's near fatal bouts with diphtheria and typhoid and others' influenza, abscesses, typhus, rheumatic fever, and tuberculosis. Many people today take antibiotics for granted. I know how lucky we are and fear going back to the pre-antibiotic era as we squandered these treasures, breeding resistance for short-term greed. Indeed, from my mother's stories I have learned that my own family's history illustrates the precarious intersection between poverty, social class, and health.

As Ma's health deteriorated, I found it challenging and painful to balance my knowledge as an experienced physician of more than thirty years—sensitive to errors by medical and nursing staff, errors born sometimes of haste, sometimes disregard—with just wanting to be a daughter, caring for my mother's emotional needs as best as I could. The balance, to my dismay, tipped toward playing physician and shepherding her care.

In her early nineties, despite being almost blind and on oxygen, Ma was fiercely independent and still lived alone in the home she and my father had purchased fifty years before. The last two years of her life, she was in and out of hospitals in the metropolitan Washington, DC, area, where I felt she was receiving frightening care. Perhaps the biggest problem, besides poor communication and inattention to detail, was that where I saw a fiercely determined mother, grandmother, and oldest sister fighting for her life, much of the hospital staff saw an ill old lady waiting to die.

I went home and put my treasured notes from my mother aside. I largely gave up my solo practice when Ma was ill, staying with her in each hospitalization as she begged me, "Please don't leave me. They'll kill me if you are gone." I suspected and feared she was right. Even in the best hospitals, mistakes happen, and as a doctor, I've been witness to too many medical errors not to have my hackles raised.

While I wish I hadn't had to play doctor, I now know that my "interference," as some saw it, bought my mother months of life, at no small cost to my family and me. I stayed with her day and night but for taking brief breaks to eat and shower and clear my head.

After my mom died, I returned to practicing medicine, but working with ICU patients became too painful, and I made the difficult decision to close my practice. Since then, I have worked part-time in clinical care, choosing to spend most of my time and energy as a writer to educate others about medicine and social justice and the many ways they are so closely connected.

Now I am fulfilling a promise to my mother: to share our family's experiences and to remember and to honor their memories.

My Journey with This Book

I had begun delving into my family history when my son was born and my husband and I chose to name him Michael, after my father, both to honor Miki and to celebrate the fact that my mother had lived to see the birth of a grandson. We also hoped that one day our son would be curious about his roots.

Unexpectedly, perhaps as a result of pregnancy hormones and to my husband's dismay, a switch inside me flipped as suddenly I began to feel it was important that our children have a Jewish education.

The next milestone in my evolution came nine years later in 1995 when our son, Michael, was in fourth grade. He had an excellent teacher, Valeria Arch, who had her students read *Number the Stars*, a Newbery Award–winning book about the Danish Resistance, which helped rescue Jews during World War II. Valeria invited my mother to speak to her class.

I was a jumble of emotions—proud of my mother for accepting the invitation, afraid of what recounting her story might stir up, and more than a little worried as I watched the young faces surrounding her and their expressions of discomfort, boredom, and innocent curiosity. One young girl asked my mother what the most valuable thing she had lost was. Without hesitation, Ma replied, "My baby."

That day, my mother shared more with these children than she had ever shared with me, and her candor stunned me. When I learned of her great loss, I was shocked and horrified, and I was a college student then. These students were so young, I worried that Ma had upset them; Valeria reassured me that she thought this class was mature enough to handle the story. She did not, however, think the next year's group of students would be an appropriate audience.

The following school year, in 1996, Ma sat for an interview for the Shoah Foundation, which was collecting oral histories of survivors.[1] I was not allowed to be present during the taping and was disappointed when I watched her interview later, as most of the emotion that she had expressed to the fourth graders was gone from her recitation. While I was conducting research for this book, I watched several other interviews of survivors. I was struck by how consistently dispassionate the interviewees were and wondered why Ma, in particular, had tamped down her emotions when speaking to interviewers for the recording. The USC (University of Southern California) Shoah Foundation's project seems to have been a turning point for many of the survivors, who for the first time began opening up about their experiences because the researchers let them know how important their participation was for history.

Then, when my daughter, Heather, was preparing for her bat mitzvah in 2000, she chose to interview my cousin Andor "Ancsi" as an oral history project. He was my father's first cousin and the sole survivor of his branch of the Glattstein family. I was taken aback by his directness and the graphic nature of his story, which I had never heard. While I worried about its effect on my daughter, this visit highlighted how little I knew about my family's experiences and further spurred my resolve to learn more.

After that, when I visited my aunts and uncles, I frequently asked if I might tape their stories to one day have a more complete family history. Each unhesitatingly agreed. In 2000, I began to more seriously gather our history, taping an interview with my aunt Klari that year and then recording the other siblings (minus Bözsi, who did not attend) gossiping at Heather's bat mitzvah the following year.

Over the years, more recordings of our chats followed, with varying levels of success. What I lacked in interviewing skills I made up for in enthusiasm and a desire to know about my family members' lives. My inquiries were casual and lacked focus because I knew so little about the Holocaust and the occasions where I might have had an opportunity to gather stories were infrequent and

Kati, Judy, Klari, and Magdus, 2001, Cumberland

fragmented. The other impediment to fully accessing the stories was that I was still working full-time as a physician and raising two young children—the distractions were many and profound.

IN 2007, when my mother was hospitalized, the day she asked me to take out my computer and start writing notes was a significant turning point in this journey. Another turning point was New Year's Eve 2007, when Miklós and Kati were visiting my mother in the hospital and Miklós unexpectedly turned to me and asked me to take him to our house so I could record his story. He was usually taciturn. Only once before had he spoken to me of his war years. That he and Kati had never shared their history with each other stunned me and renewed my sense of responsibility and commitment to compile their stories, hoping that their lives would be remembered.

We are once again living in dangerous times, and their lives hold important lessons. I am also moved to tell their stories for reasons so eloquently offered by Rabbi Jack Paskoff in his December 21, 2018, sermon: "But we do think about the marks of goodness that people left in our world. We think of the stories, and once in a while, to have a chance to tell them is a beautiful thing. And so

I hope at some point, as you think about the lives of the people you love, you'll tell their stories and you'll laugh and you'll cry. But hopefully at the end of the day, you'll be able to say of them that they left their mark, not in some heavenly life that awaits them, but in the here and now of our lives today. And then of all these folks we'll be able to say, *Zichronam livracha*, 'their memories are a blessing.' And may we aspire to live our lives in such a way."[2]

After Ma died, I began to transcribe the tapes in fits and starts; at times doing so was too painful. I reunited with Kati, from whom I had been foolishly estranged for six years. Our reunion was inspired by her "coming out" as being Jewish and immersing herself in an effort to provide Holocaust education to me—and to others.

I also visited Hungary twice and spoke with relatives in Sáránd, trying to better understand what life in that rural village had been like before, during, and after the war. And with this visit, the book started to take shape. I laboriously transcribed videotapes using a powerful program, Transana, which allowed me to mark significant clips—I wanted to make an audiovisual collage of their stories told in their own powerful words. This program also started the beginning of my creation of a database of information.

As a physician-researcher, I knew that organizing the vast amount of information I had collected would help me make better sense of it. A program called Scrivener made this daunting and considerable undertaking far more doable. My research papers had started with laboratory notebooks and index cards sorted in myriad ways. However, with Transana and Scrivener, I was able to make a database for my parents and each of their siblings, with subsections for childhood, the prelude to war, the war years, liberation, and coming to America. As I transcribed, I filled each of these folders with notes and quotes. I also added sections for research and historical data.

Everything in this book is real history, not historical fiction. I am aware that the reported dates of incidents might be slightly off, but I took every detail and vignette from my relatives' recounting of their experiences, hoping to honor each of their memories.

In 2016, I began to write in earnest, starting with my aunt Kati's story, using mostly her words rearranged to tell her story chronologically. That effort didn't work. My mother and Sanyi were storytellers. I am a physician, researcher, and science writer—accustomed to writing "explainers" rather than writing compelling stories. For a while I set the whole project aside.

In 2018, almost retired, I regrouped and began to read biographies, memoirs, and books about the craft of writing. I also consulted with others more skilled than I in personal narrative, and through many ups and downs, I struggled to puzzle out a timeline for the months immediately following my family's liberation. I discovered some seemingly irreconcilable differences, and I wanted this book to be right, to be perfect, to not disappoint either my family members or anyone who might doubt their truths and experiences because of an error I had made. Telling this story truthfully, I realized, is a huge responsibility.

I was afraid that responsibility would incapacitate me, and as I worked, I flashed back to my college years when I sat frozen during an exam, and my friend Esther whispered to me, "I don't care what you write. Just start writing." And I did, and I was all right, and I passed.

At times with this book, I felt that same frozen fear, not wanting to write because I knew all the facts weren't perfectly aligned. But I wrote all that I could about the complex and muddled chapters when, after the war, my mother, her sisters and brothers, my father, and Sanyi were finding each other. The story was and remains a tangled mess—for that, I came to understand, is what their lives were.

I remain frustrated and disappointed that I could not do a perfect job recording this history but remind myself that impediments prevent perfection and that my earlier resistance to learning about the Holocaust—fear, trauma, shyness, a desire not to know—kept me from asking for the level of detail I now wish I had when I was interviewing.

I console myself with my new mantra: "She did the best she could," the same mantra I recited when my mother pushed me to my limits and I sought for more patience with her.

My DETERMINATION to complete this project has been fueled by the rising divisiveness, "othering," and fascism that currently envelop our country and Europe. I wanted this story to serve as one more warning. It is my hope that if enough of us speak up, speak out, tell the truth about world history, we will somehow stem the tide of growing hatred.

I am not optimistic, but I comfort myself with the knowledge that I have done what I could.

Books were everything to my mother. Writing her story and her family's and mine became a way to honor her and to say, "Your lives mattered. Your legacy lives on in your children and those whose lives you have touched."

With this book, I have fulfilled my promise.

Acknowledgments

THIS LABOR OF LOVE could not have been completed without the help of many people. Particular mention should go to: my relatives, for graciously sharing family history, their life stories, and photos and allowing me to record them over past decades. My mother, Magdus, and uncle Sanyi (Alexander G. Stone) sat for hours of interviews after instilling in me their compulsive desire to collect family history and preserve lessons for future generations. Since they died, my aunt Kati (Kitty Williams) has patiently done the same, filling in many small pieces. Klari Gray, Miklós Field, Ancsi Glattstein, and Marianna Grünberger Gersch also granted interviews. Further family details were provided by my cousins Linda Elkin; Peter Gray; Mari Deutsch; David Kasik; Gloria, Sharon, and Brian Glattstein; Michael, Karen, and Florence Radkowsky; Victor Stone; and Jonathan and Erika Jacoby. Many thanks, too, to my cousins in Hungary who welcomed me with open arms and took me to visit areas of historical interest.

Drs. Julia Frank, Glenn Kashurba, and Yolanda Roth added details and perspective on families.

Gabriel Hirsch, Nancy Holden, and the H-Sig groups on Jewish Gen directed me to valuable historical resources, as did Arthur Allen and the staff of the USHMM, particularly Steven Vitto.

My friend Elise George read multiple early drafts and provided useful suggestions. Kati's friend Donna Walter from IHENE also gave me valuable advice on drafts, given her vast experience with providing Holocaust education. Friend Larry Lynam helped me with the art of storytelling, as did Larry Shotland with his stories over the years and his love for my mother.

Rabbi Jack Paskoff rekindled my attraction to Judaism with his wise sermons, the comfort and warmth of his services at Congregation Shaarai Shomayim in Lancaster, Pennsylvania, and his friendship to a stranger in their midst.

The manuscript was reshaped and molded with the sage advice of Elaine Kalman Naves, Amy Friedman, and Sharon Goldinger.

Finally, this project could never have been completed without the support of my family—especially husband Mark Skinner and daughter Heather—as well as son Michael, brother George, and friend Virginia Singer. Their encouragement, patience, love, and companionship through years of writing and life have meant the world to me.

Introduction

I'VE ALWAYS HAD A LOVE-HATE RELATIONSHIP with families and history. I have a fascination with and desire to understand the individuals and their relationships, as well as what drives them. I also have an aversion to confronting my family's history, knowing that many were deeply scarred by their experiences during the Holocaust.

Growing up, I heard little about the Holocaust; rather, the sudden silences were more telling. My parents, aunts, and uncles tried to protect my brother and me, as well as their own children, from the horrors they had endured. They never spoke of their wartime experiences in front of me or my cousins. Respecting privacy was ingrained in our earliest lessons, and we knew better than to pry.

I often sensed an undercurrent of fear, with occasional punctuations of a subconscious, almost telepathic terror, like when my mother unexpectedly saw a policeman in her rearview mirror. She was dropping me off at high school when she noticed him and quickly hit the gas to drive off. Unfortunately, my hand was still clutching the door handle, and she dragged me on the ground for a few feet. She caught herself, and then we had to deal with her guilt and her fear that she had injured me. Fortunately, I was just bruised and shaken. Other times, a glimpse of the past would slip out without warning from behind the protective walls that had been built. Mostly, my cousins and I, all children of Holocaust survivors, were sheltered from the harsh reality and had no idea what our family had suffered.

IN THEIR LATER YEARS, when I was an adult and sought out their stories, my mother and uncle began to share snippets with me. I tried to assume the mantle of family historian from them. I called my mother Anyu, which is Hungarian for "mother." My brother George began to refer to her as Ma, and I sometimes adopted that name when speaking to others about her. She was usually called Magdus by Hungarian relatives, Maggie by her nieces and nephews, and Mrs. Stone by others. This left me struggling with what to call her in writing her story. I have chosen to refer to her as Magdus in her life before she was my mother and as Ma or Anyu in our personal relationships. Similarly, my father is Miki before my existence or to those in his generation and Apu ("father") to me.

Ma had an incredible memory for detail and was the keeper of family lore on the Ehrenfeld side of my family. Similarly, my uncle Sanyi was a meticulous historian for the Glattsteins, my father's clan. I lack their memories and so relied on recording them as much as I could and writing things down.

After Ma died in 2008, I attended a conference of Holocaust survivors, hidden children, and second-generation descendants of survivors held by the World Federation of Jewish Child Survivors of the Holocaust & Descendants.[1] Since it was not very far from my home in western Maryland, it seemed a low-risk way of learning more about the Holocaust and beginning to fulfill my promise to my mother. Seeking a common bond with others, I searched for people from Hungary. I naively asked one woman, "Isn't there anyone here from outside Budapest? Is there anyone from Debrecen or smaller towns?" She looked surprised and told me that almost no one from rural Hungary had survived the attempted annihilation of the Jews. I was stunned, having had little sense of how unique and lucky my family's experience was, and I asked a few Hungarian attendees to explain more of the wartime history to me.[2]

Both of my parents were from eastern Hungary—the city of Debrecen and the countryside—and had survived, along with five of my mother's six siblings and one of my father's two brothers. During the war, they took different paths and were imprisoned in different places, yet all made it through. I realized that in many ways, their stories were different from the norm and warranted telling. Their story of survival—the extraordinary nature of all those sisters and brothers who endured so much—seemed all the more miraculous. I wanted to understand what ingenuity helped them survive and how their nondescript, middle-aged facades belied their strengths, both for surviving the war and for starting life anew in a strange land.

By learning more about them, I hoped to learn skills, too, skills that might help me in the future, for I often wonder if I lack their competence or pragmatic resourcefulness outside of my role as a physician. Not surprisingly, given our family history, ever since adolescence, I have longed to possess practical skills, such as finding shelter and food and blending in comfortably among strangers.

Except for my father, who tragically died too young, at only fifty, these survivors lived long and productive lives. Despite many trials before, during, and after the Holocaust, their lives are a remarkable testament to their resilience.

The story that follows is the biography of two intertwined families from rural Hungary. On her deathbed, my mother asked me to ensure that their remarkable story was preserved and passed on. While too many years have passed since I gave her my word, I now feel a sense of urgency to complete this project and fulfill her wishes and am now much better prepared to do so, having traveled back to Hungary, conducted more interviews with family, and read more extensively on history and the Holocaust. This book is based on more than a hundred hours of interviews with family members, the culmination of a decades-long endeavor. Some family members shared more details than did others. I know that some of what follows will likely offend some of my relatives. There were many spats in the family, and I have recounted these as they were told to me—to give a sense of the varied colorful characters we grew up with and were shaped by. I make no claims as to the veracity of any individual's perceptions. I recount only what was I was told.

CHAPTER 1

The Ehrenfelds

A SMALL VILLAGE IN EASTERN HUNGARY, Sáránd, is where my mother's family's story begins.

Visitors still often arrive in Sáránd by train, stopping at the same unwelcoming station that was my mother's portal to the bigger world. When I first visited Hungary with my mother in 1978, that station was the same as she remembered it: two stories of bleak tan stucco with dark doors and window frames, capped with a peaked roof. The stark white blinds made me wonder what dark secrets were hidden inside. The building felt forbidding, with no trim or shutters around the masked windows to soften its appearance. A sullen stationmaster stood outside, arms folded across his chest, wearing a navy uniform and red cap trimmed with a gold braid. With his cigarette dangling between two fingers, he motioned me away when I began to take a photo. I took it anyway.

After elementary school, my mother left this station every day to venture to school in the bustling big city, Debrecen, which had a population of about one hundred thousand. The village of Sáránd, 9.4 miles south of Debrecen, had about two thousand residents. In 1978, all the roads were still dirt, and pigs, cows, and chickens ran freely through the town. The Református (Calvinist) church remains the focal point of the town, demanding attention with its brown spire and clock towering above the grayish-white stone.

Mór Ehrenfeld, circa 1918

My mother said that little had changed from when she grew up there. Mór (Mozes) Ehrenfeld, the dignified and reserved family patriarch, apparently ended up in Sáránd by accident.

Born in 1879, Mór grew up in Bököny, a bit north of Debrecen, the sixth of eight children in a poor family. His father, David Ehrenfeld, was a peddler of fruits.

My grandfather Mór's first marriage was to Maria (Kupferstein) Grosz, who came from a tiny rural village in the plains region of northeastern Hungary (either Nyírjákó or the adjacent Petneháza). She and Mór moved to distant Lénártó (now Lénártóv), Slovakia, 150 miles north of their birthplaces, a region of low mountains not unlike the Appalachians. I don't know why Mór went there, other than perhaps it looked promising, being on the trade route from Poland to Galicia, and it was nestled in a lush little valley.[1] Family lore is that Mór managed an estate there for a Baron Kornfeld and learned many refined manners from him. Mór's twin boys, Istvan "Pista" and József "Józsi," were born there in 1907.

Mór reportedly wanted to go south to Hajdúdorog, an agricultural region northwest of Bököny, almost equidistant between the larger cities of Nyíregyháza and Debrecen. I don't know why it had particular appeal nor how he apparently got so lost en route that he bypassed Hajdúdorog and ended up going farther south, even beyond the *középpont*, or hub for the region's trains, in Debrecen. I suspect that perhaps he wanted to be closer to his sisters Etél and Rebi, who lived in that region. I believe his parents had already died, but despite making a trip to the Family History Library in Salt Lake City and hiring a genealogy researcher in Hungary, I have come up with almost nothing else about Mór's family.

Legend has it that the young family ended up stopping in Sáránd when they took a wrong train. They met a Jewish merchant, and Mór ended up buying the general store from him and becoming well-established in the small town.

This is not unlike the way I ended up in Cumberland, Maryland, in 1983. I first met the town when I was about twenty years old, driving alone on the old Route 40 from St. Louis, Missouri, to Silver Spring, Maryland. A tire blew out in the valley just beyond town, and as I waited for help, I looked around and thought what a lovely area it was, nestled in the Appalachians. A decade later, the local hospital recruited me to start a solo practice in infectious diseases there—as no other specialist was available in more than a seventy-five-mile radius—and like my grandfather, I built a thriving practice from scratch. I'd like to think a bit of my pioneering spirit was passed on to me from my grandfather.

Even when I visited Sáránd with my mother in 1978, decades after the war, some folks remembered Mór—for lending everyone credit in his store or for sometimes giving a child candy.

Maria and her baby died in childbirth in Sáránd in 1910, leaving Mór a widower with two young twin sons. As was the custom at that time, he then married the oldest eligible girl in the family, Maria's cousin Anna Róth, who was also from Nyírjákó, and moved her to Sáránd in 1911.

It became Anna's lot to raise Maria's sons, in keeping with local traditions and arranged marriages.

Anna Róth (18) and Mór Ehrenfeld (32) wedding, 1911

In Sáránd, Mór continued farming, a business he had learned while managing the Lénártó estate, and also ran a general store and tavern. My mother and her sisters told me that their father was so knowledgeable about farming that others often turned to him for assistance.

Growing up, I never heard my mother or her siblings say anything nice about their mother, Anna, though I could tell they adored their father. It wasn't that they spoke badly of Anna; it was more that they said so little about her. Only as an adult did I realize that their silence reflected disapproval rather than their growing up for many years without a mother. It was only after I stepped back and made a timeline did I begin to gain perspective as to why Anna was often mean to her children.

Anna was only eighteen when she was married off to Mór, a widower fourteen years her senior. She was separated from her own close family, and once married, she promptly began having children of her own, one almost every two years, except during World War I. By 1922, eleven years after marrying, Anna had five children, as well as two stepsons.

ANTISEMITISM IN HUNGARY has waxed and waned over the centuries. When Hungary was under Turkish rule (1526–1686), life was better for the Jews, as the Ottoman Empire even encouraged their settlement and allowed them to hold official government positions. Conditions for them worsened under the Hapsburgs. However, some Hungarian noblemen recognized their skills and sheltered them on their estates. In 1867, the Austro-Hungarian Compromise of the Hungarian Parliament removed restrictions on the Jews, such as those prohibiting them from living in cities. Jews became more assimilated, educated, and prominent members of the communities.[2]

In 1882, a fourteen-year-old Christian girl disappeared in a town called Tiszaeszlár. Rumors were that she was murdered by Jews so her blood could be used in rituals, a common and recurrent defamatory canard—and a lie still used today by conspiracy theorists. The teen was later found to have committed suicide by drowning herself in the Tisza River, and the accused were acquitted after fifteen months of imprisonment.[3]

This notorious episode became known as the Tiszaeszlár blood libel trial. According to the YIVO Institute for Jewish Research's encyclopedia, this was the first such ritual murder trial occurring outside of Poland or the Russian Empire since the sixteenth century.[4]

The acquittal sparked a wave of similar accusations and worsening antisemitism in Hungary. Despite this, Jews in this "emancipation period" (1867–1914) became more assimilated. They were patriotic and actively fought for their country in World War I.[5]

MÓR HAD GONE OFF to fight in the war, at times in Albania and in Montenegro. He had sustained a shrapnel injury to his neck that abscessed and had to be periodically drained; it was a lifelong, painful reminder of the war. He also was injured by mustard gas. As a decorated veteran of World War I, Mór was granted a temporary reprieve from the growing antisemitic regulations in the 1930s and early 1940s.

My mother described the first signs of danger she noticed:

[The Hungarians] started to take away business from Jewish merchants. They had to take in somebody who was non-Jewish; they were the owner by name only, the Jews. They had to give it to the new owner. . . . You had to have a partner who wasn't Jewish, or you couldn't buy anything from the wholesaler. We tried to keep a low profile, not to be outstanding in anything, because we always knew we were second-class citizens.[6]

Mór, previously exempted from restrictions because of his war service, lost his licenses to sell tobacco and liquor.

In 1938, Hungary passed more restrictions, similar to the Nuremberg Laws in Germany. The first law restricted Jews to only 20 percent of professionals. A year later, Jews could make up only

Anna, circa 1930

6 percent of those groups—including students attending universities—and none could hold government jobs. Most lost voting rights. This second Jewish law also defined Jews as anyone with two, three, or four Jewish-born grandparents.

Anna, with her brooding look and icy stare, bore a total of seven children; one girl died when only a year old. This photo stared down from the wall in my mother's bedroom until 2008. It always felt threatening.

Undoubtedly overwhelmed by her expanding family, Anna seemed to have been unhappy with her lot in life, later hissing as she complained to her youngest, "Why did I ever marry a widower?"[7]

I heard a lot about Anna's playing favorites with her children. She treated Pista and Józsi as stepchildren—which, of course, they were—and picked on them. One day, Józsi hit Magdus, Anna's eldest, on the arm with his violin bow. When Anna saw the bruise, she broke Józsi's violin across her knee, shattering it, knowing the violins were the twins' most cherished possessions.

My mother, Magdus, made her way into the world in 1912, just a year after her parents married. She must have been a challenge, having a determined and questioning nature. As she got older, Ma was tasked with household duties, giving up her education to help raise the younger children. Outgoing and helpful, she also spent considerable time in the store, helping her father wait on customers.

Another daughter, Bözsi, followed in 1914. Magdus recalled that everyone was unhappy and always hungry. With Mór away at war, Anna had to work alone in their general store, as well as care for her two babies and her young stepsons. In October 1918, when

Miklós was born, they sent a letter to the army, and Mór, then a well-regarded sergeant, was allowed leave from Italy to celebrate the birth of his son. When he returned to his unit, the war had just been declared over, so Mór returned to Sáránd. He resumed running his store and the adjacent tavern, and he and Anna went back to having babies about every two years— Klari (1920); Jolanka (1922), who died the year after she was born; Kati (1924); and Gabriella "Henduka" (1927).

Magdus (about 21), circa 1933, Sáránd

WHILE AS A CHILD I never heard anything about the Holocaust, my aunts and uncle regularly spoke adoringly about their father. They told a number of stories about their parents when we all got together for the Ehrenfelds' first big family reunion in 1992 at Brookdale, in the Pocono Mountains.

Anna was said to be good at taking care of the cows. Marcsa, a cow with infected eyes, needed daily treatment. When Marcsa came home from grazing in the field, she would go to Anna as though she were one of her own children to have her eyes rebandaged. The sisters also joked that they were named after the cows Anna loved so dearly. Miklós added that Anna was able to save a diseased tree. However, my mother bemoaned the fact although their fruit and nut trees were planted for production, they had to let them lie fallow for several years because of the Orthodox Jewish rule of *orlah*.[8]

MY GRANDPARENTS reportedly had an unhappy marriage. Most of the difficulties likely stemmed from their fourteen-year age difference and Anna's being unprepared for or not wanting the burden of producing and caring for a large family. Perhaps some of their marital difficulties also emanated from my grandmother's nature and upbringing.

When I uncovered a photo of Anna's father in 2015, I could see that Anna and her father shared the same icy stare and demeanor, and I wondered how much these traits affected their children. I wondered, too, how much of their personalities and apparent lack of parenting skills came from their hard childhoods and wartime trauma.

Anna's father—my great-grandfather—Herman Róth, a potato farmer, was not a very nice man, according to my mother and uncle Miklós. He had nine children with his first wife, Julia Grosz. After she died in 1916, he married Rózsa Rosenfeld and kicked the remaining children from his first marriage out of the house. After Anna married Mór and had children of her own, one of her sisters, Irma, worked as a *cseléd* (maid) for her, but soon she married and left. Leonka, the youngest sister (about Klari's age) helped Anna with the housekeeping and stayed with the family in Sáránd after Anna's death. She also went to school in Debrecen with Klari and Bözsi. Magdus and Miklós recalled Leonka as a talented, natural artist. She was killed at Auschwitz.

Four of Anna's other siblings also moved to Sáránd and were supported by Mór. He even bought a house on the outskirts of Sáránd where there was grass, not just dirt and dust, for two of them, Etél and Jenö, who both had tuberculosis. White leghorn chickens provided nourishment from the abundant eggs they laid. Two other siblings, Béla and Rózsika, cared for Etél and Jenö for about five years until they succumbed to the infection.

My uncle Miklós told me about visiting his grandfather Herman once or twice when he was young and how disturbing those visits were. He told me of his surprise and hurt that his grandfather never touched or embraced him. Miklós was frightened, too, as every drawer that he opened contained a gun. His aunt Rózsika also told him that Herman locked Gypsies in the icehouse, a tale that further terrified the young boy.

Kati never met Herman; he had died before she was old enough to visit. However, as a child, she visited the farm in Nyírjákó. Kati recalled that the workers lived in very small row houses on the farm. She was impressed that the family's house was two stories high, with the bedrooms upstairs, and had an "English closet"—an indoor bathroom with a chain that was pulled to flush the toilet. In Sáránd, the Ehrenfeld family had an outhouse in the far corner of the yard, and they had to skirt piles of manure from the animals. Yet Kati recognized how much better off they were than most of the other villagers.

ANNA SEEMS TO HAVE TAKEN after her father in her iciness and difficulty expressing affection, the latter trait being passed on to her children in varying degrees.

Both Magdus and Kati told me with dismay that Anna periodically stole money from her husband's tavern. My mother felt guilty for helping her mother steal from Mór. When they were paid in the store or bar with large bills, the money was put away in a different drawer that was more inaccessible. Magdus would give some of the paper money to Anna, who then gave it to her brothers and sisters. When she spoke of her mother, Magdus often sounded bitter and expressed the belief that her mother loved her siblings more—and did more for them—than her own children.

Anna also bred resentment by playing favorites with her children. Each had a unique place in her affections.

The twins, Józsi and Pista, were stepchildren and thus never in her good graces. Despite this, Anna's biological children never regarded Józsi or Pista as unequal in any way.

Magdus, the eldest, was the reliable hard worker. She had a serious face enlivened by her warm brown eyes, with thin lips and a very high forehead. Her earnest facade belied her stubborn and willful nature, which manifested itself from the time she was young. She was often in trouble, even as a young child, and was nicknamed *nagyszájú* (big mouth) by her mother, which Magdus seemed proud of. When she was four or five years old, her mother made her a doll from cornhusks and dressed it in a white frock. They went to Debrecen together one day and the wholesale business owner gave Magdus a beautiful doll, a real doll. However, on the return trip home, while they were waiting at the rail station, the doll slipped between the slats of the bench they were sitting on and was inadvertently left behind. Anna became angry with her young daughter, but Magdus said, "I didn't like it anyway. Don't bother to fight with me because I didn't like it anyway."

About six months before Anna's death, Magdus was sent to a distant village to work as a *cseléd* for one of her aunts to cook, clean, and do tasks in the apple orchard. One day, she was in a tree trying to clear a wasp nest when she saw her father walking toward her. It turned out that her parents were worried about what had happened to her, as she worked so hard that she hadn't even had time to write home.

Bözsi, dark-skinned and shapely, was the *cigány* (Gypsy), which was not a term of endearment. Bözsi is a nickname for Erzsébet (the queen of Hungary, 1867–98) or Elisabeth.

Bözsi (about 10), circa 1924, Sáránd

Bözsi, 1948, Germany

I never heard much about Bözsi's relationship with her parents. Like many children, she was displaced when the next baby came along, and she could no longer sleep with her mother. She was jealous of Miklós at the time and cried, "Dobják be a budiba!" (Throw him in the outhouse). She had dark hair and high cheekbones and was a beautiful young woman, earning her mother's approval for her looks. She was also aloof and did not have the right personality to wait on customers in the family's store. Bözsi was thus later nicknamed "Queen Elisabeth," both because of her regal bearing and her haughtiness.

Bözsi had a distinctive and grating nasal voice. As an adult, she always had her hair teased into an updo with a French twist, which was strikingly elegant with her snow white hair, and maintained her commanding demeanor.

Miklós was welcomed by Anna, being her only son, and was immediately more valued in the family than the girls were. In fact, he was so valued that he was sent away from home at the age of four so he could receive a proper Jewish education. During the school year, he stayed with the family of his paternal aunt, Etél Lindenfeld, in Hajdúhadház (often called Hadház), ten miles north of Debrecen. Hadház was a larger town and had several hundred Jews who could support a religious school. While he was allowed home for summer vacations, Miklós was otherwise exiled until the age of fourteen, when his mother died. Miklós never forgave his mother for sending him away and referred to her contemptuously as a "born-again Jew" in a manner very uncharacteristic of his usual kind demeanor. As he grew older, Miklós looked just like his father, and he had a similar calm, quiet nature, which was comforting to his sisters.

KLARI CAME NEXT and always felt neglected, "the girl after the boy." She also was the one child to share Anna's distinctive cleft chin. Klari garnered her mother's attention only because she was sickly and scrawny. Anna plied her with expensive imported foods like bananas and dates that were too costly to be shared with the other children. Klari complained that her mother and older

Magdus, Klari, cousin Magda "Mártonfalvi Magda" Ehrenfeld, and Bözsi, circa 1930

sisters would force-feed her like they did the geese. Anna would take waif-like Klari and the baby, Henduka, with her to vacation at warm baths in Hajdúszoboszló. In 2008, I was taken to visit these famous healing mineral spas by my cousin András. I could picture my grandmother and her daughters there, enjoying the warm waters, the children playfully splashing each other. They also went to spas near Nagyvárad (now Oradea, Romania), where Anna's sister Irma lived.

When Klari was a child, her father privately referred to her as his *fa kutya* (wooden dog) because she was impassive, like a statue of a dog. By the time Klari was in her late teens, Mór noted that she was always *szomorú*, sad. Perhaps he recognized himself in her.

I wonder when Klari changed, because I was always struck by how malleable her face was, with an ever-changing array of expressions.

Kati was said to be homely by her mother—which later saved her life as a child. I don't see the homeliness in the rare photos of her and find it ironic that Anna was ashamed of her daughter, given that Kati reportedly looked like Anna's side of the family—the Róth side.

Kati seems to have suffered the most from her mother's poor parenting skills. In the hierarchy of Anna's favorites, Henduka (the baby) and Miklós ranked at the top and Kati was at the bottom of the scale. Anna called her ugly

Kati (10), 1934, Sáránd

and always left her young daughter behind when she traveled. Just seven when her mother died, Kati had only hurtful stories about her. When I asked about their relationship, Kati remembered her mother spanking her twice.

The first time was when she was about five years old. She had been playing in the town square with other children but dawdled, lagging behind. A young Hungarian peasant, dressed in the old attire of the Hortobágy (plains) shepherds, with loose, almost skirt-like pants covered with an apron, picked Kati up and carried her to a nearby wooded area. While gently cradling her, he lifted his apron and placed his penis in Kati's hands. "Here's a doll for you," he said. "Kiss it. That's it. Play with it." Later—a child has little sense of time—perhaps much later, he brought her back to the town square, where Anna and a crowd were gathered, wailing about the lost child.

"Look what I found in the woods," the young man said, depositing Kati in front of Anna. Instead of embracing Kati with relief, Anna grabbed the small girl, lifted her dress, and began hitting her in front of the villagers. All the while, Anna humiliated

Klari (about 11), Henduka (about 4), Anna (39), and Kati (about 7), circa 1931, Sáránd

her, telling Kati what a bad girl she was and spanking her in front of the neighbors.

The second spanking was also for something unavoidable, when young Kati, who was ill, soiled her underwear at school.

Kati always remained afraid of her mother and yearned for her love.

Kati was built more stockily than her sisters, which came in handy for the hard work she had to do most of her life. She became the "good," obedient child, later caring for her father and sisters.

Kati grew up outwardly the most pleasant of the sisters. Being the youngest, she had a special closeness with her father, and after Magdus left, she was his right hand in the store.

Then there was Henduka, the baby and everyone's favorite, even among nearby villagers. She accompanied her mother everywhere.

Anna had a photo with her younger daughters enlarged to display on the wall of her home. Kati was pictured in the original, but Anna had Kati erased from the photo, inflicting a wound that festered for the rest of Kati's life.

The sisters didn't speak much about their parents, but when they did, it was consistent with the adage "It's always the mother's fault."

All the children spoke reverently of their father—about how well-read he was and multitalented, being skilled in farming and running his store. He spoke six or seven languages, including Czech, German, Yiddish, Albanian, and Slavic languages, and often helped villagers with applications or business dealings.

A 1924 business directory lists the following professionals in Sáránd: six shoemakers, five boot makers, four wheelwrights, four blacksmiths, three butchers, two grocers (though curiously, Mór is not listed, perhaps because his was a general store), two carpenters or furniture makers, two innkeepers (Mór and Ignác Leitner, a Jewish man on the outskirts of town), two barbers, one tinsmith, and one midwife.[9]

Besides the general store and tavern, his major business, Mór managed a small farm in Sáránd, growing vegetables and melons between the rows of grapes, as well as raising cows to provide kosher milk. Mór also had a seven-acre vineyard east of town, en route to the nearby village of Hajdúbagos.

Mór was generous in extending credit in his store or feeding any beggars who came by. Until the past few years while researching and writing this book, I hadn't appreciated how generous Mór was to extended family, Anna's and his own, and how many people he was quietly supporting without complaint or recognition. Learning this made me even sadder that I never knew him and that the younger members of our families have grown apart. Hearing these details about Mór and realizing how remarkable he was also made him a real person in my mind, rather than just a faded two-dimensional photo. I am remorseful that until August 2018, I did not even know when he died and so could not properly observe his Yahrzeit (anniversary of his death).

CHAPTER 2

The Glattsteins

THE STORY OF MY MOTHER'S FAMILY, the Ehrenfelds, is but half of my own, as the girls' lives became intimately intertwined with two of the Glattstein family's sons and their mother, another unlikeable matriarch.

My uncle Sanyi (Sándor), clean-cut and fair, the obsessive keeper of family records, traced the Glattsteins back to the mid-1700s, when Wolf Zev and his father, Azriel, were in the northern Abaúj megye (county) village of Szina, south of Košice (Kassa). They were among the first Jews there, according to tombstones. Taxpayer records from 1768 note three Jewish households whose heads made their livings from peddling and selling their wares in the Abaúj markets surrounding their homes.[1]

As with Mór Ehrenfeld, I have no idea what attracted the Glattstein patriarchs to this area of northeastern Hungary, an agricultural region where many worked on estates, nor why they later moved. Almost all of my knowledge of the Glattsteins comes from multiple interviews with Sanyi over the years and his own very detailed notes. My recording him started seriously in 2003 in Los Angeles.

Wolf Zev and his father migrated sixty-three miles south and made the larger town of Mezőcsát their permanent home. Azriel even had a house recorded in his name there in the early 1800s. His children and grandchildren spread throughout Hungary, with several becoming prominent rabbis. In about 1872, one grandson,

Anton (Antal in some records), a grocer, married Pesl (Pepi) Czucker, who became my great-grandmother. About fifteen years after they married, she died, leaving behind five children, including my two-year-old grandfather, Zsigmond.

Anton remarried in 1887 and moved with his three young sons to Tiszadorogma, a small nearby village on the banks of the Tisza River, as it was his new bride's hometown. Anton and Rachel Leah Horowitz raised their two daughters and four sons there, in addition to the three boys from Anton's first wife. The couple had a general store with a bar in their house. I knew two of their children, my great-aunt Etél (and her husband, Emanuel "Mano" Kramer) and her brother, Samu, who lived in New York City in their later years. I met them in the late 1950s when we visited the big city to see my father's few surviving family members. Samu and Mano worked in the Horowitz-Margareten Matzoh Factory.

Like many teens, Zsigmond had no desire to stay in a small village nor to work in the family's business. He moved to Debrecen, where he became an apprentice and later a journeyman in a grocery store. Sometime between 1906 and 1909, Zsigmond took a job at Grünberger & Glück, a wholesale and retail grocery store. One of the owners was Sándor Grünberger, who had a sister named Ella, ten years his junior.

Zsigmond and Ella married on March 8, 1911, in Hajdúszoboszló, a small city near Debrecen, where Ella and her family lived. Ella and her twin brother, Jakab (generally called Jakus), were the eighth and ninth children in their family. Their mother had died when they were fourteen years old. Jakus went to Debrecen to attend high school. Ella stayed home until her father remarried, then she went to Debrecen to learn dressmaking, since sewing was a common trade for women at the time.

Zsigmond and Ella started their married life together by renting an apartment on Bethlen utca (street) in Debrecen. Zsigmond had enough money saved to be able to buy a small house at Bercsényi utca 35. They moved there and opened a small general store in the house. Their lives were uneventful until the war came. They had

Wedding of Ella Grünberger (21) and Zsigmond Glattstein
(26), 1911, Hajdúszoboszló

two sons before the war: Jenö, born in 1912, named after Ella's young brother who had died of typhoid fever a few years before, and Miklós ("Miki"), my father, born in 1913.

When World War I started in 1914, Zsigmond was drafted into the army and served until the end of the war. While he was home on leave, Ella became pregnant with Sanyi, who was born in January 1916 at their house. Only two weeks later, tragedy struck Ella's family again. Her sister Hermina died of a stroke at age thirty-four, leaving an eight-year-old son, who was also raised by her brother Jakus.

Ella's family. Her brother, Jakus, became the patriarch
of the family after Zsigmond died. *Back row*: Ella's sister
Hermina (Grünberger) Schwartz (born 1882), brother
József Grünberger (born 1889), sister-in-law Sarah "Sári"
Lowenheim Greenburger (born 1876), twin brother Jakab
"Jakus" Grünberger (born 1890). *Front row left to right*: Ella's
nephews, Jenö "Jancsi" G. Schwartz (born 1908) and Sanford
Jerome Greenburger (born 1903)

Family lore is that Zsigmond was desperate to get out of the
army so he drank a lot of coffee to cause palpitations. He soon
became ill and was forced to sell their house and the general store
on Bercsényi utca, downsizing to a rented apartment at Csapó utca
29, with only a medium-sized room, a small entry hall, and an
even smaller kitchen. He was not discharged but reportedly died

of heart disease precipitated by his heavy caffeine intake in 1919 at age thirty-four, leaving Ella, only twenty-eight years old, widowed with three young sons between the ages of three and seven. Her life shattered, she struggled to make a living and raise her sons, first working at home on her own sewing machine as a seamstress, making ladies' dresses. Since her income was not enough to support the family, several of the Grünberger brothers pitched in to help her. Sándor, who had the grocery store, pledged to give her groceries every month, equivalent in today's dollars to $35 to $40. Her twin brother, Jakus, a lawyer, paid the rent. Zsigmond's brothers also helped the family.

Ella's apartment building had four units surrounding a courtyard, typical of Debrecen design. Her only living sister, widowed Ilona (whom we called Ilonka *néni* ["aunt" or a term of repsect, like Mrs.]), also lived there with her children. Bachelor brother Jakab (Jakus *bácsi* [uncle; bácsi or a term of respect, like Mr.]) helped both his sisters. He and Ilonka adopted Hermina's son, Jancsi, and raised him as their own. The families remained tight-knit. Although young, Jancsi was killed in World War II. Thirty-odd years later, his widow, Irén Schwartz, became like an aunt to me.

When I was a lonely freshman student far from home at Washington University in St. Louis, Irén unhesitatingly adopted me into her family, and I spent many weekends with her.

Jakus served as the father to his four nephews—Miki, Sanyi, and Jenő (Ella's sons) and Jancsi (Hermina's son). Jakus remained the patriarch of my father's side of the family for the rest of his life. We visited him regularly after he immigrated to New York City in 1958. He was a strict, conservative penny pincher. He spent no money on anything nonessential but paid ungrudgingly for whatever he considered necessary, such as Ella's rent and his nephews' studies.

Helen (Hella), Ilonka's daughter, became Jakus's wife. It was not uncommon for such relatives to wed where finding a suitably religious partner was difficult as it was in rural settings and the Orthodox community). This is called an avunculate marriage and was not prohibited.

Ella (Grünberger) Glattstein, Jancsi G. Schwartz, and Irén
Schwartz, circa 1940

Most of the ancestors on both sides of my family were religious
and clannish. While that clannishness led to the occasional
intermarriage, it also meant that family members took care of one
another. We visited the elderly Glattstein-Grünberger family in
New York once or twice a year. After my father died, they and their
children supported me. This value system influenced so many of
my life's decisions—for example, the place I chose to do my medical
training and where I established my practice. I wanted to be within
reasonable driving distance of my mother in case she needed me.
This connection was conspicuous enough that the two Indian
women physicians I trained under commented about it and asked
me where my family was from. They saw my family values as not
typically American.

Later, my willingness and need to take care of family became
critical in my choice of a life partner.

My father, Miki, and his two brothers attended the elementary
school of the Orthodox Jewish Congregation, located on Reál Iskola
street between Hatvan utca and József Kir. Herceg utca. Sanyi told

me that being too young and too poor to take the streetcar by themselves, they walked the half mile.[2]

In 1920, a year after his father died, Jenö came down with meningitis and was left with learning disabilities and a bent back. He could carry on a conversation, but he could never learn a trade nor hold down a job.

After finishing the fourth grade, Miki and Sanyi entered *polgári*, middle school, and then attended the new religious high school, the Debreceni Zsidó Gimnázium. Classes were held six days a week, Sunday through Friday, from 8:00 a.m. to 1:00 p.m., and each day the brothers studied five subjects, including math, geography, history, language, and literature.

On Saturday, the students were required to attend morning services in the synagogue. They conducted the religious services under the supervision of the teachers. Sanyi often served as a Torah reader. Other students chanted as cantors.

Sanyi described himself as a perfectionist, very bound by rules, and Miki as "normal," never hesitating to bend the rules. My father was described as a *csibész*, a mischievous rascal who charmed everyone.

Sanyi was a good student who became, in turn, a lawyer, a watchmaker, an orthotist with Miki, and then a mathematician and computer programmer at NASA's Jet Propulsion Laboratory. He also enjoyed studying the cello, which he played in the Debrecen Philharmonic Orchestra.

My father, on the other hand, was as smart as his younger brother but had no interest in studying or music. Miki was handy and could fix anything. He was very sociable and an avid soccer fan, a passion he passed on to my brother.

ON OCCASION, Grandmother Ella and her brood would travel to visit the Glattstein family in Tiszadorogma, a village west of Debrecen. The train crossed the Hortobágy, Hungary's Great Plain, to Egyek, leaving them to navigate the Tisza River to reach the tiny village. In the summer, they traversed the river by a ferry large enough to accommodate three or four horse-drawn wagons and many pedestrians on its broad, open deck. One man operated it by hand, using a long pole with a hook at the end. This enabled him to grab a cable that stretched from one bank of the river to the other and pull the ferry across. In the winter, they crossed the frozen river on foot.

As a boy, Miki spent many long summer vacations in the countryside by the Tisza River. Sanyi was three years younger. During his one summer in Tiszadorogma, Sanyi went to cheder (Hebrew school) every day. There, he learned to chant portions of the Torah and the Haftorah and attended services in the synagogue to help prepare him for his bar mitzvah. He spent the entire two-month vacation in Tiszadorogma like Miki did but lamented the fact that in subsequent years, he was not invited back. Sanyi was very serious and strait-laced as a youth. He suspected he wasn't asked back because he wasn't as entertaining as his mischievous and charming older brother, Miki.

I think Sanyi's insight is accurate; while he was warm and friendly, I saw only his studious, usually data-driven manner. In contrast, Miki was known by both sides of the family for his playfulness and as someone who could set people at ease and make them laugh. He was invited to spend every summer vacation in Tiszadorogma with his uncles and aunts until he flunked out of school and was not allowed—by law—to repeat that grade.

While Miki was bright and initially did well in elementary school, he did not want to study—his mind was on everything else. In the high school, he was always playing tricks on the teachers such as rigging their chairs so they would fall or pulling their coats when they walked by. Surprisingly, he was never caught!

Because of his failing grades due to his disinterest in school, Miki had to drop out and seek an apprenticeship. To his dismay, after he started his vocational training, he could no longer take time for the long summer vacations in the countryside by the river.

JANCSI AND SANYI both graduated from high school and then the University of Debrecen for undergraduate studies. Both obtained

Etél (Glattstein) Kramer, Florence (Kramer) Radkowsky, Emanuel "Mano" Kramer, and Samuel "Samu" Glattstein (Etél's brother), circa 1953

doctor of law degrees, Sanyi on June 28, 1940, in the midst of the growing uncertainties of war. That month, Italy entered the war, invading France, and Romania was forced to cede swaths of territory by the Soviet Union to Ukraine; the Soviet Union occupied the Baltic States, and France surrendered to the Germans.[3]

BY THE LATE 1920S, the Glattstein family scattered farther. Zsigmond's brothers Herman, Samu, and Ferenc "Feri" moved to Edelény to work in the offices of the coal mine (Edelényi Kőszénbánya), which was also owned by the Horowitz-Margareten family.

Although dispersed then throughout north-central Hungary, the families remained close, visiting each other regularly before the war. The few survivors helped each other after the war. In fact, Etél néni and Mano bácsi were integral in getting my parents settled after they immigrated in 1949. When I was about six years old, we began driving periodically from Silver Spring to New York City to visit my great-aunt and uncles who lived on the Lower East Side.

While I enjoyed the visits, I hated the drive and often got sick from the fuel smells as we passed through New Jersey, which was thick with oil refineries. I was also overwhelmed by the noise, poverty, and filth of New York. Every year, Mano bácsi sent us a care package with matzoh, gefilte fish, and coconut macaroons for Pesach (Passover). I especially appreciated the macaroons as my birthday often fell during the holiday, and cakes were prohibited at that time of year. My mother's cousin Florence was attentive to my mother, who was twenty years her elder. When I was young, I took these close family ties as the norm and never questioned the family's history. With everyone's aversion to speaking of the war or their losses, for years and years I heard only bits about the village life and their family closeness.

I remained close, too, with Jakus and his daughter, Marianna, whom I called Mari, and with Ancsi, the son of Feri and the sole survivor of the war in his entire family.

I grew up regularly visiting Jakus, Hella, Mari, and Ilonka in New York City. Uncle Jakus's thriftiness was legendary, as was his hoarding. I still have a small copper-colored custard cup he got for opening a bank savings account. I think of him fondly and with amusement whenever I see that cup. He was a remarkable character. He would repeatedly open accounts to get the sign-up gifts, which he shared liberally with family, then later close the accounts, moving the funds to another bank offering a sign-up bonus. He had piles of newspapers stacked against the living room walls in his tiny one-bedroom apartment in the public high-rise development on FDR Drive. I hated the green walls of the claustrophobic elevator and the pervasive smell of urine in the long, gloomy hallways.

As a child, I always found the three older relatives odd in appearance. Jakus was very thin, with white stubble on his chin, deeply sunken eyes, and tightly drawn skin under his jaw. In contrast, his sister Ilonka was matronly and nondescript, except for her yellowish white hair and soft, wrinkled double chin, which hung like crepe, all but hiding her neck. She, too, had deeply set eyes, but they were softened by her chubbiness. Hella looked like a softer version of Jakus, except for having full wavy hair and hooded eyelids that made it look like she had been crying.

Grünberger family: Hella, Mari, Jakus, and Ilonka, circa 1960, New York City

Miki and Sanyi were uncommonly close brothers and except for short periods remained together from childhood, through the war, and until Miki's unexpected death in 1964. Sanyi often commented to me late in his life that he was surprised at their closeness, given their extremely different personalities. But often opposites attract and complement each other.

My father's family, the Glattsteins, lived in the city of Debrecen, with its urban amenities such as electricity, a trolley, and cultural events, as well as a large Jewish community. In contrast, my mother's family, the Ehrenfelds, lived in a small village where they were isolated socially and did without similar amenities. From my childhood on, I pestered my mother to tell me about her life in the "dark ages" before electricity and modern conveniences.

CHAPTER 3

Early Life in Sáránd, 1910–1930

ALTHOUGH EVERYONE WORKED HARD, according to reports from each of the siblings, the Ehrenfeld family was relatively comfortable in the 1920s. Cousins, aunts, and uncles often visited. Anna's sister Leonka lived with the family for some time while going to school and working as a maid after Anna died.

The house was L-shaped and sat on a corner lot. Wooden fences surrounded all the neighborhood yards. The Ehrenfeld home was also encircled with sweet-smelling acacia trees, their heavy creamy white panicles exuding a honeylike scent. When my mother's sisters visited me in Cumberland in spring 1988, after my daughter was born, and smelled the locust blossoms, they were transported back to their yard.

In their Sáránd home, the tavern was closest to the main intersection. Next came the general store, followed by the parents' bedroom, which was shared with the latest baby. Anna and Mór's bedroom, with two iron beds along the wall, also served as a dining area. There was a stove near the door that led to the store. A large wooden table filled the middle of the room, and Mór's desk was on the front wall toward the street. No space was wasted. I learned many of the details through interviews with family members as well as my visit to Sáránd and interviews with Irén Bakó, who knew my family and lived across the street from the Ehrenfeld family. I learned still more in later interviews with Kati as I pestered her for more and more particulars.

31

A covered walk on the outside of the house faced the courtyard and connected the rooms that were farther from the corner. The yard was graced with a flower garden and a mulberry tree. The girls shared the room adjacent to their parents', and beyond it was the twin boys' room. Toward the courtyard was the *kamara* (pantry) and kitchen, then the cold room and woodshed. The kitchen was large, with a wood stove, two ovens, and a large *teknő*, a trough carved out of a log for mixing bread—up to forty pounds of flour at a time. A second trough was used for doughs containing milk, as the family kept strictly kosher, with two sets of dishes—the *tejes* one for dairy and *húsos* one for meat—and different work surfaces. Behind the house was a barn and barber shop. On the far side of the courtyard was the silo, an outhouse, and an outdoor bowling alley, which provided entertainment for the tavern's customers.

Anna and her maid did the bulk of the cooking, which was no easy task with so many mouths to feed.[1] They baked huge, heavy loaves of bread in the big *kemence*, or wood-fired oven. To know if the oven was hot enough, Anna would scratch the floor of the oven, to see how it *szikrázot*, or sparked.

While the courtyard had a well, the water was too hard from minerals and wasn't suitable for cooking or doing laundry. The sisters hauled drinking water from the main village well, which was a few blocks away near the town square behind the church. They needed a lot of water, as the milchig (dairy) and *fleischig* (meat) dishes were all handled separately and even washed in separate tubs.

With the large family, a lot of laundry needed to be done as well, but this chore was undertaken only monthly in a two-to-three-day process. During the week, the girls wore dark blue cotton school uniforms that buttoned in the back, topped with a white collar and dark blue bow where it tied in the back. At home, they each wore a colorful patterned dress, covered with an apron to keep it clean. All their clothes—even underwear—were handmade for them, often by the Lindenfeld cousins in Hadház. For Shabbos, the Sabbath, they had finer clothes. Most of the dresses were cotton, so in colder weather they wore warm sweaters and heavy cotton or wool thigh-high stockings held by garter belts. A large wooden hamper in the *spájz* (pantry) next to the kitchen held all the dirty items.

The family could still afford hired help then, and a laundress would come for one week a month. She washed the clothes with brushes in a big wooden tub. Kati said that hauling water for the laundry was a big social event, as they met their classmates at the well and gossiped while they worked. Shirts had separate collars so that just the collar could be washed or changed, rather than the whole shirt. Heavy, wet laundry was hauled up to the attic to dry in the winter, where it often froze first.

I heard many of these stories when the siblings got together and reminisced about their youth. Since childhood, I have been fascinated by the strength of pioneer women. The Little House series of books I read as a young girl prompted many of my earliest questions to Ma. Late in her life, I pressed my mother for more details about her village life. Awed by all they were able to do and accomplish despite being relatively poor and having no electricity or running water, I wanted to understand.

More recently, I've continued to pester Kati, the only surviving member of that generation, for every little detail she can remember. I've asked her to compare the family's experience with stories I've read in other books about Hungary in the first half of the century. I regret not capturing more details earlier from my mother and her siblings. Naturally, my perspective on what is important in life has changed as I've grown older.

While the Ehrenfelds were still better off than many of their neighbors in Sáránd, when they went to the *polgári* in Debrecen, the girls became aware of significant disparities between their classmates and themselves. Kati, for example, told me that she always took a lunch of bread smeared with goose fat. How she longed for the pretzels or baked goods sold at school that her friends could afford! Those city girls took piano lessons, learned French, and went out on dates, but being the only Jews in their small town, the Ehrenfeld children didn't have any social life.

Required school subjects were mathematics, geography, history, composition, Hebrew, and German. Students also had mandatory physical education, art, and music classes. Kati jokes that the singing class marked another tragedy in her life, as she couldn't carry a tune and failed the class, marring her academic record.

The girls shared beds, Bözsi with bony Klari, and Kati with Magdus, a dozen years older. The bedrooms had no heat, so the girls wore heavy flannel pajamas in the winter, sewn by their cousin Ilona Lindenfeld, and they slept on a straw mattress under heavy quilts with a satin cover. Now and then, a peddler would walk down the lane selling feathers. Usually, the family plucked their own, using the coarser outer feathers to make pillows and the down for quilts. To her death, my mother felt guilty over the cruelty of plucking feathers from the living birds and stuffing feed down their gullets to fatten their livers to be made into paté. She occasionally commented that perhaps the abuses she later suffered in Auschwitz were retribution for what she had done to the geese.

Life in a small rural Hungarian Village presented challenges for everyone, but for homes of Orthodox Jews, everything was made more difficult by the dietary laws of kashrut, keeping food strictly kosher. For instance, the preparation of a chicken culled from a small family flock for a strictly observant Jew was complicated. As Magdus explained, "The Gentiles had it so much easier compared to us. They would just wring the chicken's neck and throw the bird in a pot of hot water. This meant all those feathers would come loose and could be easily plucked. But not for the Jews. No, it was much more complicated for us because if you put the bird in the hot water before you drained the blood, the blood might remain in the meat instead of flowing out, and then the chicken was not kosher and not fit for Jews to eat. So our family had to wait for the *shochet* (ritual butcher) to arrive. Even the killing had to be planned because the shochet had to come from Mikepércs, a neighboring town. He had other towns to visit, too, so we had to plan ahead."[2]

Even with all this preparation, things could go wrong. Magdus especially enjoyed telling one story. A chicken was to be killed for

Yom Kippur, the day of atonement. For that holiest of days, there was an additional ritual—the family would say a blessing and ritually swing the chicken around over their heads, to take away their sins before butchering the chicken.[3]

But that day, the plan went all wrong. As Klari told the story,

The shochet who was sent to preside over the ceremony was Goldstein bácsi, a rather unique individual who had a purplish beard. Our Kati, who was known for her schoolgirl crushes, had an obvious crush on him. Perhaps that affected his professional duties—who knows?—but on more than one occasion when he performed the ritual at our home, he was a bit clumsy. On this day, his ineptitude was memorable. As the family said the ritual prayer as usual, the shochet was expected to quickly swing the bird over our heads before butchering the fowl for our holiday meal. But on this day, the shochet was more unskilled than usual: the blow to cut off the chicken's head was not a clean one, and to everyone's horror, the chicken jumped up and began to run all around the yard with blood spurting from the neck and the head hanging askew.

Once everyone was over their initial shock, someone quickly caught and finished killing the poor bird, but since it was no longer kosher, we couldn't eat it. We couldn't waste food, of course, so that day, just like on the other occasions when the shochet got clumsy, we gave the bird to the Gypsies. They lived as transients on the outskirts of the town and were pitifully poor and more in need than anyone else around us.[4]

Typically, the shochet was scheduled to arrive on Thursdays to perform the killing. No refrigeration was available, so meats were lowered into the well to be kept cool. A chicken killed on a Thursday would be safe to eat through Monday. The *tepertő* (cracklings) would keep longer without spoiling. Before Anna died, when the family needed beef, they made the trip to Debrecen for kosher beef on Thursday or Friday so they would have it for Shabbos, and they ate the liver fresh from the butcher with mashed potatoes. The meat would be cooked into *fasírt* (meatballs) or added to *cholent* (beans).

A noon meal was often *bundás kenyér*, which was like French toast without the syrup.

The women baked once per week in preparation for Shabbos. Anna would usually prepare *mákos* (poppy seed) rolls and *túrós béles*, which was like a cheese Danish. The enticing scents of baking often wafted onto the street, attracting neighbors, who often received a small portion. When the baking was done, the *cholent* would be placed in the still warm oven to cook overnight.

Butter was made twice a week, as well as cottage cheese and sour cream, which were kept in the *kamara* or *spájz* (pantry) or in an ice cellar. Cottage cheese was a staple, and dairy products made up the main meals midweek.

(The Hungarian words *kamara* and *spájz* come from the German *Speisekammer*, a small room like a pantry, most of the time accessible from the kitchen. A *kamara* might also be used to store firewood.)

If the family ate meat for lunch, the main meal of the day, then they had to wait six hours before they could have anything with dairy, another rule of kashrut. This comes from the practice of not mixing milk and meat, based on the biblical prohibition against boiling a kid (goat) in its mother's milk.

When my mother told me stories about their meals, she wryly recounted how even eating the liver and potatoes became a ritual reflecting the different sisters' personalities. Bözsi ate the liver immediately, as soon as she got it. Ma covered her liver with potato and saved it for later. When they were older and had a little spending money, the sisters would go shopping in Debrecen. Bözsi immediately bought what she wanted. Ma would walk around, agonizing over what to do, feeling guilty for squandering money on silly things. But Bözsi enjoyed whatever she had; Ma always saved for later. "People never change," she observed. As I learned to be a more careful observer of human nature, I saw that truth both in others and in myself.

For many years the family's kitchen floor was earthen and had to be freshened each Friday in preparation for Shabbos. A different type of soil, tinged with yellow, was imported to Sáránd from Karcag. The family would wet the dirt in a dish and then apply the clay-like mix to the floor, finally topping it with some dry sand for decor. Eventually, Anna had the surface changed to cement, which was easier to maintain. Magdus and Bözsi still had to scrub the cement floor each week.

My mother attempted to instill this Sabbath cleaning ritual in me and taught me to scrub the kitchen floor each Friday. I was probably about ten at the time, and it made me feel grown-up to be learning such lessons and helping her. Ma and her sisters also had to sweep the dirt in the entryway and courtyard into zen-like patterns to welcome Shabbos.

Then, of course, the family bathed. They would stand in a huge wooden, barrel-like tub in the kitchen and stoop down to wash themselves. Around 1930, the tin maker made them a real bathtub. Rainwater from the cisterns was used for bathing. Magdus said that she and Bözsi would break the ice and bring the water into the toasty kitchen but not heat it, as they felt bathing in cold water was healthier. The others opted for water warmed in a large cauldron on the wood-burning stove.

A traditional Shabbos dinner was held on Friday nights, with two chickens, geese, or ducks—enough to feed nine or ten people. The family would then read and pray before the maid turned off the lights. On Shabbos morning, they would have pastries for breakfast; then Mór would walk almost three miles to the next town, Hajdúbagos, for services, often accompanied by Kati. If the fire in the oven was still burning, they would add a little more wood, but they would not work or build a fire from scratch that day. Lunch was the traditional *cholent*, beans baked in the embers of the oven, and a beef dish that had been prepared earlier. Meats were preserved by smoking them. Goose breast was a favorite. Poultry might instead be baked until it was very dried out, which helped it keep a little longer. Foods like stuffed cabbage would keep for a couple of days.

The Ehrenfelds' lives followed this weekly routine of school, work, and Orthodox observances before the war. While this relatively comfortable and peaceful way of life would soon come to an end, I found the echoes of it and the rhythms of the rituals—from simply preparing for Shabbos and going to the synagogue, to the more elaborate holiday observances that were a part of my childhood—comforting and grounding.

CHAPTER 4

Grandfather Mór

MY GRANDPARENTS ALL DIED long before I was born, and the concept of what a grandparent was, or what a relationship with one might feel like, has always been beyond my imagination.

I didn't have a strong image of my grandfather Mór until I was in my late forties and began to delve into our family's oral history; I had only glimpses from rare photos. He was a tall, handsome, but stern-looking man even at his wedding. On that occasion, he wore a fancy long tailored coat over a starched, stiff-collared white shirt; his pocket watch chain was peeking out from his vest, and he was holding a pair of gloves. But that picture of him is marred by the somber visage of the bride at his side, a much younger woman who showed no sign of joy on her wedding day.

Another image I had of him was the erect World War I soldier guarding a group of villagers. The final image? A well-respected, devout man, more knowledgeable and worldly than many in the village, and a father who, while being a man of few words, radiated love toward his children that they still felt well into their old age and that they each shared with me.

As I grew older, occasionally I heard my mother and uncles and aunts make reference to my grandmother's meanness and selfishness, but I never heard a whiff of negativity about Mór. His Hebrew name was Mozes, which was apt. He was wise, and his knowledge and bearing commanded respect.

Miklós, Judy, and Mark, June 17, 1984, Cumberland

Whenever I asked what Mór was like, the sisters (as his daughters were called) would say he was very much like their brother Miklós, both in appearance and mannerisms. As adults, both father and son had prominent, slightly curved noses, thinning hair parted on the side and combed over the top to mask their balding, and trimmed mustaches. Miklós said very little, at least compared to his sisters, but I always felt a gentleness from him and the affection I longed for, especially after my own father died abruptly. He was a bit chubby, but that reinforced his softness. On rare occasions late in his life, I liked to feel his soft cheek or gently hold his plump hand, reminiscing how Kati's thrill as a child was walking with her father, holding his hands, or being held by him. Miklós was, in those moments, the father and grandfather I didn't have. I had asked Miklós to walk me down the aisle at my wedding, incurring my mother's wrath for breaking tradition and not giving that honor to my father's brother, Sanyi. But at that time I craved Miklós's gentleness. It helped fill the void in my heart I had felt since my father died. Sanyi was gracious about my decision and gave me his blessing to have the ceremony I wished. In the end, Miklós escorted me to the chupah (wedding canopy), and Sanyi chanted the blessings over the challah and wine. My mother, thrilled with our "storybook" garden wedding in the mountains, never again mentioned her initial upset.

Some descriptions of Mór stand out in the stories I heard about him. One was the widower, left with seven children to raise after his two wives and young daughters had died, sitting by the window on Shabbos, tears streaming down his face. My mother, Kati, and Miklós all had that image seared into their memories and on occasion over the years shared it with me.

Mór was a devoted father, doting on his youngest daughter, Kati, and walking hand-in-hand with her to shul (synagogue). I can picture him trying to placate his tantrum-throwing child after her matzoh broke, a pious man so distraught that he violated the religious prohibition against work on the Sabbath by trying to sew her matzoh back together with a needle and black thread. He was not very successful except in consoling her with his valiant effort. How helpless he must have felt with an inconsolable child then—or a bit later when she was thrashing about with a high temperature from scarlet fever and he wrapped her in cool, wet sheets to try to break her fever.

Of all the children, Kati had a particularly special bond with her father, and they had an alliance that was especially obvious at mealtime. After Anna died, Magdus took over the role of mothering her youngest sister. She was very strict, insisting that Kati eat the weekly bean soup, which she detested, before she could enjoy the main dish of *mákos tészta*, egg noodles with ground poppy seeds and sugar. When Magdus turned her back to the table, Mór quickly exchanged bowls with Kati, giving her his empty bowl, and ate her portion of soup. I was amused by Mór's allying himself with his youngest daughter and was reminded of my own family and how my young daughter similarly had her father wrapped around her little finger. Mór and Kati had a kind of private signal for situations like that, much as my father had with me. A quick two squeezes of my hand and I knew he was sending love and kisses or telling me he understood my feelings. It was our secret code.

Mór's children adored him. Although isolated in a small village, the girls absorbed his love of reading, staying up too late at night to read by the faint light of the kerosene lantern on the table between the two beds. Kati complains to this day that her poor eyesight resulted from being pushed farthest from the lamp while trying to read.

The girls vied with each other to be closest to the light, as reading was a vehicle to travel and explore the broad world beyond Sáránd. The daughters would sometimes fall asleep as they read late at night. When the kerosene in the lamp ran out and only the wick was burning, Mór would smell it in the next room and come to snuff it out after they had drifted off. This late-night reading instilled a lifelong love of literature, poetry, and learning in each of the children.

While I enjoyed reading, I was never as avid a reader as my mother and my brother were. It bothered Ma, too, that I didn't delve into serious literature as she had. My mother was not expressively proud of me for becoming a physician, but when I authored my first book, seven years after my brother had written one, and when that book was adopted by some universities as a text, her pride was palpable. Nothing was more respected than literacy and authorship. Indeed, when I published my book, I saw her attitude toward me change. I had finally achieved something worthwhile. "My daughter, the author!" she would murmur, and she placed my book, *Conducting Clinical Research*, next to my brother's *Suicide and Attempted Suicide*, on her living room coffee table, where no visitors could miss seeing them.

As THEY GREW OLDER, the oldest and youngest daughters liked to help their father in the store by waiting on patrons and measuring out and packaging the dry goods. Both told me about the way they would carefully roll paper into a cone, fill it with salt or flour, twist the bottom and crimp it tightly, and then fold over the top to make a lid. As a child, I stood in the kitchen and watched my mother rolling wax paper and filling it with salt for my school lunches, and I was mesmerized, not realizing then that she had learned this skill all those years ago.

After working in the store or on the farm, Mór enjoyed listening to his sons playing violin and reading in the evenings with his neighbor and close friend, Tóth bácsi (Mr. Tóth). In addition to the Budapest newspaper, Mór especially enjoyed reading Zane Grey and other westerns. He must have been generous with his children, as Kati said she always had a few *pengő* in her pocket with which to buy a book in Debrecen.

Mór always leaned toward formality and gruffness, in keeping with his having been a decorated officer in the First World War. He always wore long-sleeved shirts, heavy trousers, a vest, and a hat. In Bözsi's wedding photo, he looks older and stockier. That wedding photo was in his coat pocket when he was forced to strip at Auschwitz before being sent to the left, to the gas chambers.

As I've learned more, I've reflected on how progressive my grandfather was for his time. He provided for and encouraged education and literacy in his daughters. Later, when they fell on hard times, he was pragmatic and flexible. He allowed the girls to go to Debrecen to learn a trade of their choosing and paid for their apprenticeships, despite being Orthodox Jews (who are generally more rigid in their thinking and practices). His daughters all became accomplished seamstresses, each with her own niche. My mother's skill became fitting and constructing orthopedic corsets.

My grandfather also allowed Magdus and Bözsi to choose a love match rather than, as was tradition, insisting on an arranged marriage. Given how insulated he was in rural Hungary, except for his forays during World War I, and how steeped in Orthodox

Jewish traditions he was, my grandfather Mór seems to have been a worldly and broad-minded gentleman who reared well-educated and self-sufficient children who were well-equipped to survive in the world. It was these lessons—independence, practical skills, and a broad education—in part, that helped them survive what was to come.

Despite his gruff visage, Mór possessed an underlying tenderness that I heard about as well. For example, when his daughters were young, he would walk ahead of them, making a path through the snow for them to get to the train station, three-quarters of a mile away, to go to school.

Other stories I heard from my mother and aunts about the final days in Sáránd are forever welling up in my memory. One is of my grandfather taking valuables such as jewelry and watches from his store, as well as woolens he was safeguarding from the bombings in Budapest for Bözsi, and placing them in a big wooden box. Then, one pitch-black night, with only Kati as a frightened and solitary witness, he buried the treasures in the backyard next to the flowerbed as she stood watch. Mór hoped these items would provide them a renewed start when they came home after the war. But then, a few days later, he had overwhelming guilt, feeling he was breaking the law, so he dug the box back up—and found it was empty. Although he worked in darkness and Kati was watchful, someone witnessed Mór's actions that night; Kati thinks it was a neighbor's workman.

Another trait Mór's daughters remarked on was his stoicism and how hard it must have been for him, as a proud and decorated World War I soldier—a hero—to slowly lose his rights to own a business, to vote, and even to move freely in his own town. The family had felt secure, confident that Mór's war service had earned him full citizenship status and respect. Kati explained that as they self-identified far more as Hungarian citizens rather than as Jews— not even bothering to learn Yiddish—they failed to recognize that they were still viewed as the "other" and less worthy by most. They were in denial about the rabid antisemitism and what could happen to them in their homeland.

Yet it seems that by March 1944, Mór must have known what was to befall them shortly. A man who had escaped from Treblinka found his way to Sáránd and to Mór's home, attracted by the mezuzah (a scroll of parchment in a case attached to the doorpost, containing, in Hebrew, the passages from Deuteronomy 6:4–9 and 11:13–21). Mór took him in, fed him, and hid him in the attic for a number of days, until someone from the village warned Mór that he had noticed the unusual activity in the attic and he would be reported to the police if that continued. My mother learned this from Pista, her older brother, after the war. Mór, ever protective, had hidden the news from his daughters. "It was much worse to know than not to know," my mother told me and my daughter's high school history teacher, who came to speak with her in 2006. One of the neighbors described her father being taken from his home, walking next to the horse wagon, as "Jesus Christ going to the cross . . . Proud . . . straight . . . but he couldn't do a thing."

Then my grandfather Mór was taken to Auschwitz, where he was murdered.

CHAPTER 5

My Grandmothers

I HAD ONLY TWO CHILDREN, both when I was in my thirties, yet I felt overwhelmed by the work and responsibilities. So when I began to put together this book, I started to better understand Anna. Plotting out a timeline helped me be much more sympathetic toward her. Indeed, I cannot imagine how she coped, marrying at eighteen and then having a passel of children, including two stepsons. Because I never met my grandmothers, only as an adult did I learn that they were the antithesis of my fantasies of sweet and loving women. My mother and all her sisters had difficulties with their mother—but my compassion for Anna has grown over time.

On my father's side, Sanyi described his mother as "primitive," or coarse, and emotionally unstable. Ella's mother had died when she was fourteen, she married at twenty-one and then rapidly had three children. By twenty-eight, she was a widow with three young sons. Ella was said to be overly protective of them and very jealous of Miki's attention to my mother.

When I was young, my mother would say, "You look so much like your grandmother." I thought that was a compliment. I was too naive to know that she despised her mother-in-law and that she blamed Ella for having ended up in Auschwitz instead of with her family, who was deported on the earlier train from Debrecen to Strasshof, in Austria.

Ella Glattstein (50), 1940   Anna Róth (30), 1922, Sáránd

But I am, in so many ways, clearly my mother's daughter. These days looking more closely at photos and speaking with Kati, I understand that I look more like Anna.

I occasionally half-joke that I inherited my mother's outlook and my father's lipids; how I wish it were the reverse!

I saw firsthand how poor parenting skills can be passed down from one generation to the next where there is a dearth of role models. I've recently come to understand, too, that some of my mother's negative behavior toward me had nothing to do with me. Instead, I now understand, I reminded her of the two powerful women in her life who were hateful toward her. And my own experiences as a parent have helped me to become more understanding of my mother's failures as a mother, as well as my own.

Now when I ruminate about some of the hurtful things Ma did, I remind myself of my own mantra and I offer it to her: "She did the best she could."

CHAPTER 6

Magdus's Childhood

M<small>Y</small> <small>MOTHER'S EARLIEST CHILDHOOD MEMORIES</small> were of hardship and hunger. Born just before World War I, she recalled general unhappiness. Her father was away fighting in the Hungarian army, leaving her mother home to work at their general store as well as to raise four children—her two stepsons, young Magdus, and baby Bözsi. Food was so scarce that Anna was forced to measure out and slice the bread carefully for each of her children.

When Mór returned from the war, he was a decorated hero, earning him considerable respect in a long-antisemitic country. The family had a Gentile maid. Strangely, it was this *cseléd* who taught the young children to say the Hebrew morning prayer. The Modeh Ani gives thanks to G-d for having returned one's soul after the night and enabling one to awaken to another day. After the prayer, the children rose, washed their hands and face in cold water, and ate their modest breakfast of milk with bread and butter or a *túrós béles*.

Magdus went to a nursery school, where she enjoyed singing songs and dancing with her teacher, Ottomanyi néni. She also learned to play hopscotch and jump rope, which she later taught me as a child.

When she graduated to elementary school, Magdus had her first taste of corporal punishment and antisemitism: teachers would strike across her nails with a stick or beat her more than her Gentile classmates. She attended a Calvinist school only a block away from home and had to take part in its church on Sundays. In her recollection, it did her "no harm" to do so. Classes went from 8:00 a.m. until 1:00 p.m.; then she did her homework, played, and helped her mother. After helping with the cooking or cleaning or caring for the younger children in the family, all the children were free to play with other neighborhood kids. The girls made dolls from corn cobs and furniture from scraps of wood and spools. They especially liked climbing up into the *góré* (corn crib) to make up plays. They also enjoyed playing ball, with either a *gumi labda* (rubber ball) or one made from rags, and playing jump rope.

Being a quick study, Magdus was bored at school and skipped a grade, moving on to the *polgári* in Debrecen. She loved her teachers there. She often said that her education was far better than mine or my children's, particularly in geography, history, and literature.

Anna and her eldest daughter had a strained relationship at times because Magdus often balked at her mother's orders. Anna was a fanatic for cleanliness, and everything had to be in perfect order—an unrealistic goal with seven or eight children and no electricity or running water.

Magdus's biggest complaint about her chores was that she needed to scrub the floor until it was so clean you could eat off of it. She and Bözsi washed the cement floor with dangerously toxic lye every Friday in preparation for the Sabbath. They always wound up with red knees and hands and some of their skin might disappear in the process. When I was young, my mother taught me, too, to scrub our linoleum on hands and knees, but we used Spic and Span, and she wasn't very strict with me.

My mom wanted to be a physician—something she never told me as I was growing up in an effort, I believe, to allow me to make my own choices. I was impressed at her restraint. She told me of her dream only after I graduated from medical school, and I understood she did not want to try to live her dreams through me. Her parents had promised they would support her ambition but then decided they could no longer pay her way. As a consequence, Magdus stopped studying and began skipping school and forging excuse notes from her father. By age fourteen, she had to drop out of school altogether to help her father in the store and her mother with the raising of all those kids.

I suspect that this situation contributed both to my mother's choice of apprenticeship and profession and to her intense and long-lasting hurt a half-century later when none of her sisters came to my medical school graduation.

But Ma's love of reading never abated. In her later years, even when she was almost blind, she spent much of her days listening to news and *Washington Post* stories read to her over the telephone through the Metropolitan Washington Ear. Even in the hospital the months before her death, my mother struggled to read Sándor Petőfi and János Arany, word by word, with her magnifying glass. When I tried to read one of their poems with my broken Hungarian, she promptly took over, reciting lines she first learned more than eighty years before. I felt a twinge of envy because my memory is increasingly a disappointment. I also felt sad that I am not as well-read as she was. I admired how sharp she was at ninety-four and that she maintained such a broad range of interests. She has become a role model all these years later, giving me something to aspire to.

CHAPTER 7

The Watershed

I've grown to view my grandmother Anna's death as a watershed in the family. There was an era of happiness and light before and a dark veil of despair clouding everything after, much as my own father's death wreaked on our family decades later when I was a child.

Early in the summer of 1932, Anna took three of her daughters—Magdus, Klari, and Henduka—to a wedding for their first cousin, Béla Lindenfeld. Each of the girls had a fancy dress sewn for the occasion—dark red velvet with a white collar with tiny red polka dots. Kati got one as well, which she viewed as her consolation prize for missing the wedding.

Kati, only seven, was not taken to the wedding because her mother thought she was *csúnya* (ugly): she wore glasses, she was *kancsi* (cross-eyed), and her ears stuck out. Anna often left her behind when she took trips to the healing thermal baths or to special occasions, like this wedding. This time, Kati was left with her older cousin Ilona in Hadház to care for her. Kati felt abandoned, left alone with the Lindenfelds all summer, with no word from her family.

Kati told me the story of where she went that summer, though Magdus and Miklós filled in the details about life at the Lindenfelds, as they both spent considerable time there over the years. Mór's sister Etél had married Dezső Lindenfeld, who had been a Hungarian cavalry officer in World War I and was now a poor tailor. They had five sons and one daughter.

Dezső was an expert at going to the market and being able to select the chicken or goose that would provide the most meat, as it needed to last the entire week. When satisfied with his decision, he took the bird to the shochet for ritual slaughter. The family made soup, *tepertő*, and *fasírt* from a single bird. As they had no refrigeration, they would lower the meat into the well to keep it cold. Episodically, thieves stole their food during the night.

Magdus was awed that Etél could feed her entire family and Magdus from a single chicken. She said Etél could magically manage to make a meal out of nothing and nobody was left hungry. When twelve or thirteen years old, Magdus would take the train to visit the Lindenfelds for a weekend. Her cousin Géza would meet her at the train station and walk her the two miles to their home, arm-in-arm. The house, which had a dirt floor and thatched roof, was cramped. Rooms served multiple uses.

Magdus recalled that the boys slept together in a "box" that was used in the daytime as an ironing board or cutting table and that the family had an older woman boarding with them. While her younger siblings—Miklós, Klari, and Kati—all thought that Etél didn't like them, Magdus felt very loved and was spoiled by her aunt. For example, in the summer, Etél would awaken her in bed with a small dish of fresh raspberries. Magdus also liked visiting the Lindenfelds because they would all sit outside in the evening and their father, Dezső, with his beautiful voice, led them in many folk songs.

Miklós, who spent the school years in Hadház with the Lindenfelds, resented his time there. His aunt Etél greeted him with cold apple soup, which he detested. His uncle Dezső made him a fine winter coat of English wool when he arrived at age four. It was so long that it reached the ground and lasted him until he was twelve, though it was more like a jacket by then.

Etél and Dezső were strict. When Miklós did not like the food that was prepared, he was locked in the pantry, which was dark and dungeon-like, until he became hungry enough to eat anything. While his life there was difficult, Miklós became close with his cousins. Whenever they came to Sáránd, they would go back to Hadház with a lot of provisions from Mór's store.

SOON AFTER THE 1932 WEDDING of Dezső and Etél's oldest son, the Ehrenfeld family was stricken with typhoid from tainted food at the celebration. All four, who had attended the reception—Anna and her daughters Magdus, Klari, and Henduka—were hospitalized in Debrecen at the university hospital for weeks. My mother, who was twenty at the time, told me a few more details of that horrid summer that broke her family.

She had fallen ill while caring for her mother, who died on August 23, 1932, shortly before Magdus herself was also hospitalized. She never spoke of her own bout with typhoid nor what she experienced as she cared for her mother, but as an infectious disease physician, I know deaths from typhoid involving a perforated bowel and sepsis can be terribly painful. Severe sepsis can cause respiratory failure and shortness of breath, bleeding, and shock. Every breath and movement hurts. As I learned about my grandmother's death, I felt professionally detached, but I was sad when I heard about how ill my aunt Klari was; I love her deeply, and learning about how she and Henduka, charming, joyful, and everyone's pet, had suffered broke my heart.

Klari, Magdus's twelve-year-old sister, lay in the bed next to Magdus and was unconscious for more than a week. Tragically, the youngest, five-year-old Henduka, died in my mother's arms. Reflecting on what a hard life she had and how resilient she was has pushed me to tell this story of inspiration and resilience and has instilled in me the belief that it is a story others should know.

Only Klari and Magdus made it home from the hospital that September and were cared for by their sister Bözsi, who had stayed home from the wedding to help her father in the store.

Anna's death affected each of her children differently, as might be expected given the wide range of ages and roles in the family. Her daughters seemed more affected than her sons by her death. I've long wondered if the boys felt a glimmer of relief. After all, Pista and Józsi, her twin stepsons, had been poorly treated and by then were in their midtwenties, and Miklós was allowed to return home to live with his family only after his mother's death.

My mother told me how hard it was to grow up without a mother. I am certain that she used to tell me she was only fourteen when her mother died, but in fact, she had just turned twenty the prior week. Unprepared, she was suddenly thrust into the responsibilities of running the household. Perhaps in her mind's eye, she was still only a fourteen-year-old schoolgirl.

Bözsi, then eighteen, also had new adult responsibilities she was unprepared for as well and had to help nurse her sisters back to health.

Miklós, fourteen, had been exiled to Hadház for most of his life. He hated it there both because he missed his family and because the Lindenfelds were very poor. They could ill afford the burden of the extra mouth to feed, and Miklós regularly took them food or other supplies from his father's store to contribute. Miklós, who as an adult was quiet and mellow, with rarely an unkind comment about anyone, vehemently told me that he could never understand how a mother could send her four-year-old son away to the cheder in Hadház.

Klari, age twelve, had always been sickly, and this condition was compounded by her critical illness. Being a middle child, she was more lost after her mother's death and was too young to be much help around the house. Her older siblings had to assume more responsibilities in the house, the store, and the tavern, leaving them less time to pay attention to her. Kati, now the youngest, received more nurturing.

While all the sisters felt very close to their male Lindenfeld cousins, especially Ernö, who was intelligent and affectionate, staying in Hadház was difficult for Kati. The Lindenfelds were very poor, and Etél seemed to like only Magdus. Kati also didn't like having to sleep with the sole daughter among five sons; Ilona was much older and had so much facial hair it frightened the young girl. Kati found Etél to be very bitter about her lot in life, living in a *nyomortona* (a world of misery). The family was also more religious and strictly observant than the Ehrenfelds were, perhaps believing that they would be rewarded in an afterlife, sustaining them in their impoverished existence.

That summer in 1932, Kati wondered why Etél would make regular trips to the hospital in Debrecen on the train, carrying jars of chicken soup with her, when she had so many mouths to feed at home and her husband was so poor.

In September, when school was to start, Kati was sent home by train. Instead of being greeted by family, a neighbor and the father of her childhood friend Irén Bakó picked her up at the train station and walked her to their house, where they told her that her mother and young Henduka had died. Her father couldn't bring himself to tell her. Kati remembers jumping up and running across the street to her home, screaming, and then her father sitting her on his lap, gently stroking her hand.

Now the youngest child, Kati took the news of her mother's death perhaps the hardest.

After Anna's death, the home seemed to have no life. Mirrors were draped in black for a year. Music and laughter vanished. And for years, Mór would welcome Shabbos not with joy but with tears streaming down his face as he sat by the window.

THE SAME EXTREME RESPONSE to grief and mourning was reprised a generation later in my own family when my father died unexpectedly in 1964 when I was twelve. As with my grandfather's family, ours lost all joy. My mother became profoundly depressed, and we stopped celebrating anything—even holidays and birthdays. Not being in perpetual mourning, even years later, would have seemed disloyal to Apu's memory and respect for my mother, recapitulating the tragedy a generation before.

After my father died, relationships in the family shifted. My brother, always favored by Ma, grew more godlike in her eyes. Sometimes she lashed out at me when I wanted to be a normal young teen with adolescent interests or showed any interest in hair or makeup.

MAGDUS HAD HELPED AROUND THE HOUSE, but although grown, she had never learned her way around the kitchen, to cook or bake, because she was charged with raising the younger children and helping her father in the store and tavern. Anna did all the cooking with her *cseléd*.

After her mother died, Magdus was suddenly forced into the role of mother and became responsible for feeding the household and running the family. This was not a smooth transition.

Once, her father rushed into the smoke-filled kitchen after she poured cold water into a pan of hot grease while making soup. Another time, trying to slide a twenty-pound loaf of bread into the oven was too unwieldy for her, and she upended the dough off the paddle and into the ashes. Despite many such misadventures, with practice and guidance from their maid, all the girls learned how to cook and clean and became superb bakers.

As if the loss of Anna and Henduka wasn't already bad enough, the family also ran out of money in 1932. The prolonged hospitalizations for Anna and her three daughters were costly, as were the two funerals. The family's financial difficulties had started earlier, but the region was now experiencing the Depression, and the townspeople didn't have money to go shopping in the family's general store. Mór had to sell cows and horses and lay off many of his workers, the stable hands and *kocsis* (teamsters), and some maids.

Magdus and Bözsi, the two eldest, recognized that they had little future. Money that was to have been their dowries had been lent to their mother's siblings so they could buy a farm in Nyírjákó and was never repaid, causing an ugly rift in the family. Now impoverished by the hospital bills and funerals, the sisters knew that a good marriage was unlikely to be arranged. They decided that they would need to learn a skill to be able to support themselves—which I find rather remarkable for young Orthodox village women.

56

Bözsi found a divorcée, Lily Reichman, who had her own salon in Debrecen, sewing corsets and brassieres. Mór paid for Bözsi to have a six-month apprenticeship there because sewing was an easy trade to learn. Soon after, Bözsi went to Budapest to find a job, which she quickly did. Deciding that Klari needed to take over the housekeeping, Magdus went to the city for training, apprenticing at a corset and orthopedic shop for six months. She soon fell in love with the store owner, Miki Glattstein, but they did not marry, in large part because of her having such a small dowry. Ever the pragmatist, Miki was finally able to persuade his mother and uncle Jakus that Magdus's hard work would be far more valuable than a dowry in the long run—but it took him six more years to do so.

CHAPTER 8

Miki's Shop

LIKE MY MOTHER, my father, Miki, and his brother Sanyi were
scarred by their father's sudden death at age thirty-four, when
they were seven and three respectively. Compounding the tragedy,
shortly after Zsigmond died, Jenö became ill with meningitis,
leaving him severely intellectually disabled. Their grieving mother,
Ella, was unable to raise the boys by herself, either financially or
emotionally, so Zsigmond's siblings all pitched in.

After Miki flunked out of school, he had to learn a trade, so
at age fourteen, he searched for an apprenticeship. The first
opportunity he found was a job in an auto body shop. Every night
he came home dirty and oily from head to toe, so after the trial
period, he didn't accept the job.

Miki next applied to Sándor Schön's, a glove, corset, and
orthopedic appliance maker. He was accepted and stayed there for
seven years, first as an apprentice and later as a journeyman.

Feeling exploited there, he borrowed money from his uncle and
set up his own shop in 1935, when he was only twenty-one, and his
mother continued to sew dresses part-time. Their small apartment
on Piac utca now included the living space for the entire family as
well as their business.

Miki needed labor for his shop, so he took in apprentices, who
paid him for their training. After Bözsi had learned a trade and
moved to Budapest, it was time for Magdus to learn a skill that
would allow her to support herself. Bözsi's boss recommended

Mór (57), Magdus (24), Kati (12), and Miki (23), 1936, Sáránd

the Glattsteins' shop and Magdus and her father went to assess it. Miki was olive-skinned and handsome with a magnetic personality. Mór complained that Miki looked too young and didn't like his daughter's choice for vocational schooling.

I wonder how much of Magdus's choice of profession was driven by her inability to become a physician. She was always a helper; working with an orthotist (brace maker) was likely the closest she would be able to get to her dream. Nursing, a more subservient role in the 1930s, would not have suited her as well as the more independent orthotics profession.

Perhaps Mór didn't like the idea of Magdus having intimate physical contact while fitting patients for corsets and braces. I suspect he also likely recognized and worried about Miki's intentions toward his chaste eldest daughter.

Nonetheless, Mór reluctantly agreed to pay for six months of training. From the beginning, Miki addressed Mór, who was by

Magdus and Miki, circa 1939, Debrecen

then in his midfifties, as Apuka (Father).

Soon, Miki told Magdus that he wanted to marry her but he had too many responsibilities. He needed both to support his mother and brothers and to repay his debt. Miki begged Mór for a large dowry: "But Apuka, I need the money to expand." But Mór insisted that he could not afford more than 5,000 pengő ($1,000) as he had other daughters to provide for as well. I heard from Sanyi and my aunts how Miki tried to persuade his uncle Jakus, the patriarch who raised the brothers, that Magdus was such a devoted and tireless worker that she would be more valuable in the shop than any idle wealthy young woman who only brought a dowry.

At one point when they were courting, long after Magdus's apprenticeship with him was over, Miki gave her a watch inscribed, "For so many bad hours, one good one . . ."

It would be six years before they wed.

ONLY THREE MONTHS after they wed in 1941, Miki was called up into forced labor, leaving his wife to manage their shop. Although Magdus had passed the examination to be a journeyman, a competitor complained that she was working without a license. She recognized the handwriting on the complaint, although the official wouldn't share the complainant's name.

Miki (28), 1940, Debrecen

Magdus (about 28), circa 1940, Debrecen

A metalworker whom they worked with to make braces and body casts told the official that he couldn't continue without her help, so she was allowed to do that small part of her business. Then she added making backpacks for the forced laborers. One backpack was for Ancsi Glattstein, Miki's cousin. His backpack came to America with him. Another was for Imre, a childhood classmate of Miki's.

CHAPTER 9

Prelude to War

ANTISEMITISM WORSENED AGAIN in the interwar period. By the end of World War I, the Austro-Hungarian Empire, forged in 1867, dissolved, and Hungary lost two-thirds of its land as border regions were broken up and given to Serbians, Croatians, and Slovenians as parts of Yugoslavia, Czechoslovakia, and Romania.

In March 1919, a short-lived Communist government took over. It tried to regain territory lost to Romania (Transylvania) and Slovakia and restore Hungary to its pre–World War I borders. That effort failed. Fighting heightened between the primarily urban Communists and the people from rural areas. The many killings became known as the Red Terror.

My mother explained to me that those who had factories or businesses were considered capitalists, so they were shot. When the Communists were ousted, the White Terror or White Guardists, led by Admiral Miklós Horthy, retaliated and carried out mass murders against the Communists. Horthy became regent of Hungary in 1920 and remained in that position until the next world war.

Fueling ill will was that while Jews made up about 5 percent of the Hungarian population, they included a disproportionate number of professionals—48 percent of doctors, 34 percent of lawyers, and 43 percent of technological students, for example—and owned or operated up to 90 percent of Hungarian industry through banking families.[1]

Horthy was antisemitic and promptly passed a *numerus clausus*, which limited the proportion of Jewish university students to 6 percent or less, matching their percentage in the general population.[2]

Magdus noted that some teachers punished her more than non-Jewish students, and she was bullied on the train to school in Debrecen. Kati, born in 1924, was more acutely aware of antisemitism and being called a "dirty Jew" as a child. She said her father would tell her that this was nothing compared to what their ancestors had gone through and that she should accept their destiny as part of G-d's will. Kati ascribed her lack of playmates and a social life in the town to being Jewish.

WHILE MÓR PREVIOUSLY had been exempt from any restrictions because of his World War I service, around 1926–1928, according to my mother, he lost his license to make alcohol. A Gentile challenged him. That man had the advantage of having a good lawyer and a telephone; Mór had neither.

Before then, Mór had made kosher wine, first dancing in his bare feet in the barrels of grapes from his seven acres of vineyards, and then fermenting the mash and distilling it to make *pálinka*, a strong fruit brandy. As he was the only one in town with the special machine used to make *pálinka*, villagers brought him debris from their own grapes to make into brandy for them.

Kosher wine was reserved for family and other Jews. Non-kosher wine for the tavern was bought from Tokaj or Debrecen, and hard liquor was also purchased and resold in the bar.

The only advantage of losing the distilling room was that the room, with its large stove, was converted into a bedroom for the twins. No one can remember where they slept before that happened.

Although antisemitism was growing in Germany in the mid-1930s and Jews were deprived of citizenship by 1935, the sisters said they were totally unaware of the threat. The first concentration camp, Dachau, was established in Germany in 1933.[3]

The 1938–39 period marked a turning point in worsening antisemitism in Europe. First came the Anschluss, in which German troops occupied Austria on March 12, 1938, and promptly incorporated the country into Germany, forcing it to adopt Germany's antisemitic laws.[4] Aryanization followed in Germany in 1938, whereby Jewish properties were taken or forced to be sold to Gentiles. Concentration camps were established in Austria in 1938. Kristallnacht, the "Night of the Broken Glass," occurred that year on November 9–10. Thousands of German synagogues and Jewish businesses were attacked and markedly damaged, and thirty thousand Jewish men were sent to concentration camps.[5]

The first signs of danger my mother remembered was the taking away of businesses from Jewish merchants. With this Aryanization, the Jews in Hungary became owners in name only and had to have a business partner who wasn't Jewish.

In May 1938, Regent Horthy passed more restrictions on Jews, limiting their participation in the professions, education, and even voting.

Jenö, Ella, Sanyi, and Miki Glattstein, May 28, 1940, Debrecen

In February 1939, Miki was drafted into the artillery. Later, however, Jews were no longer allowed to be in fighting units and were demoted to menial, tough, and dangerous work in forced labor battalions.

Over the next two years, Miki's younger brothers were also taken into the military, Sanyi into the artillery and Jenö into the army.

World War II began with the German invasion of Poland on September 1, 1939, followed by Britain's and France's declaration of war on Germany. Soon Poland was occupied and surrendered to Germany.

By the second half of 1939, Kati saw many soldiers coming through Sáránd. Mór's tavern became a busier and more popular venue.

The tavern had tables and chairs, in addition to a bar where men stood as the bartender poured their shots. There was hard liquor at the counter, a barrel of wine, and a machine to add carbonation to the wine and adjust its strength.

Mór's sons sometimes helped in the bar. Mór also hired a bartender, Jóska Szegedi, to work in the evenings and on Shabbos. Szegedi had lost a leg in a railroad work accident, so he sat on a stool behind the bar and measured the shots.[6]

Kati said the tavern smelled so strongly of tobacco and booze that she could detect the odor from the next room. (She was too young to be allowed into the tavern.)

Sometimes Gypsies came to the tavern and played music. Other times, the entertainment was provided by the bowling lane Mór and his sons had built in the back of their yard. Customers often got drunk and peed or vomited in the yard; poor Kati hated to have to go to the outhouse at night because of them.

One night the military customers were rowdier and more aggressive than usual. Kati said a "Hungarian captain . . . wanted to rape me. I was fifteen. I hid under the bed in the guest room. I crawled out the window to get into the hall" and get away from him. Kati heard their maid, Erdös néni, say to this captain, "Why don't you screw me? I'm here; she's just a child." Kati was terrified. The officer, who was staggeringly drunk, backed away after this challenge. This group of soldiers soon moved on, and Kati wasn't bothered by them again.[7]

IN 1940, the Germans had taken over other countries in Europe; Hungary formally allied itself with Nazi Germany.

CHAPTER 10

The Brother I Never Knew

ONCE, WHEN I WAS IN HIGH SCHOOL, I lamented my lack of breast development, as young girls do. Ma was climbing the stairs from the basement, carrying a basket of laundry, and I was standing at the head of the stairs, looking down upon her rounded form. I teased Ma that she was more amply endowed than I and asked when I would blossom into womanhood. Without catching herself, she blurted out, "Well, when you have had three children," and I startled. *Three?* I was shocked, knowing only about my one brother and myself. Who was this phantom child?

I pressed Ma for details, but as she so often had, she closed down and gave me no explanation of her comment. Only five or six years later, when I was in college and I pressed her again, did that wall of silence finally crack.

I wish I remembered more about how her unexpected revelation came about. I think I felt so bad about the hurt I had caused her then that I have repressed the memory. It was likely when I was a senior at Washington University in St. Louis. While they didn't often have a chance to visit each other, my mother remained close to Irén (Schwartz) Abrams, Jancsi's widow and one of her friends from *polgári*. She relished the opportunity to visit Irén and thank her for having helped me navigate being so far away from home.

On one of those visits, Ma and I sat in my tiny room in the tower dorm, on the floral coverlet she had sewn for me, surrounded by a plethora of small potted plants, echoing the plants she surrounded us with in our home. She began telling me her story, breaking down and crying as the memories tumbled out.

Ma confided that she must have been crazy, wanting to have a child in the early 1940s, knowing that her husband might well be killed in the war while he was in a forced labor unit. After all, the Jews were often sent ahead, like bomb-sniffing rats, to be sure an area was safe for the Hungarian soldiers. Her older brother, Józsi (József) had by then been blown up when he stepped on a landmine in Belogorye, Ukraine. By laboriously plotting timelines, I figured that she became pregnant while my father was home on a brief leave. Then, in March 1944, the Jews were forced into ghettos, and even in Debrecen, she had to move from one restricted area to another.

While in the ghetto, my mother saw two rabbis speaking with German officers. She couldn't hear them but found it remarkable that they were speaking like friends rather than enemies. One was the chief rabbi of the orthodox community, who had married her and Miki, Rabbi Salamon (Shlomo) Strasser. The other was much younger, Pál Weisz. She soon learned that both men and their families were allowed to go to Switzerland and freedom on the Kasztner train. Decades later, when visiting Pista's family in Israel, Ma saw that Weisz was teaching at the University of Jerusalem. She told me she wanted to spit on his name. She felt he had betrayed the community to save his own skin. Weisz later publicly claimed that he had no idea what the fate of the rest of the Debrecen Jews would be.

My mother said that she went into labor in the ghetto, and when it was time to deliver her baby, she was placed in a room with another woman in labor. They had no one to help them nor anything to ease the pain. Eventually, a doctor came to sew up the lacerations she sustained in long, hard labor. Policemen came to search everyone for valuables, but with the doctor's intervention, she was spared being strip-searched. She named her newborn József, after her beloved brother.

Even in these crowded, dirty ghetto conditions, a self-appointed rabbi appeared on the eighth day, wanting to perform the Bris, or ritual circumcision, on my brother, but my mother adamantly refused. "No way I will let anybody touch him because we don't know where we are going." The mohel was furious but retreated, being no match for a protective new mother.

A few days later, the ghetto dwellers were taken by a horse-drawn wagon to the Serly brick factory on the outskirts of the city. Baby József was in a small clothes basket, but the dilapidated building was full, so he and Ma were forced to stay outside, on the ground, with no protection from the wind and driving rain.

That day, sitting in my dorm room, my mother revealed that she shielded him with her body as best as she could, but her baby had developed pneumonia, and they had no medicine. So she moved to a secluded corner of the brickyard because she didn't want to be seen; József died in her arms, still sucking at her breast. She teared up as she told me about his tiny nails turning blue, and then his forehead, as she watched him die.

While she was holding him, a gendarme came over and said, "We're going. You have to go." She replied, "I want to stay with my baby," but he said no. So she covered her baby, put a note on him with his name, asking someone to bury him in the Jewish cemetery. The gendarme took the baby from her and she was forced to leave József in the brickyard.

The Palm Reader

Late in her life, I heard an unusual story from my mother. One day in 1944, Ma and Bözsi went to see a palm reader. The palm reader told my mother, who was pregnant at the time with József, that the child she was carrying would save her life. The woman was prescient: if Ma had arrived at Auschwitz with a newborn, she and the baby would have immediately been sent to the left, to the gas chambers.

She also recounted this story to Julia Frank, a psychiatrist friend, and gave Julia permission to share the details and her perspective with me. Julia told me she was impressed that Ma had found positive meaning in such a terrible loss, in seeing her child who died as someone who mattered and had made a difference in the world.

This story was also remarkable to me because the mother I knew was not known for being a glass-half-full kind of person.

CHAPTER 11

My Son's Birth

AFTER MY HUSBAND AND I MARRIED, I was driven to get pregnant as quickly as possible. My odds of getting pregnant were not favorable. A few years before, when I was in medical school, I went to an ob-gyn to have him check my irregular periods. The doctor, a Catholic, gave me a blood test—an incorrect test as it turned out, given my symptoms. Afterward, he told me I was likely infertile and should promptly tell anyone I was dating this news, implying, of course, that this fact lowered my value as a potential spouse.

I desperately wanted to have a baby for my mother, hoping that would ease her pain. While she never directly pressured me to have a child, I felt an unspoken expectation among Jewish mothers who seemed to live for grandchildren. Ma's sisters hadn't lost their husbands, and all of them had grandchildren they adored. I felt an unquestioning need to follow in my cousins' footsteps, and I was keenly aware that my biologic clock was ticking. I started my solo practice in Cumberland in 1983, and one year later, in 1984, I got married. Two months later I was pregnant.

The pregnancy was stressful due to my local obstetrician's archaic and paternalistic beliefs; he did not believe in natural childbirth. In prenatal classes, I was told that women were strapped down during delivery, which I found appalling. He described my pregnancy as "premium" because of my age and indicated his preference for a Caesarean delivery. I had a lot of trouble gaining weight during the pregnancy—the only time in my life that has been a problem—and I believe it was due to the stress of all he was telling me. In my second trimester, my obstetrician told me I asked too many questions and said that he would no longer see me and that I was not to see the cross-covering physicians. He instructed me to go out of town to deliver my firstborn.

I found a nearby family practice physician and midwife who would do home deliveries and made a backup plan with the hospital—although I warned the administration that if I had a complication and went to the emergency room and none of the OBs came to care for me (since my first obstetrician had asked them not to), the hospital would have an abandonment suit on their hands. The idea of a home delivery was not uniquely mine and reflected the caliber of local care. In fact, a female pediatrician, one of the other two physicians who delivered that year, also chose a home delivery. We did not make this decision casually, and the decision weighed on me, though ultimately I decided giving birth at home was safer than giving birth in the local hospital.

The last two weeks of my pregnancy required me to be on bed rest due to a complication that made me susceptible to infection. My pediatrician's group sent me a message that I risked child abuse charges for refusing an elective C-section and instead adopting close monitoring for any early sign of infection. I suspect it was my stubbornness (and perhaps something in my DNA) that kept me in town after these nightmarish experiences. I didn't want to succumb to defeat.

In the end, I delivered a healthy baby at home with a midwife and family practice physician in attendance. Like my mother, I had a difficult labor that carried from one early afternoon to the following morning, and I was not allowed so much as a Tylenol to diminish the agonizing pain. At one point early in the process, I got up and found my mother huddled surreptitiously on the stair landing, wanting to be with me but not wanting to incur my wrath, knowing I would have lashed out at her. From my teenage years on, whenever I was angry or frustrated with someone, she bore the

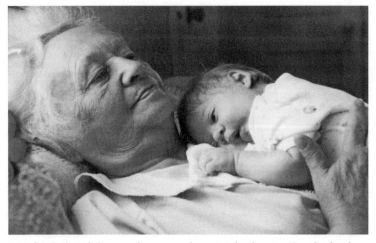

Magdus (73) with her newborn grandson, Michael, 1985, Cumberland

brunt of my (misplaced) anger. I knew, of course, that she would never abandon me.

And now I understand how my pregnancy and her hearing me scream during labor must have triggered memories of her own childbirth. A decade had passed since she shared her secrets with me, but after she had, she once again hid them away.

When my son was born, I felt some unspoken pressure not to break with centuries of religious tradition regarding ritual circumcision. However, my mother never pushed me on this. My cousin Ancsi told me the only time I had hurt him was when I did not invite him to a Bris or *pidyon ha ben* (a Jewish ritual for the redemption of the first newborn male). He was disturbed when I told him that it was because we had not observed either tradition. He never mentioned it again.

My husband, who had converted to Judaism before his prior marriage, strongly opposed circumcision, and ultimately I, too, refused to have a Bris, both because I could not bear to expose my child to any unnecessary risk or pain and because I wanted him to be able to hide that he was Jewish should the need arise.

Fear—an inherited legacy of the Holocaust.

CHAPTER 12

The Sáránd Ghetto

MARCH 19, 1944, was the day the Germans invaded Hungary—the day Kati and Mór knew they were in serious trouble, as the Hungarians welcomed the Germans as saviors. First, the town crier came to the town's square and announced that the Jews were subject to progressively more restrictive curfews. They were ordered to wear a yellow star on their outer clothes. Their valuables and radios were confiscated and eventually they were confined to their homes.

The Early Days

Before conditions in Sáránd worsened and the noose around the Ehrenfelds' freedoms tightened to house arrest, a neighbor girl of similar age, Juliska Rácz, occasionally came to keep Kati company and provide respite from the growing restrictions.

One day, Juliska suggested going to the movies. Even though they were mostly German propaganda films, the invitation offered a welcome change of scenery.

Kati recounted to me how she and Juliska walked to the theater arm in arm. Kati's yellow star, which by then all Jews had to wear to identify them, managed to become obscured, and this crime was reported to the authorities.

The next day, gendarmes came to the house and handcuffed and arrested Kati for going out without the yellow star, despite her tears and begging and Mór's stature in the community.

Kati (18), November 7, 1942

Kati and Mór were so obedient, they wouldn't have dreamed of breaking such a rule. But the gendarmes didn't believe Kati, so at the age of eighteen, she was taken and jailed in Derecske, a town five miles away, for two days.

Mór was able to send a message to their old housekeeper Zsófi néni, who was Mrs. Leitner's sister, and she took a bribe to the jailers and bought Kati's freedom, enabling the women to walk home to Sáránd together from Derecske.

Kati never saw Juliska again. Decades later, in 1985, when she returned to Hungary, she asked about her old neighbor and was told that the twenty-year-old had suddenly died "of "natural causes" right after Kati's arrest. It's clear that Kati doesn't believe that and suspects that Juliska's death was retribution for her consorting with Jews.

AFTER THE GERMAN OCCUPATION, food was rationed to all, but Jews received only half the ration because they were considered subhuman.

In March 1944, the Germans made Mór close his bar, and soon after, the store was forced to shut its doors. Mór had to give the officials the key to the store, and they sealed the area so he couldn't get in.

All the young men had to register with the authorities, and they were all taken to labor camps; only 10 to 20 percent of those young men survived the war.[1]

Even tiny Sáránd had its own Kristallnacht a few nights after the Nazis took over Hungary. In the town, the houses were right on the street, with only a narrow muddy lane where people walked on the edge of the dirt road, which was usually filled with animals and wagons. The Ehrenfeld home's windows opened right onto the street. One March night in 1944, people began yelling and throwing stones, and Kati and her father heard the sound of splintering glass as young Hungarian men shattered all the family's windows.

The next day, Mór boarded up the windows. From then on, he and Kati lived in almost complete darkness. From about March 21 until early in June, father and daughter did everything by the light of a faint kerosene lamp. Despite rationing, Kati recalled that Magdus sent her and their father matzoh from Debrecen with which to observe Pesach, which began on April 7 that year. Kati told me they almost felt relieved when they were taken from the town, likely around June 1–7, as best as I can piece together from the limited records I have found.

Hiding at Tóth Bácsi's

The night after Sáránd's Kristallnacht, the village hoodlums knocked on the boarded-up windows and door of the Ehrenfeld home. They yelled at Mór, "We brought the German soldiers, and you bring Kati out; the Germans want her." Of course, the Germans wouldn't have known that Kati existed unless they were guided to her by the young and very drunk Hungarians.

The German soldiers demanded that Mór fetch his daughter for them. All the while, Kati was shaking as she hid under the bed in the guest room, which had a bedspread that reached the floor.

Fortunately, Mór, who could speak German, was able to convince them that Kati was visiting her sister in Debrecen, even inviting them to come in and look. They finally gave up and left.

TÓTH BÁCSI WAS A GOOD FRIEND of Mór's and lived across the street from the family. He was an old man by that time, probably in his eighties. He was tall with an angular jaw and cheekbones, softened by his wavy steely gray hair and a bushy white mustache.

Mihály Tóth with daughter, and wife, Zsófi, 1930s, Sáránd

The widower used to cross over to the Ehrenfelds' every evening after dinner to pass the time with Mór and Kati. As they sat around the stove, Kati's task was to read him the editorials from the *Buda*, a newspaper. Mór was the only person in town who subscribed to the Budapest paper. Tóth bácsi would sit on one side of the stove and Kati would sit on the other side, reading to him. That's how they spent each evening, reading by the fire until it was time to go to bed, and then Tóth bácsi went home.

After the drunks came looking for Kati, she never dared to sleep at home. She and Mór were afraid that the men would return and next time not believe Mór. Until they were deported, every night when darkness fell, Kati walked across the street with her pillow and blanket—even though she was breaking the law by leaving her home—to sleep in Tóth bácsi's house.

Kati told me and Miklós in 2007 that she slept under Tóth bácsi's bed because he had only one bed in his small one-room house. The chickens were on one side of the room, sitting on eggs to hatch, and the bed was on the other side. The fireplace, where he cooked, was on another wall. Tóth bácsi's wife, Zsófi néni, had already died. The bed that the couple had shared was no wider than a single bed. The night Zsófi died, her husband woke up and found her cold. He wondered, "What can I do in the middle of the night?" Realizing there was nothing to be done, he simply went back to bed next to her and slept the rest of the night. The next day, he called the undertakers.

Kati left her blanket and pillow when she and Mór were taken out of Sáránd. Later on, Kati heard from her sister Magdus that Tóth bácsi said that he was waiting for Mór to return—that he could not die until then. He was very old and very weak by then, but he fought dying. Klari gave virtually the same description of Tóth bácsi's resolve.

The story about Tóth bácsi is one of Kati's favorites and one she always shares in her talks. She emphasizes to audience members that "I just wanted to show you that there were decent people, and there are still. I always believed there were good people in the world, despite all the horrors that happened to us."

Tóth bácsi died the summer of 1945, shortly after the sisters were liberated. Klari and Magdus recalled seeing him, a frail old man, still waiting for his best friend, Mór, to come home. He couldn't wait that long.

Kati was deeply moved by the fact that Tóth bácsi had jeopardized his life by offering her his home and hiding her. It would have been a certain death sentence for him if the authorities had found out. She desperately wanted him to be recognized by Yad Vashem (the World Holocaust Remembrance Center) for his courage and decency.

The lack of recognition for him and two others who had risked their lives to help her and her father weighed heavily on Kati's conscience. In July 2016, when Kati was ninety-one, I reached out to Yad Vashem as I did not have all the information I needed to fill out the online forms for Kati, who is not computer literate. Gili Diamant, Yad Vashem's reviewer, was kind and helpful with my submissions.

Diamant told me she watched Kati's Shoah Foundation testimony, which helped her prepare the submission to the Commission for the Designation of the Righteous. While she had warned me that the process would likely take months, Yad Vashem expedited this request, given Kati's age.

Mihály Tóth was posthumously awarded the title of "Righteous Among the Nations" in July 2017, a year after we began the process. Kati felt great relief as a huge weight was lifted from her shoulders. Helping Kati accomplish this recognition was a great honor.

Others in the Sáránd Ghetto

Even during this stressful and uncertain time, when Mór and Kati were under house arrest, Kati was still young and at times girlish. Always the romantic, she was affectionately known among the sisters for her frequent infatuations. Just as she had developed teenage crushes before the war, Kati again fell in love, as she embarrassedly confessed to my daughter and me.

As German soldiers were retreating from Russia, passing through Hungary en route back home to Germany, they dropped off the injured ones who couldn't travel, placing them in different homes along the way. In the spring of 1944, they commandeered the guest bedroom at the Ehrenfelds' for an injured officer.

This officer, Gunter, lived with the family for several weeks. He kept telling Kati and Mór not to worry—that the Germans were losing the war and it wouldn't last much longer.

The soldier was very kind and reassuring. Gunter had both leg and arm injuries and couldn't care for himself at all, so Kati and Mór attended to his needs. Kati used to clean the wound around his knee and change his dressing. She also cooked for him and fed the young man, sitting on the side of his bed. As the weeks passed, Kati found herself falling in love. The young couple promised they would meet in Düsseldorf, fantasizing about living happily ever after together.

Kati and Mór were happy to grasp at the promises of good news and to believe the war would soon be ending. Perhaps more

Denial

I have repeatedly asked Kati about her—and many other Jews'—deep level of denial, as it is one of the things that has been most difficult for me to understand.

As I neared the completion of this book, I discovered a helpful and accessible explanation of the psychological aspects of the Germans' strategy, including denial, resistance, and complicity. Dr. Peter Hayes's book *Why? Explaining the Holocaust* gave me a much greater understanding of the no-win situation the Jews were faced with.[3]

Hayes observes that Germans assigned Jewish Councils the task of carrying out their instructions. The "choiceless choices" led to cooperation, as the Jews played for time, even as they were pitted against each other and forced into increasingly untenable options.[4]

Another strategy the Germans employed was liquidation of the ghettos in a slow, staggered way, preventing the Jews (particularly in Poland) from recognizing what was happening. This also enabled the Germans to continue to deny that it was. Further, "the urge to grasp at straws of hope was powerful within the ghettos because mass murder seemed not just unimaginable but downright irrational. Why would the Germans kill people who could be useful?"[5]

Finally, Hayes notes that the Germans camouflaged what they were doing, even sometimes exempting ill or elderly Jews from deportation to deepen the illusion that the trains were taking people to work camps, rather than to their execution. This latter strategy was particularly effective with those who were young and unworldly, like Kati.

importantly, having the German officer in their home offered protection. It kept the Hungarians from harassing them, and Kati could stop going to Tóth bácsi's house to sleep at night.

Kati kept Gunter's address and name on a little piece of paper where he had written the information down before he left later that spring. She told me she still had it even when she was taken to Auschwitz. "I was holding the scrap of paper even while taking a shower at Auschwitz. . . . I remember seeing it going down the drain, thinking everything seemed so hopeless and desolate. There's no point. We became not even human."

AT FIRST, ONLY KATI AND HER FATHER, the only Jews in town, were confined to their home. A few weeks later, after Gunter left, the Germans started gathering the few Jews from nearby areas and made a ghetto inside the Ehrenfeld house.

Anyone who had a drop of Jewish blood or had married a Jew was forced into the Ehrenfelds' home. A wealthy widow, who came with her furs and jewelry, kept crying that she wasn't Jewish. But it didn't matter. Then there was the Leitner family, who lived on the far side of town. Mrs. Leitner wasn't Jewish, either, although her husband was. Their daughter, Ica, was Kati's age and was striking in appearance with her curly red hair, thick lips, and many freckles. The two girls became close friends.

CHAPTER 13

Kati's Friends

AS ANTISEMITISM WORSENED in Hungary, two old family friends offered to help Kati. One was Irén Szabo, who had grown up with Magdus in Sáránd, then married and moved to Debrecen. Irén offered to hide her friend's sister.

Just after Germany invaded Hungary, Mór arranged for Kati to go to Debrecen with someone taking goods to market. Kati hid in the back of the wagon among the chickens and produce. She took off her glasses and put on clothes and a headscarf like the *paraszt* (peasants) wore. A soldier stopped the wagon, lifted the canvas covering the back, and waved them on.

Kati stayed with Irén for a few days, hiding in a dark little room. She felt like she was imprisoned, only allowed out to go to a shared bathroom in the hallway. When one of the neighbors noticed Kati, Irén was afraid she would be reported, as hiding a Jew was as good as a death sentence. So Kati returned home, again hidden in a wagon.

Bözske Losonczi, a close friend who had been Magdus's apprentice in Debrecen, came down to Sáránd and offered Kati her ID papers. Kati was blondish and blue-eyed and was often mistakenly assumed to be Christian. Kati declined the offer, having decided that she would never leave her father again.

Károly Kövesdi

When Kati and Mór were under house arrest in Sáránd, Károly Kövesdi and a few others brought them food and comfort. In earlier days, the two ventured out for vegetables and milk. They bought milk from a neighbor, Lovasz bácsi. Kati would go over with her bucket and rag so that she could properly clean the udders of the cows to make the milk clean and kosher. Now, unable to milk the neighbor's cows or leave the confines of their fenced yard, they relied on kindly neighbors who would, on occasion, lower pails of fresh milk over the wall or pass eggs through gaps in the wooden slats.

Károly was a young man, a teacher in the town with four daughters of his own. He would collect money from some of the people who had bought their groceries from Mór on credit. (Other people felt they had no need to repay a Jew.) More important than the money or small amount of food that he brought was the solace. Early each evening he would visit, sometimes climbing over the wall at the back of the yard if they had not seen him coming. He sat with them, bringing news of the outside and encouragement. They would do crossword puzzles together and chat, and he would try to reassure Kati and Mór that the war would soon be over.

As a Jewish sympathizer, Károly was risking his life to help Kati and her father. When she returned to Sáránd in the 1980s, she asked what had happened to him. The townspeople told her that just after she and Mór were taken for deportation, Károly went to the cemetery and shot himself fatally. I wondered if this was because he was in love with her. Kati thinks not, but I'm not so sure as I think about how he tried to comfort her. Kati wonders whether he had been threatened for having helped the Jews or was distraught over their fate. Or perhaps the culture of "Gloomy Sunday"—named for the popular but melancholy 1930s song linked to a rash of suicides in a country that often had the highest suicide rate—caught up with Károly, as it had for so many other Hungarians.[1]

CHAPTER 14

Obedience

LIKE MOST JEWS, my family was unable or unwilling to see the warning signs of the approaching catastrophe. Kati made clear to me that many Jews had no idea of the hatred and cruelty that was soon to be unleashed upon them. They put their faith in German civilization and culture. Like German Jews, Hungarian Jews were highly assimilated, and they viewed themselves as Hungarians first and foremost. The majority no longer spoke or even understood Yiddish, the language common to many Ashkenazi Jews.

Every evening, Tóth bácsi visited Kati and Mór. After Kati read the newspaper aloud, they listened to the radio, hearing Hitler's voice and propaganda. Kati says there was no formal news of the antisemitism or the pogroms. Now and then, people, mostly those escaping Poland and trying to find their way to Palestine, stopped by the store. Mór hid one escapee from Treblinka so carefully that even his daughters were unaware. Whether because they were in deep denial or because they had heard so little news from outside, the sisters certainly were unaware of the magnitude of the growing threat.

With the advantage of hindsight, I am dismayed by my understanding of how staunchly they believed that if they obeyed the country's laws, they would be rewarded. To this day, Kati is haunted by an incident she remembers from the Nagyvárad ghetto. Guards chose Kati and her friend Ica Leitner to go to houses abandoned by the Jews who were already transported to Auschwitz to fetch the food left in the empty dwellings.

The Jews from Sáránd and surrounding villages were forced to walk, with their belongings on a wagon, to a larger town, Berettyóújfalu, centralizing the deportees from the *vidék* (countryside). From there, they were almost immediately transported to Nagyvárad, the next larger collection point en route to Auschwitz.[1]

When my family was deported from Sáránd, they were told what and how much to pack; they were allowed twenty kilograms (forty-four pounds) of food and clothing per person. They were able to prepare dried pasta, bake bread, and select other things to take with them.

In contrast, the two girls recognized that in the Nagyvárad ghetto, people had no such warning about when they were going to be taken away. They found it heartbreaking to see children's clothing scattered all over the floor, an isolated baby shoe in one corner, and a piece of bread, now molding, left on the table. "It looked like they were wakened in the middle of the night and taken from their homes. The sight of it, it still chills me," Kati recounted to me.

She recalls hearing noises up in the ceiling and telling the gendarmes guarding them about the sound. The policemen investigated and brought down two young Jewish boys who had been trying to escape. With great remorse, Kati told me, "I was so naive that I thought, 'Here they are. They're not obeying the law like we do.' If they tell us, 'You pack your things. You can take twenty kilos with you, and you will be taken somewhere,' we followed, absolutely blindly. I went back to the ghetto and told my father and he, in turn, told the other people. They all thought I was a hero because they thought, 'That's why things happen to us, because of some people not obeying the law.'"

More than anything, six decades later, she dwells on this and feels guilty, and hopes that those boys lived despite her unwitting betrayal.

UNTIL ACTUALLY DISEMBARKING from the packed cattle cars at Auschwitz, Kati and others believed the Nazi lie that all would be well. They were told to pack their best food and sturdy clothing to go to a work camp. They obediently followed the rules. Only after their arrival did they learn that they had been deceived.

CHAPTER 15

The Shoes

A WEEK HAD PASSED with the Jewish families packed into the Ehrenfeld home when the town crier again notified Kati and Mór to get ready to move.

By that time, Kati and her father weren't able to get out of the house except for two hours a day. They heard whispering and rumors that all the Jews would be taken "to work" because Germany needed laborers. They desperately wanted to believe that and welcomed the idea that they would be taken out of the country and would be safe.

Kati and Mór struggled to prioritize what little they might take with them, not knowing where they were going. They had to bring sturdy clothing and food, so Kati prepared noodles that could be dried, salty *pogács* (biscuits), and some potatoes. She wanted to pack all the tinned sardines from the store, as her father loved them, but he insisted that they leave some so that they would have something ready to eat when they returned.

While they wanted to believe that they would be safe, working somewhere in the Dunántúl (western Hungary), Mór and Kati worried. Mór decided to hide some money in the soles of his shoes. He had a close friend, Hagymási bácsi, a shoemaker, who went to their house on the Sunday afternoon before they were taken and removed the outer part of the shoes' soles, placed Mór's 5000 pengő in paper bills in each shoe, and stitched the shoes back together. He did this for his friend, despite knowing it could have meant a death sentence for him.

Doing this was also very much against Mór's law-abiding nature, but he told his daughter, "Who knows? Maybe it will buy a loaf of bread, and maybe it will save your life."

LATER, THE TRAIN DEPORTING THEM from the Nagyvárad ghetto north was stopped before passing the Hungarian border near Kassa (Košice), a crosspoint for the railroads. German soldiers opened the door of the wagon and told the deportees to surrender any valuables and that anyone found to be hiding anything risked being shot.

Mór and Kati hastily talked about their limited choice. What should they do about the money in the shoes? They decided to give it to the Germans. With some kind of pocketknife, Mór pried out the cash sandwiched in the soles of his shoes.

The rest of the people in their cattle car wagon were divided in their opinion as to whether what Mór and Kati had done was right or wrong. Some angrily blamed them for all of them being in trouble. They lashed out, feeling that if only everyone obeyed the rules, they all would have been safe. Other people were sympathetic. Mór handed the German soldiers the money.

The soldiers left, and a few hours later, they came back—carrying long loaves of French bread, likely enough for each person in that wagon to have a whole loaf for themselves. By that time, the prisoners were entirely out of the food they had brought from home. The soldiers also gave them water! Theirs was the only car that received food and water, and provision continued for the rest of their several-day journey.

Once the bread and water appeared, the other prisoners did a turnabout: Mór was great for doing this. What 10,000 pengő and a few loaves of bread had done for their morale on the arduous trip into the unknown.

AFTER LATER BEING SEPARATED from Mór and until long after liberation, Kati believed her father was alive and was haunted by the worry that he was cold every time it rained. It was always muddy in Auschwitz. She had visions of her father walking in the mud, his soles torn off of his shoes, suffering from the cold. She blamed herself, as he had disobeyed orders to protect her, and anguished over whether they should have done that. But she "could not believe that he could have been killed and he never needed the shoes."

CHAPTER 16

Bözsi and Tibi

IN BUDAPEST IN THE MID-1930S, Bözsi enjoyed a more active social life than she had been able to have in Sáránd or Debrecen, with more music and theater and dates with friends to the movies or soccer competitions. There she was introduced to Tibor Goldféder, a handsome young man with thick, wavy hair, dark eyes, and a quiet smile. The couple particularly enjoyed going to the swimming pools in Nagyerdö Park in Debrecen and the elegant, vast thermal pools at the Szechenyi Baths in Budapest, with its man-made sandy beach.

Everyone in the Ehrenfeld family liked Tibi. When Tibi approached Mór about marrying Bözsi, Tibi stressed that he didn't want a dowry. He felt they didn't need one, as he was working as a shoe salesman, Bözsi was sewing bras and corsets in a factory, and Mór still had three other daughters to marry off. That earned him considerable respect.

Sometime later, my mother recalled that the attractive young couple was like the Kennedys, and people would turn to watch them on the streets. She added that Bözsi's mother-in-law, Sári, wanted to exchange partners. She thought Magdus should marry Tibi because, while comparatively plain, Magdus "was good," and Magdus's own mother-in-law wanted the swap because Bözsi was beautiful and elegant, reflecting Ella's priorities of what she sought in a daughter-in-law.

Bözsi and Tibi wed in October 1939 in Budapest, with about fifty family members in attendance. Most of Bözsi's siblings were

Wedding of Erzsébet "Bözsi" Ehrenfeld and Tibor Goldféder, 1939, Budapest. Mór
is in the second row of adults on the left. (A little girl partially obscures his right
arm.) He is short and stocky and wearing a double-breasted wool coat and hat.
(Just behind his right shoulder is Pista, who is wearing a bow tie and bowler hat.)

there, but Kati and Józsi had to stay in Sáránd to run the store. In
the photo of the wedding, almost all the guests, men and women,
are wearing dressy suits and hats. My grandfather is standing erect,
wearing a heavy overcoat. This photo is the only one of Mór with
his children. He carried it in his coat's pocket to his murder at
Auschwitz.

Within a few months of marriage, Tibi was drafted into the
Munkaszolgálat (forced labor service). Deemed untrustworthy
to bear arms, as of 1940 Jewish men were drafted into specific
labor battalions where they were assigned to the lowliest, most
unpleasant support jobs for the army.[1] At first, like my father
and Sanyi, Tibi was allowed home for brief intervals between
deployments. Hungarian men were loath to use condoms, the
only form of contraception other than the rhythm method.[2]
Bözsi became pregnant but had an abortion, a common surgical
procedure in Hungary.

The Hungarian army allied with the Germans to fight the Russians. The Germans established a staging area in Voronezh, Russia, to help support their attack on Stalingrad.

Tibi was sent to the Eastern Front in 1942 to an area near the bend in the Don River, near Voronezh. This was not far from where Józsi, the only Ehrenfeld sibling to die in the war, was fighting at Belogorye and about 250 miles south of where Miklós was barely enduring.

By the winter of 1942, the laborers were starving to death and freezing. In Novij Gran Hresztiki, Voronezh, Russia, one of Tibi's guards shot and killed him for his warm clothes. Tibi was only twenty-nine.

Bözsi received a terse notice from the Hungarian Red Cross: "I regretfully inform you . . ." Tibi's brother, a detective, later tracked down his killer, who was tried, convicted, and hanged in a public square in Budapest.

CHAPTER 17

Bözsi in Auschwitz

BÖZSI WAS THE FIRST SISTER to be sent to the concentration camps, and she was there the longest. She never gave me details of her story personally; I gathered it by watching her Shoah testimony, listening to snippets from her sisters, and conducting research.

Within six months of Tibi's death, Bözsi became engaged to Pista's brother-in-law, a widower with two young daughters. Even in mourning, Bözsi was elegant in her tailor-made black dresses, but the German invasion of Hungary derailed her second chance at a normal life.

Unaware of the immediate threat from the Germans, Bözsi went on vacation along the Danube with some friends. On March 19, 1944, the very day the Germans occupied Budapest, she was arrested as she got off the train. A man she was with was also detained, but another friend escaped. Almost none of the hundreds caught up in this roundup knew why they were arrested and packed into large trucks. A few were Communists who worked in factories and actually wanted to be arrested to get an insider's view of what was happening in the country. They got more than they bargained for.

Bözsi, along with many others, was taken to Kistarcsa, a transit camp nine miles northwest of Budapest that had been used for "enemy aliens" and political prisoners before the war. They were locked into large rooms that were empty except for straw given to them for a thin bedding. Unlike at Auschwitz, those detained at Kistarcsa were allowed to keep the bags they had traveled with.

Bözsi thought that as the widow of a dead soldier, she would have special privileges, but she quickly learned how mistaken she was.

Bözsi was in the first group sent from Kistarcsa, on April 29, to Auschwitz, arriving with many Serbians on May 2, 1944. Two-thirds of the group failed the "selection" process on arrival that determined whether they might be able to work and live a bit longer or be immediately murdered. Further transports were delayed pending completion of a spur of the railway within Birkenau to an area that would allow more efficient use of the gas chambers for "extermination" and crematoria.

Bözsi's first memories of the camp were similar to those of her sisters: being greeted by yelling Häftlings (inmates) and watching Josef Mengele, an SS (*Schutzstaffel*) captain and physician, determine each person's fate with a flick of his whip. Bözsi, however, was most struck by the horrendous smell. When she asked what it was from, the guard said, "You don't want to know." The smell stayed with her day and night.

If you looked young and healthy, as Bözsi did, you had "the privilege of going to the right," to live at least for the time being. During the processing, Bözsi had to strip and be examined, and some Häftlings tattooed the number 80059 on her arm with a triangle underneath. By the time Kati and Magdus reached Auschwitz, the Nazis were in a greater hurry to kill Jews and didn't take the time to tattoo numbers on them to identify them after they died. The women in Bözsi's *csoport* (group) were also allowed to keep their hair.

They were taken to cheaply built barracks with triple-decker bunks, but each spartan bunk held seven or more women. The thousand women felt packed in like sardines. Bözsi recalled that the thin soup they received daily had a funny taste, which she later learned was "brome," used to suppress the women's periods. (Potassium bromide was likely the chemical used to stop the monthly bleeding.) Many women were frightened by the change in their bodies and the assault on their womanhood and feared that they had been sterilized.

Bözsi recalled that after being processed on that first day, she lost all hope and thought she would never survive. She added, "You just do whatever you have to. . . . You don't live just for one day at a time but for one minute at a time . . . in a place like that."

The next morning, Bözsi was assigned to help build the new railroad spur in the camp, which she did for some time.

Bözsi's *csoport* was used to trick the new arrivals. With their hair intact, their "normal" appearance kept the newcomers from becoming more frightened and rebelling as they came off the train.

The women in Bözsi's group also had to write postcards home to reassure their families that they were well treated and working in "Waldsee." This was a fictitious "woodland lake." The cards were used as a ruse to placate people and get them to cooperate when they were later being deported, believing they were joining their families.

After working to build the railroad, Bözsi was reassigned to work in Kanada, the sorting part of Auschwitz. All the clothes and baggage from the incoming prisoners were sorted to be sent back to Germany. The women found lots of jewelry sewn into the hems or shoulder pads of coats or in jars of jam or butter. One Wehrmacht (Nazi armed forces) soldier told the women that rather than turning in the gold, as they had been instructed to do, they should throw it into the latrine—as every piece of jewelry lengthened the war by a day.

Late in June 1944, Bözsi had a horrible vision, just as Magdus had when her brother József was blown up in Belogorye, Ukraine, in September 1942. She woke up screaming, having seen her father burning at the stake. The next day, while sorting clothes in Kanada, her friend found Bözsi's wedding picture in the pocket of a man's coat and recognized Bözsi. Her reassuring propaganda postcard from Waldsee was tucked in with her wedding picture, safely in the coat pocket. Bözsi's nightmare led her to presume that her premonition came almost exactly at the time her father was being gassed and burned.

Years later, Bözsi confided to Kati that she wondered all her life about how strong her father had been. When the gas chamber was opened, the victims were piled into a dome, where they had climbed on top of each other, trying to reach air. Bözsi wondered, "Was he on the bottom, or had he, too, clawed his way higher?"

My aunts and uncles never spoke of such gruesome details. I had always avoided reading or thinking about such specific details until I began working on this book. Now I frequently have nightmares about my family and the Nazis. I hope one day to be able to again repress these images, even as I hope to make vividly clear to those who read this book the reality of what individual human beings endured.

Bözsi's next assignment was horrific, as she witnessed what had happened within the gas chamber and then the "processing" of the bodies. She had to dig ditches to hold the mountains of ashes from the crematorium. To survive that, Bözsi told me she focused on the fact that maybe she would get a piece of bread after her terrible and terrifying work. She couldn't think about what she was doing or she would have gone mad.

The women who worked in Kanada were given slightly better rations than those in the rest of the camp. They also were able to eat some of the food they found hidden in the clothes they sorted. Bözsi recounted in her testimony that one of her friends, Regina Simsovits, was even able to sneak out small bits of gold in an oversized shoe and exchange that for food from some of the Polish civilian workers.

My mother later commented bitterly that those in Kanada had a comparatively good life because they had more food. Bözsi's son observed that Magdus and Bözsi had an ongoing rivalry their entire lives that extended to who had suffered more. Kati tells me she never noticed that their feuds included their suffering. She did tell me, however, that when Bözsi managed to sneak over to her part of the *Lager* (camp) just before Kati was to be transferred out, she looked "damned good" with her black wavy hair and relatively normal appearance in her uniform, in contrast to the bald, raggedly clothed women Kati and her camp mates had become. I never picked up on the deep rivalry between them until after my father died.

FROM KANADA, Bözsi was transferred, still within Auschwitz, to the Weichsel-Union-Metallwerke, an area where munitions were manufactured. She was supposed to check that parts of a revolver were working smoothly, but she didn't, hoping to sabotage the works.

Four other young women were more successful saboteurs, smuggling small quantities of gunpowder from the factory to workers in the camp's resistance movement. Hidden in scraps of fabric or paper stolen from Kanada, the explosive was passed on to the prisoners who worked in the crematoria, the *Sonderkommando*. On October 7, 1944, they revolted, attacking their SS guards and setting fire to Crematorium IV. Seeing the flames, the *Sonderkommando* in Crematorium II soon joined the uprising. The hundreds of prisoners from Birkenau who participated in the insurrection were captured and executed that day.[1]

The four women who smuggled the gunpowder were arrested and tortured. On January 6, 1945, these saboteurs were hanged in front of the camp women. Bözsi was horrified as they were all forced to watch until the bodies stopped moving from the wind before they were allowed to return to their barracks. This scene was one of her most vivid and disturbing memories and became one of mine after watching her taped testimony and reading about this episode in history books.

BÖZSI'S COMMANDING STYLE persisted to the end. In her Shoah tape, after a disturbing exchange in which she tells the interviewer that Miki and Sanyi were in a camp where "they ate, they gnawed on bones . . . human bones," when the interviewer asks, "To survive, they chewed on human bones?" Bözsi abruptly tells the interviewer to ask another question: "Next one. I'm the boss."[2]

THE NAZIS KNEW they were losing the war and that the Russians were approaching. They didn't want to leave the prisoners behind, so on January 17, 1945, anyone who could walk was evacuated from the camp.[3] They mostly walked in the snow in the freezing winter weather. Occasionally they rode in open freight car wagons. Bözsi recounted being horrified to see blood in the snow from prisoners who were shot for trying to steal a potato from the ground or those simply unable to keep up.

Bözsi told her Shoah Foundation interviewer that her group of prisoners marched through Mannheim, Germany, during the bombing on March 2, when three hundred British Royal Air Force bombers attacked the city, causing a firestorm. Bözsi said she enjoyed these fireworks and hoped she would be struck, but she was spared.

The women were taken to Ravensbrück, but there was no room for them to be left there, so they kept traveling. Bözsi became so weak that she wanted to give up, but two young women saved her by urging her on and carrying her part of the way.

The next place they came to on this death march was Mohlhof, Germany,[4] which they reached on April 1, Bözsi's father's birthday. For a month they stayed in the woods, sleeping on the ground and eating grass or anything else they could find.

Hearing Bözsi's story, I have a little better understanding of her later cold, harsh personality and am more sympathetic to her. While I liked her the least of my aunts and was afraid of her sharp tongue, I am amazed that she was able to survive, reunite with her family, and go on to have a full and relatively normal life.

ON APRIL 30, a beautiful sunny day, the surviving twenty-seven young Hungarian women reached the Mulde River at Russian-occupied Grimma, Germany, near Leipzig. The other side was American-occupied, and the SS asked them which way they wanted to go, whom they wanted to be liberated by. Having heard about the Russians' reputation for rape, they opted for the Americans.

A makeshift bridge reached halfway, then the Americans made a rope ladder that they managed to get to the prisoners. Bözsi weighed only sixty-six pounds by then, but the women helped push each other up this ladder to the "beautiful Americans."[5]

Although the women were cadaverous, filthy, and lice covered, the soldiers were wonderfully kind to them, giving them clean clothes, bedding, medical care, and a modest amount of food. The women were angry they couldn't have more, not understanding then that being fed too much too quickly might kill them.

From Grimma, the women were sent to what was once "an SS recreation place" to recover some strength. They still felt hungry all the time. As they regained health, an enterprising young Yugoslav woman, Adele Moskovits, decided that they should work as fortune-tellers. Armed with cards, they would tell the local German women that they knew their husband was in the service: "He's on his way home now and is on the far side of the river"—always the same type of story. The gullible German women believed them and rewarded them with bacon, sausage, bread, or even gold for bringing them good news.

Through Sanyi, Bözsi was able to learn where Kati was—at the American air force base in Fritzlar, Germany—and soon joined her sister.

CHAPTER 18

Mór and Kati Reach Auschwitz

THE TRAIN CARRYING KATI and her father arrived at a railroad station in Poland late in June 1944. The first thing they saw was a massive iron gate with a sign on it: *"Arbeit macht frei"* (Work Makes You Free). Finally, they thought, they had arrived at the place where they had been promised they would work. They still believed all would be well. The doors of the wagon were opened, and they felt a welcome rush of fresh air.

Sign at entrance to Auschwitz, "Work Makes You Free" (photo by Dnalor_01, Wikimedia Commons, CC-BY-SA 3.0)

In the next moment, Kati and Mór's sense of reassurance was shattered. A sudden swarm of skinny, unkempt young men in striped uniforms screaming, "Los, rasch, los." (Come on, faster!)

They were the infamous *Kapos*, prisoners who were appointed to supervise lowlier inmates. Hardened Polish Jews incarcerated already for many years, they received more privileges than ordinary prisoners and were known for their cruelty and brutality toward other prisoners. The Kapos carried leather straps in their hands, and they would lash at the new arrivals if they didn't move fast enough.

The newcomers were told to form rows of five, the women in one line, and the old people and children in another. The suitcases and parcels had to be left on the train, and the prisoners were told they would get their belongings later. At first, Kati was sandwiched between her father and another girl from Sáránd, Ica Leitner, and her parents.

A German officer in a uniform with snow-white britches stood on a platform. Beautifully groomed, he was the very antithesis of his new prisoners. German shepherd dogs were at his side, and he held a whip ready in his hand. Only later did Kati learn that this was Josef Mengele, soon to be known as the "Angel of Death."

Mengele, tall and handsome and wearing his immaculate uniform, directed the arrivals with his whip, pointing this way and that. He motioned for Kati and Ica to go to the right and for Mór, Ica's parents, and a younger girl from Sáránd to go to the left. Kati and Mór embraced and kissed as tears poured down their faces. Kapos rushed to the scene, striking them. Shoving Kati toward the right, they taunted her, "You want to go with him? So go." In that moment Kati believed that wherever fate pointed her was the right way. So she didn't go with her father.

The men were segregated from the women, and then they were separated by age. The young people, healthy enough to work, went to the right, allowed to live for another day. The older people, very young people, babies, and mothers with children were sent to the left, to be murdered in the gas chambers, though at that time no one knew what would happen to them.

Kati kept looking at her father—and at all the old people—the mothers holding their babies, and little children hanging on to them.

Reeling with shock, nobody dared to yell or disobey the orders of the Kapos. Most of the women stood sobbing in disbelief, while the Kapos lied smoothly, "You will see them on the weekend" or "They're going to the family camp and you're going to work because you're young. But you will see them." Kati and the other new arrivals still wanted to believe the promises. They couldn't imagine that one day they would look like the skeletons surrounding them.

As the women were marched away, leaving all their belongings, Kati thought again of the sign at the entrance: "Work Makes You Free." That played on her naiveté, and in that moment, she summoned up the hope that all would still be fine.

The women marched to a cavernous room where they were forced to strip and were shaved by *Häftlings*, female Kapos. These women were bitter toward the arriving Hungarian Jews, as they themselves had already endured Auschwitz for years. Looking for valuables, the *Häftlings* even searched all of the women's body cavities.

Even then, the young Hungarian women were deceived. They were told to put their clothes in a pile and to remember where they had left them. They were to tie their shoes together so they could find them after their shower. The shorn, naked women entered another room, and some of them whispered that there would be gas coming from the showerheads. Kati still believed that people are inherently good and that such a thing couldn't possibly happen. In fact, unlike some of the new arrivals, they did indeed get a shower with cold water, which felt wonderful after their arduous journey in the boxcars. When they got out, however, their clothes were nowhere to be found.

Instead, they found a heap of dirty rags and some wooden shoes, which were thrown at them to don. They had no underwear.

Then the women were disinfected and herded to their barracks while being constantly beaten by the Kapos.

When the young women looked at each other, they cried. All of them were bald. They were hardly able to recognize each other and were humiliated by the lack of privacy. Kati felt "ripped beyond any humanity." They had been reduced to animals "or worse."

Herded along to their new home, all they could see were miles and miles of barracks of every size. Everything was a drab gray or brown. Not a speck of green, nothing growing, could be seen.

But a species of creature seemed to be everywhere—but they were really not like people. At first, Kati couldn't figure out what these creatures were. They resembled walking skeletons much more than human beings. The new arrivals never believed that one day they would look like them. It was all beyond comprehension.

Kati's barracks was vast and barnlike and had been quickly built out of wood to accommodate the new wave of prisoners. It had no windows and only a dirt floor. Earlier barracks had bunks. There might have been twenty people to a bunk, but they were elevated and at least gave the appearance of a normal bunkhouse. Now one thousand Hungarian Jewish women between the ages of eighteen and forty were shoved into this makeshift space, forced to lie on bare dirt or mud, with nothing to protect them from the elements. The rain felt incessant; the ceiling leaked.

The women were given a tin dish to use for their meager rations. The same bowl served as their pillow when they didn't need it as their waste bucket at night. They were not allowed out to use the ditch behind their barracks, which served as their daytime latrine.

During the day, the women were not allowed into the barracks. Except during the roll calls, which lasted hours, and lining up for their soup and evening ration, the women wandered within their compound or sat in the dirt or mud, talking. No work assignments were made for these Jews who arrived relatively late in the war.

That first night in Auschwitz was also the first time Kati heard someone die. These thousand women from the *vidék* (countryside) were too cramped to lie down, so they sat on the dirt floor, falling over on top of each other as they dozed off. Kati heard somebody next to her moaning. After a bit, the sound stopped, and somebody announced that the woman had died from diabetic shock. They added her to a line of bodies outside. Then they tossed her body onto a cart piled with corpses pulled by the Jewish Kapos. Kati saw a leg, an arm, a head hanging down off these makeshift wagons. That ghastly sight, Kati's first experience with death, soon became an ordinary, daily event. Some bodies—for example, when someone touched the electrified wire—lay where the person died until the collection wagons came along. After a while, the women became numb to what they were seeing. Kati was sustained by the belief, beyond all logic, that her father was still alive, though she is now puzzled as to how she might have thought so.

CHAPTER 19

Grandfather Mór's Death

ONE OF THE MOST POIGNANT STORIES about my grandfather is that of how his daughters learned of his murder. I am not certain when I first heard about it. I believe it was in 2001 when I was visiting Klari the year before she died. I do know for sure that Kati told Miklós and my daughter, Heather, the story on New Year's Day 2008 when they were taking a break from visiting my mother's bedside in the hospital, and I heard it that day as well.

Kati told us that on arrival at Auschwitz, everyone went through an immediate "selection," where Mengele, in impeccable white britches, directed people to go to the left or to the right with his whip. Pregnant women, children, the elderly, and the disabled were all sent to the left, to immediate death in the gas chambers and the crematoria. Those young and hardy, like Kati, were chosen for a slow death from starvation, disease, and working in the concentration camps.

At sixty-five, younger than I am now, Mor was doomed, as "old" people and others failing Mengele's selection were considered expendable parasites on society. But Kati and the other prisoners did not know that. They were told the elders were being sent to watch the children while their parents or older siblings worked and that they would see each other on weekends. The murders were a well-kept secret, except to those who worked the killing machines, and when there were inklings of the truth, no one could believe the horrors.

Kati was unaware that Bözsi and Magdus were also imprisoned in Auschwitz when she arrived there.

Although they were all at Auschwitz, Kati and Magdus didn't know of their father's death until after the war, when Kati was working at Fritzlar air base in Germany in 1945, almost a full year after Kati and her father's arrival at Auschwitz. Bözsi—who knew her father's fate—had learned that Kati was at Fritzlar and went to join her.

Bözsi and Kati, circa 1945, Zennern

Kati, revealing the power of denial, recalled, "I remember being very proud of the fact that I was saving food for my dad, if you can imagine how naive I had to be that I thought he was still alive. He loved sardines, and the Americans just showered us with care packages besides our regular food. I always saved my sardine cans, and I had a stack of them in the closet. I was so proud of it, and I said [to Bözsi], 'Look, this is what I'm saving for dad.' And she looked at me like I was crazy and she said, 'Oh my little sister . . . Don't you know that he is dead?'"[1]

Then Bözsi showed Kati the priceless wedding picture that she had miraculously managed to save through Auschwitz and the death march.

Magdus learned the truth that December when she reunited with her sisters in Germany. None of the sisters know the date of their father's death. Not knowing when to observe a Yahrzeit and say Kaddish, the ritual prayer of remembrance for the dead, has increasingly troubled and saddened me, especially in the past few years since I have regularly attended services in Lancaster, Pennsylvania. My aunts and uncle never mentioned this, nor do I remember lighting a candle for their mother or sister. I only remember a Yahrzeit candle for my father. Survivor Manya Friedman expressed a longing familiar to me after she discovered a grave in Savannah, Georgia, that contained the ashes of some Holocaust victims and was covered with pebbles (a sign of remembrance in Jewish tradition). She noted, "At least their ashes are buried where one can come and pray for their souls" when she could "only envision the smoke from the chimney rising toward the sky and a handful of ashes from the ovens of Auschwitz scattered around in the fields and blown away by the wind. . . . How can I put a pebble on the headstone in the air?"[2]

Kati, too, is understandably bothered by not knowing when her dad died. I have tried to fill in gaps for her and have been extremely frustrated at my inability to find records. I have spent hours trying to puzzle out this information with no luck. I have made timelines, but the sisters' hazy recollections of the exact dates when they were being marched and transported do not exactly reconcile with published data, and even those records are occasionally inconsistent. I checked records of transports from Nagyvárad and the "Kassa train" records of all the trains that passed through that checkpoint.[3] I have corresponded with the USHMM (United States Holocaust Memorial Museum) and the International Tracing Service in Bad Arolsen, a German records repository, all to no avail. I find it maddening—infuriating—that the Germans, such notoriously meticulous record keepers, have no records of him or my cousins or millions of others. They didn't count. They weren't human.

I believe my grandfather was killed on July 29, 1944, or within a few days before. Although I never knew him, it still matters to me. At the only synagogue that has ever felt like home to me, Congregation Shaarai Shomayim in Lancaster, Rabbi Paskoff always has the entire congregation rise to recite the Mourner's Kaddish together for those who have no one left to recite the Kaddish for them—a reminder, too, that we are all one people and that we must remember all those whom the Nazis tried to erase. We must never forget.

CHAPTER 20

Magdus's Arrival at Auschwitz

MY MOTHER AND OTHERS being transported from the ghetto still had suitcases holding their most durable clothes, as they had been instructed to pack for work camps.

In late June 1944, after the gendarmes tore my mother's newborn from her arms, she and the others in the brickyard ghetto were herded onto crowded cattle cars. Magdus was with some doctors and the woman with whom she had shared a room during childbirth.

The woman had no diapers for her son, so Magdus tore up the eyelet tablecloth she had embroidered for her trousseau into diapers for this woman's son, as her own baby wouldn't need it.

Sixty or seventy people were crowded into a hot, closed cattle car in Debrecen, filled with the stench of their ripening urine, stool, vomit, and sweat. They were crammed together so tightly they were unable to lie down or stretch out. They had one bucket of drinking water for everybody and one bucket to use as a toilet. At first, they held up a blanket when someone had to use the toilet; later, they no longer cared about modesty. They instead used the blankets to cover the growing number of dead. The German guards occasionally opened the locked door, threw out the corpses, and gave them a new bucket of water.

High in the wagon there was a tiny window, covered with wire. The doctors, who were well-traveled, peeked out and recognized that they were not going to western Hungary, where they had been told they were being sent to work, but were heading north, through the Czechoslovakian mountains.

They traveled that way for several days, with no food and scant water, despite the summer heat.

On July 1, 1944, the doors were flung open, and they, too, saw the now famous sign "Arbeit macht frei" and a clump of German SS and Kapos awaiting their arrival at Auschwitz.[1] My father's older brother, Jenö, was the first to step out into the half-light. The newcomers heard piercing screams, shouts, and the snarling of dogs.

The SS and Kapos chased everybody out of the boxcars. Selection by Mengele followed. Jenö and my grandmother Ella were sent to the left, to be gassed and burned the same day, as my grandfather Mór had been. Magdus was selected to go to the right. She never saw her in-laws again.

As Magdus walked with the other young women in rows of five, she heard beautiful music and thought perhaps all the musicians in Europe were gathered there playing for them.[2] In truth, Jewish musicians were forced to play for the new arrivals to lend an air of normalcy and improve their compliance—but then came the dogs and the guards and the whips, breaking their momentary reverie and making them move more quickly.[3]

Magdus and the other new arrivals marched from Auschwitz I two miles to Auschwitz II-Birkenau, where they were warehoused. Birkenau had different sections, including the infamous gas chambers and Kanada (the sorting area) and other areas housing Roma (Gypsy) families and those from the Theresienstadt ghetto.[4] These were separated from the barracks where Magdus and Kati were by gates and guarded checkpoints. Kati said the women had to walk back weekly to Auschwitz I to have their blankets and bodies deloused.

When they arrived in a processing building, Magdus said she needed a pad for her postpartum bleeding. The guard said, "Oh, you will have it. Take off everything now." Magdus took in the scene unfolding before her eyes and muttered under her breath, "We need only a number painted on our forehead to be like cows" in a slaughterhouse.

As others before them, this *csoport* of women was stripped, shaved of all their body hair, and then thrust into the shower. Going out, they were told they could keep their shoes and eyeglasses but none of their clothing. They were handed clothes from a pile, and Magdus was given a ragged black wool dress that reached the ground and was so tight she could barely walk in it. Magdus begged the Kapos for a different one and was sent back to the collection of clothing, where she was handed a beautiful white dress decorated with a blue pattern. When she put it on, the woman giving it to her commented that she must have been beautiful in her previous life.

Screaming SS guards marched the women to Birkenau, urging them along with rubber whips and dogs. Magdus was assigned to barracks in Lager 8, Block 7, but there was nothing but the floor to sit or lie on. The fetid odor of the barracks, from the nearby latrines and the unwashed bodies of the women crowded together, was intense.

As the women huddled on the floor, a Kapo came and explained that whenever they heard a whistle, they should immediately jump up and do whatever they were told to do.

The women were parched. In the absence of drinking water, some women begged Magdus to allow them to drink the milk that continued to drip from her breasts to ease their thirst.

Magdus and her fellow inmates didn't have enough space to fully lie down and slept halfway on top of each other. They were awakened in the middle of the night with a whistle in the dark and forced to stand for *Zählappell* (roll call) for hours, five to a row.

The new inmates didn't receive a meal until the following day. Their rations were some black water that was passed off as coffee for breakfast, a thin watery soup with a few strands of grass or leaves for lunch, and a slice of dark coarse bread that tasted like sawdust, along with a piece of bologna, wurst, or margarine, at night. Rumors were that the meat and vegetable spread came from the Red Cross. The women treasured that solitary piece of bread and rationed it to last for at least a full day. That scant portion was their sole allotment of food and water for the day. Magdus said it was "not enough to live on but not enough to die. It kept us going, or at least alive."

CHAPTER 21

Finding Family at Auschwitz

NOT ONLY WERE THE NEW PRISONERS stripped of their clothes and hair, along with their dignity, they were also stripped of any vestige of individuality and reduced to bald, numbered women, each one dressed in dirty rags. They were barely recognizable to each other.

Daily new transports reached Auschwitz, and the women would rush to the fence, yelling to the new arrivals, "Where are you from?"

After about a week in camp, Kati learned that her oldest sister, Magdus, was there. Another prisoner who had been an apprentice in the orthopedics shop with Magdus spotted Kati at the latrine and told both sisters the heartening news that the other was nearby. At the time, the sisters didn't appreciate how important that chance encounter was. They—especially Kati—were simply grateful. I don't think my mother cared about anything at that point in her life; she was so devastated by the death of her newborn, József. He was also the reminder of her beloved brother's death and her last hope that if something happened to Miki, she would at least have his child.

While doing research for this book, I learned that sometimes having a parent or sibling with them was even more traumatic for survivors, as seeing their loved one's suffering could be more painful than experiencing their own. More often, though, those connections were a lifeline, giving them something and someone to live for. Years later, my mother and Kati both said that having each other was the greatest thing that could have happened to them at that desperate time, and that it was critical to their survival.

Once she knew her sister was also in the camp, Kati was determined to find a way to be with her, although moving from one barracks to another was strictly forbidden. Ignoring the danger, Kati sneaked into Magdus's bunkhouse and was stunned to see her older sister bereft and weak. That is when she learned that Magdus had just lost her newborn son.

Returning to her own barracks, Kati begged her friend, Ica, to join her in moving in with Magdus, but Ica, not wanting to challenge her fate, insisted on staying where she had been assigned and implored Kati not to leave.

Kati cried, "I can't do that! She's my sister."

Kati was able to slip into Magdus's barracks because the Germans couldn't possibly keep track of all the individuals, and another woman agreed to swap places with her. Prisoners were dying left and right so at roll call, the German soldiers just counted numbers.

Though torn by her earlier pledge to stay with Ica, Kati knew that she had to look after Magdus. As she later told me, "All of a sudden, here I'm twelve years younger, and I became the mother; Magdus became the child."

What she could not have known was that by this act of compassion for Magdus, she had saved her own life. When she returned to check on Ica in their original quarters, she found nothing; overnight the barracks had been emptied. A thousand Hungarian Jewish women vanished without a trace, presumably up in smoke. And so it was that while Kati's decision saved herself, she inadvertently caused the death of the woman with whom she had changed places. She mourned the loss of Ica and forever felt burdened that another woman had died in her place.

Kati tried to take care of Magdus as best she could. Once a day, a water tank, pulled on a cart by prisoners, would come through the camp. Thousands of people brawled to get a drop of the precious fluid. Kati, who had never been aggressive, found herself fighting for water to save her sister. One time, she came back from her foray bloodied and frantic because a Kapo had struck her face and she had spilled most of the water intended to sustain her sister. Kati emphasized the fact that "whenever I was hit, it was by one of us [a Jew, her *elteste* (head of her barracks), or a Kapo]. I was never hit by a German." She stressed this to say that anyone, even fellow Jews, could be turned into evil monsters under the right circumstances. Power, fear, and anger corrupted them.

Magdus's Beatings

Even in the midst of these impossible conditions, Magdus's friends from Debrecen rallied around her in support.

The prisoners' toilet was a massive hole in the ground, with a wooden plank on top, behind the barracks. There was widespread diarrhea and some bloody dysentery among the inmates, who needed to use a waste bucket in the barracks at night. The stench was unbearable. Epidemics were fueled by the inmates' inability to wash their soiled hands.

A slow moving trickle of fluid was present in one corner of the Lager, with a gray film covering it so thickly no one could see that there was water underneath. Some of the prisoners who had been there longer warned newcomers not to touch or drink the liquid, that it was poisonous. But some of the women, desperate for any fluid, still tried to drink it. Only later did they learn that this stream was coated by the ashes of those who had been cremated.

One early morning, Magdus had to use the latrine. As she was squatting over the trench, a Kapo suddenly started raining blows at her back until she could barely move. She developed a fever and was so sick that she simply wanted to die. Friends dragged her to the *Zählappell* because anybody who failed to report for roll call was killed.

A couple of days later, the women were taken to a shower. When the female SS guard saw Magdus's badly bruised back, she beat her some more on the assumption that she had to be "guilty of something."

Several of Magdus's friends, including schoolmate Ella (who later married brother Miklós), formed a protective shield around Magdus to hide the sight of her bruises from Kati, who would have been even more distraught to learn her sister had been abused.

The *Zählappell* was a twice-daily form of torture, beginning with reveille at 4:00 a.m. Each time, the women were forced to stand for hours on end to be counted, whether it was raining or scorching hot, wearing only rags for clothes and shoes, and with empty bellies. If somebody collapsed, the guards beat her. Magdus was able to endure because she was young and had been in excellent physical shape beforehand. She attributed her survival, in part, to her strict upbringing and endless chores from her demanding mother.

All the sisters held onto the hope that they would see their father again and that their nightmare would someday end.

WHILE IN AUSCHWITZ, most of the women did not have assigned jobs, and when not standing in roll call, they wandered about aimlessly in their fenced yard. Now and then—to get out of the confines of the barracks for a short while—they volunteered to work. On the road, some of the women called out to men who were working, digging trenches, and they learned from them of other nationalities imprisoned as well.

Magdus and Kati wondered what had happened to their father and why they hadn't seen him as had been promised. Other young women brooded about their parents as well. A young Czech *elteste* who had been imprisoned since she was twelve brutally informed them that their elders had been killed and burned and had gone up in smoke. The sisters were immobilized in disbelief; it was unimaginable that human beings could treat other human beings in such a way.

Magdus and Kati Find Bözsi

Magdus and Kati had no idea what had happened to Bözsi after she disappeared without a word in March 1944. One day they unexpectedly saw their sister walking in the distance, a shovel balanced on her shoulder. Magdus later said that Bözsi still had her long, wavy black hair, which allowed Kati and Magdus to immediately recognize her, and was wearing a beautiful blue polka-dot dress; Kati remembered seeing a blue kerchief around her neck, although Magdus didn't recall such an item.

Bözsi was housed in a different section of the camp, seemingly having been arrested initially as a political prisoner. Some of those women were allowed to keep their hair so that the new arrivals on the transports would be less frightened and more compliant upon seeing more normal-appearing women.

The sisters started shrieking, "Goldféder Bözsi, Goldféder Bözsi!" Bözsi turned her head at the sound of her name. She saw two shorn scarecrows wearing a gray blanket and she stared blankly at them, without any sign of recognition. "But we knew her," Magdus later said. "She walked like a queen."

CHAPTER 22

The Night of the Gypsies

THE GYPSIES OF AUSCHWITZ, who lived together as families and worked at the gas chambers, pulling out bodies, had been prisoners in the death camp for years. Unlike the Jews, unwitting about their impending fate, the Gypsies knew what happened to people. And then their turn came.

Usually, the Jews had to be outside their barracks all day, no matter the weather. On August 2, 1944, they were suddenly confined to their barracks.

That night, the Gypsies were rounded up on the orders of Reichsfuehrer SS Heinrich Himmler and taken to be gassed. Piercing screams of "Hilfe. Hilfe" (Help. Help) and "Bitte, Gott, hilf uns" (Please G-d, help us) awakened the sisters. Despite the chilling, agonized cries of people begging to be saved, nobody went to help. Nobody could.

The women looked out from their barracks and, not far from them, saw the whole sky lit by fire from the flames of the burning bodies that had been thrown into an adjacent pit.

Kati can still see the intensely red and yellow flames rising so high that they seemed to reach the sky. That was the night that they burned the Gypsies.

Inside the barracks, the smell of burning flesh and hair was overwhelming. "They are burning, they are burning people," the women kept repeating in shocked tones. Only the fervent hope that her father still lived kept Kati from accepting what was going on around her. But she still couldn't imagine that anyone could do this to people. She desperately wanted to believe that her father and others were fine.

The horrifying smell and anguished screams remained vivid to all three sisters for the rest of their lives.

CHAPTER 23

Another Selection, Another Separation

KATI CARED FOR MY MOTHER for about nine weeks while they were together at Auschwitz. She was encouraged to see Magdus getting a little stronger emotionally under her loving care and surrounded and shielded a bit by other friends and classmates from Debrecen. Kati was buoyed at having been together with her sister and having seen Bözsi in passing as well.

One day in August 1944, the women were told to form a line to go again to the baths for disinfection. The Germans were fanatic about hygiene and disinfected regularly in an attempt to keep epidemics down in the camps. The women were forced to walk the two miles from Birkenau to Auschwitz almost weekly to be deloused.[1]

Kati spotted Bözsi on one such occasion. Kati was walking one way and Bözsi the other, and Bözsi was able to throw her sister a little packet with treasures—a comb, a pocketknife, a hankie, and even a needle and thread that she had scavenged in Kanada.

In mid-August, just before they were to go for another selection, Magdus sent Kati off with her own portion of bread for the day, with the threaded needle gifted from Bözsi hidden in it. Kati wonders now if maybe Magdus suspected she wouldn't pass the selection to be sent to work, so she gave her sister her piece before they were examined.

For the selection, the women had to parade naked in front of a German doctor or nurse to be examined for their fitness to work.

LATE AT NIGHT, a sharp-eyed female German officer noticed that Magdus had milk leaking from her breasts, so she was immediately yanked out of the line. Kati, behind her in the queue, fell apart. How would Magdus survive without her? Kati was devastated.

BÖZSI HEARD THROUGH THE GRAPEVINE that there would be a selection and then a transport, transferring a group of women from Auschwitz to work camps, and that Kati was going to be transported out. Bözsi's *elteste* allowed her to try to visit Kati but urged her to not let on what barracks she was from.

Bözsi, a daredevil even as a child, marched through the lagers from Birkenau determinedly and almost defiantly, as though she was on a mission. None of the soldiers stopped her as she passed through multiple gates. When she reached Kati, showering before her transport, many of the women from Debrecen recognized Bözsi, although she didn't recognize them, since they were bald. Bözsi and Kati cried about Magdus, fearing that she had been killed after being sent back.

PIECING THIS TOGETHER from stories the sisters told me over the years, I learned that soon after Bözsi's visit, Kati left on a work transport to Allendorf, Germany. After bidding her young sister farewell, Bözsi returned to her Lager.

Surprisingly, Magdus, too, was sent from Auschwitz to a work camp, though Kati and Bözsi assumed she had been killed when she was discovered to be lactating.

Bözsi remained in Auschwitz until the end of the war.

ON THE TRAIN CARRYING HER and the healthier young Hungarian women from Auschwitz, Kati wept and wept for both herself and Magdus.

Magdus, twelve years Kati's senior, had been more of a mother to her than their actual mother had been and had raised Kati after Anna died. In Auschwitz, their roles were reversed, and Kati had fiercely protected and lovingly watched over her older sister.

This latest separation haunted Kati relentlessly as the war dragged on.

CHAPTER 24

Argus and Magdus's Death March

AFTER BEING TORN OUT OF THE LINE of women being transported to Allendorf to work, Magdus returned to her barracks, bereft. Fortunately, a woman from Hajdúbagos adopted her and assumed Kati's nurturing role. A few weeks later, Magdus was selected for transport, but this time the cattle cars had open doors, and the prisoners were given water. The women arrived in Germany early one morning, surprised at the beauty after the starkness of Auschwitz, where nothing green lived and few people survived. The sun was shining, and the women saw neat white houses brightened with vibrant flowerbeds. Magdus thought she had reached heaven! But this charming neighborhood was for the Germans, not the Jews.

Instead, the women were taken to outside Ravensbrück, in northeast Germany, where they slept on a street covered with powdered coal. It was so hot and they were so parched that they could barely even open their mouths to receive water offered to them from a hose. The women were deeply tanned from their exposure, forced to be outside all day in the Lager and were now covered with coal dust. Because the women were so dark, the blue-eyed, blond woman giving them water asked if Hitler had occupied Africa. My mother told me that when she heard this, she smiled for the first time since the invasion in March.

The Germans took the women to shower and gave them striped uniforms with a yellow Star of David patch and wooden clogs. Then

121

the women climbed onto another cattle train for a short trip to Reinickendorf, the northwest borough of Berlin.

Once they reached the train station, they were unloaded and lined up in formation. Walking across Berlin, they had to cross the Kurfürstendamm, a broad, elegant boulevard like the Champs-Élysées in Paris, to reach the Lager. They passed bombed-out shells of buildings, one with a bathtub hanging from the remnant of the upper story. The road was full of broken glass. Magdus found it beautiful, the glittering shards just retribution for Kristallnacht. The women arrived at their new quarters, where they had rooms with triple-level bunk beds, rather than only a dirt floor to huddle together on in the cavernous barracks at Auschwitz. It felt luxurious to have a hard bed with a thin blanket, even though only a few months before, Magdus had snuggled under a beautiful down comforter covered in satin and silk.

The next day, German civilians came and assigned the thousand women to various jobs, divided into two twelve-hour shifts.

Magdus became controller of a machine, checking the work of other women cutting holes in metal on an assembly line at the Argus Motorenwerke GmbH airplane factory in September 1944. The work was stressful and backbreaking, as the slave laborers had to stand for long roll calls in addition to their twelve-hour shifts. Magdus and her *csoport* toiled on the outskirts of Berlin throughout the winter.

While the women didn't experience as much physical cruelty as they had endured at Auschwitz, there was regular humiliation and psychological torture. Three prominent women, including a philosophy professor from Pécs, Hungary, and a physician, had their heads shaved and they died, in part, of exposure. Eventually, the workers were allowed to use scraps of rags from the factory as head covers. Finding a remnant of a tallis, the ritual Jewish prayer shawl, or the velvet bag it was kept in desecrated and used for grease rags was particularly painful.

One time, while standing in *Zählappell*, they saw an intense red flame and smoke nearby, and the Lagerführer (camp commander) said, "What are you looking for? Don't worry. That's not your parents. They are gone." Some of the prisoners were made to perform a show in a theater, with some of the women in lesbian roles. At the theater, the fürher taunted the prisoners about their appearance, asking why they were wearing tattered uniforms, wooden clogs, and no lipstick or makeup.

One day while working on the assembly line, Magdus asked her foreman for a needle and thread so she could make some gloves to keep her hands from freezing. He was so excited about her having sewing skills that he not only asked her to make a pair of gloves for his son but also did her work on the line at night for some time so that she could sew.

After the gloves were ready, he gave Magdus three cigarettes and three apples—a sizable reward. She naively gave the cigarettes back because she didn't smoke. She shared the apple with women who had shared their bread with her in Auschwitz. When others in the camp heard that she had given back the cigarettes, they were furious. The booty could have been bartered for food from the kitchen, but Magdus hadn't recognized the opportunity.

The bombing of Berlin intensified during the winter. Magdus and her friends enjoyed the sights of the lights flashing around them, knowing that the end of the war must be nearing. They didn't care if they died; they wanted to watch or to sleep, but the women were forced to go to bunkers.

By April 1945, the Americans and British were bombing by day and the Russian Red Air Force by night. The airplane factory was attacked twice. The first time, it could resume production, but the second bombing stopped work, so the women were sent to dig foxholes or camouflage other areas.

Soon afterward, the women were herded into long rows to evacuate the area. This was the beginning of their death march. As they walked, more prisoners were added from other camps. Magdus was so weak and her legs were so swollen that she could barely walk. Another woman, whom Magdus had known before the war, was in similar shape. As they always had to be in rows of five, three younger women made sure to take the outside positions in the rows so the weaker ones wouldn't be as visible to the guards. That kindness saved their lives. People who couldn't keep up and dropped out of the line were shot. A key to survival in the camps, as well, was to become invisible—never do anything that would cause the guards to notice you.

The march lasted seventeen days, during which they were given no food, and covered almost 150 miles. The women tried to eat grass or an occasional potato they found in the ground or stole from a pig's trough. They slept on the ground, surrounded by soldiers, never knowing where they were going nor why. When they reached Rostock, near the Baltic Sea in northern Germany, people shouted that they should stop, as the Russians were coming. Not sure what to believe, the guards assembled them all together in the forest, rather than in their neat rows of five, and threatened them with a machine gun, but the women didn't care at that point. The prisoners could see the sea. They later learned that the Nazis had intended to exchange the captives for medicine from Scandinavia, but no ships were waiting.

Afterward, the captives were led to a big barn to sleep. When they awakened in the morning, the guards were gone, having abandoned them. Many had left their uniforms. The starving women found bits of moldy cheese the Germans had discarded and ate that. They also rooted through horse manure to pick out pieces of grain to eat.

The women scattered in different directions, but Magdus, weak and feverish, stayed in Rostock with the four other women from her line. As they stood on the road, a group of Russians, pulling horse wagons full of wounded and dead soldiers, passed them. The soldiers threw them a loaf of bread, gesturing how they should tear the coarse bread apart into pieces to share.

Magdus could barely walk, but the group found an empty house, where she collapsed from exhaustion and fever. The other women laid her on some straw and left her alone while they searched for food. She awakened to see a handsome young Russian soldier with dark, soulful eyes. He asked her if she was sick and then left. Magdus doesn't know how long she was alone in the house before her companions returned.

When she came to, she and her friends went from one empty house to the next. In one home they found sugar and a side of bacon. They gorged themselves on the bacon but became intensely ill, with vomiting and diarrhea, from the shock to their bodies. Magdus found a pair of shoes to replace her wooden clogs but remained in her striped dress.

The friends started walking, part of a wave of refugees filling the roads. They were unsure of where to go. They ended up walking back 120 miles to Oranienburg, near Berlin. They saw Russian soldiers emptying houses of everything valuable, especially useful items like sewing machines, loading them onto trucks to take back to Russia. As the city was ransacked, it was burned to the ground. Magdus still had on her threadbare striped dress. The Russian soldiers told her to take the yellow star off, that everyone was the same.

As they neared Berlin, they were able to board a train. It didn't matter where it was going, as long as the doors of the cars were open. They were desperate to go home, to find anybody from their families who might have survived.

The refugees struggled to get home, walking and hitching rides on anything that moved, zigzagging back through Poland and Romania before finally reaching Debrecen in an open cattle car. I often wonder how they had the strength to find their way home, traveling hundreds of miles, still emaciated and weak. I'm uncertain about what they did for food besides foraging for remnants in the fields or stealing what they could from abandoned homes.

Magdus's childhood Hebrew teacher was at the Debrecen train station with a list of known survivors, trying to reconnect families. None of the Ehrenfelds nor Glattsteins were on his roster. I can hardly imagine how devastating that news must have been for Magdus on top of her other losses and how she kept going at that point or had the presence of mind to seek out a friend.

Magdus went to where her apartment and store were, on Piac utca, before the war. Their sign was gone, and a man who had coveted that space before the war had appropriated it. Not knowing where to go, she went to look for her childhood friend, Irén Szabo, who had hidden Kati early in the war.

CHAPTER 25

Allendorf

IN THE PAST FEW YEARS, I've spoken in depth with Kati about the sisters' entire story, but she has given me particular insight about her experience in Allendorf. The sisters' descriptions of their experiences have been remarkably consistent except about what Bözsi was wearing in Auschwitz and whether the women kept their shoes. I read more on the subject and then reinterviewed Kati about specific details of the camps. Kati was the only sister to be transferred to Allendorf, so all my information about that work camp is from her and my research. Each time I spoke with Kati, I gleaned new tidbits. The thousand young Jewish women left the barren compound at Auschwitz, where not a blade of grass survived, and rode through the lush, sweet-smelling countryside, a patchwork of fields and forest. They traveled almost six hundred miles west to the heart of Germany, eighty miles north of Frankfurt.

Kati was inconsolable after having been separated once again from her sister. She had lost her sense of purpose—caring for Magdus and nursing her back to health—and was convinced that Magdus, with her fragile mental health, would not survive Auschwitz alone.

The cattle cars taking the group from Auschwitz to the work camp at Allendorf weren't as crowded as the ones that had carried them to Auschwitz, and the door was open so they got fresh air and could see. They were treated to new gray uniforms that made them look halfway human. Most importantly, the women received water and a small amount of food for this trip to sustain their strength as laborers.

Whenever the train stopped, Kati was stunned to find towns appearing untouched by the war. At these rail stations, people were going about their mundane lives. Well-dressed women wearing hats and carrying handbags stood on the platform patiently waiting for trains, displaying every sign of normalcy. There were babies in carriages and young children at play, a world she had once known and taken for granted. Was it possible these people had no clue as to who the women in the cattle cars were? Was it possible the Jewish women were invisible to the rest of the world?

The prisoners arrived at the picturesque town of Allendorf (officially Stadtallendorf), its streets lined with white stucco houses embellished with half-timbers and reddish ceramic roofs. They then walked a few miles to their new confines at the camp, Münchmühle. They passed through the town, always in rows of five, filling the roadway. Their wooden clogs echoed on the cobblestone streets. Surely the townspeople could not pretend to not know of the Jews' presence.

Kati remembered arriving at Allendorf on her birthday, and it looked idyllic. Flowers surrounded the neat wooden barracks. Although there was a barbed-wire fence, it was not electrified. The buildings had floorboards rather than the dirt they had slept on in Auschwitz.

The barracks had actual windows. Opening one, Kati caught sight of her reflection in the glass pane and was shocked and frightened by the sight of herself, with her head shaved bald and protruding ears exposed.

My research revealed that Allendorf had the largest munitions factory during the war, and it was critically important to the Germans to protect it and the workers, who handled very toxic chemicals. Kati soon saw the effects of the poisons firsthand.

Twice daily, the women marched through the center of town to reach the munitions factory, where they worked as slave laborers, returning each night to their barracks in the pine forest. Compared to Auschwitz, their lot had improved, yet the young women feared what might lie ahead. When they heard a plane buzzing overhead, Kati said she and some of her friends wished again that bombs would drop on them and quickly end their misery. (I heard the same wish from my mother and Klari, and on Bözsi's tape, though all were in other places.) But the factories were well disguised, housed in buildings with flat roofs with trees growing on top, planted there for camouflage.

The women at Allendorf were not worked as hard as at some concentration camps and were relatively well fed, receiving a few turnips, rutabaga, and other root vegetables with their coarse dark bread and a daily glass of milk. They also had bunk beds with woolen blankets. There were only two women to a bunk, and Kati chose to sleep with Magda Klein, who preferred being with Kati to sharing a bunk with her own sister. Magda became a close confidant and supporter, as Kati spoke of her love for Sanyi and her despair over having lost Magdus.

When I was about sixteen, I met Magda Klein in Detroit. She appeared well-off, with stylish makeup and hair, very different socially from my own family. But Magda had been in Auschwitz with my mother and Kati, and then she, too, was transferred to Allendorf. I remember asking my mother why we were visiting, since it seemed she and Magda had little in common. She replied, "She was very good to me in Auschwitz." At the time this made little sense to me. Now I understand.

The women's better treatment at Allendorf was not out of the kindness of their German captors' hearts but because the slaves needed to remain healthy enough to work with toxic chemicals.

For some time after her arrival, all Kati did was work and cry, mourning Magdus, whom she could only assume was dead. She did not think that her sister had been gassed but rather that she was not strong enough to fight for herself and survive. Even after the night of the Gypsies, Kati was sustained by denial—never believing that her father might have been killed—and her belief that, as the youngest daughter, she had to stay alive so that she would be able to care for her father in his old age.

Her first job at the factory was working on an assembly line. The women took unexploded bombs, shells, and grenades and chiseled material out of them to reuse. The poisonous chemicals, TNT and Hexa, would then be remixed for new explosives.[1] The women developed yellow skin (jaundice) from liver damage, oddly colored coppery hair, and some had bluish-purple lips. This discoloration was from methemoglobinemia from the chemicals, which causes lack of oxygen in the tissues and bluish lips and nails as early signs of poisoning.

Kati was spared much of the toxicity because, with her sturdy build and square face, she looked stronger than the others. The German *Aufseherin*, or female officer, also favored Jewish women with light complexions and hair when selecting those for better work. So after several weeks in the munitions factory, Kati was chosen to work outside, in the fresh air, digging ditches and graves for the Russian prisoners of war.

Another *Aufseherin* seemed to take an unusual liking to Kati, who thought it was perhaps because she was fair and more Germanic in appearance. Hilda selected her for a peculiar project— to knit a bathing suit for her. A log building in the forest housed the toilet facilities. Hilda parked Kati on the benches in the entryway and brought her the yarn and needles. Kati set to work knitting for this rather plump woman but had no idea how to knit a bathing suit. Instead, she kept knitting and then unraveling her work, so as never to finish the project. The German soldier took care of her pet, bringing Kati sandwiches and other treats.

Kati had remarkable freedom in this part of the camp, even being able to walk around a little. She met other prisoners, men of different nationalities, who also shared some freedom of movement. These men would periodically bring Kati delicacies, like a piece of coffee cake. Some of these men worked on nearby farms and would receive extra food from the farmers' wives. Kati would share the treasures with her roommates, with everybody getting a sliver. Flirtations bloomed even here, and Kati soon had photos of a Serbian and Frenchman, their addresses, and offers of marriage after the war.

In later years, my mother and aunts teased Kati about her tendency to fall in love at every turn. Just as they teased Kati about her crush on Gunter, they would tell off-color jokes at Kati's admission of stolen kisses with the Frenchman, Pierre. Stories of the gifts of food from the male prisoners of war were told and retold. And Kati's punchline, which led to much teasing by my mother, was, "All I know is that when I was liberated, I was the only one that had to go on a diet!" As they jested with the youngest, Kati's being "on vacation" at Allendorf became a running joke among the sisters.

CHAPTER 26

Miklós's Story

AFTER MY FATHER DIED, I occasionally visited my uncle Miklós and Ella, taking the bus by myself to New York from Silver Spring. Their home in Queens felt like a quiet refuge, comfortable in an old-shoe kind of way. Miklós worked long hours as a New York cabbie; Ella was a salesperson at Sears and later owned a dress shop with a friend from the war. Ella then focused on raising their one daughter. Until I was in my fifties, and he was eighty-five, Miklós never spoke of the Holocaust to me. I don't recall Ella ever opening up about it either.

Miklós told me about his childhood. He was born in 1918, toward the end of World War I. Because he survived the Spanish flu pandemic, which killed millions, he was given a second Hebrew name, Shaya Benjamin, or "gift from G-d." He spoke contemptuously of his mother, though she prized him as her only natural-born son, a recurrent theme whenever he spoke of Anna. He never forgave her for sending him away at the age of four to live with the impoverished but pious Lindenfeld relatives in Hadház.

Later in life he referred to Anna with disdain as a "born-again Jew" for her determination to make a rabbi of him, even at the cost of a normal childhood in his own home.

At family gatherings, Miklós recalled some of Anna's more superstitious beliefs. Once, for instance, she visited the rabbi of Bodrogkeresztúr, revered as a miracle worker among Chasidic Jews (a very devout, mystical branch of Judaism)—and he blessed the sugar cubes she had brought with her. Miklós joked, "My mother had them always in her pocketbook so that nothing bad would come to her or her family," something that obviously didn't work out all that well. We chuckled together at the irony of her misguided superstitions.

Rather than become a rabbi, Miklós wanted to go to *fémipari*, a technical school that offered classes on machinery and tools, like a junior engineering school. Anna overruled him in the matter; her brother and uncles were bankers, and if he wouldn't be a rabbi, she wanted him to follow in their footsteps. After his mother's death, Miklós wound up in a *keréskedelmi* (trade) school and learned a trade at a machine shop.

In contrast to his scorn for his mother, Miklós had only respect for his father. After Anna and Henduka died in 1932, every Friday night, Miklós would see his father sitting by the window, tears streaming down his cheeks.

The gloom lifted in the house only after my father began courting Magdus in about 1936. Miki was full of life, and his ability to bring sunshine and laughter to their otherwise despondent father was remarkable.

War Years

In 2003, during a visit to Miklós in his Queens home, he opened up to me about his wartime experiences for the first time. I would have liked to ask him about them earlier, but it was ingrained in me as a child both to respect people's privacy and specifically to not ask about the Holocaust. The subject just wasn't discussed among the family until some of them did the Shoah Foundation interviews in 1995–96. Even then, I heard only my mother's story until I started interviewing seriously in 2000. Yet my mother transmitted a strong fear at times. I occasionally felt her upset on a visceral level.

I had avoided reading much about the Holocaust or watching any movies about it as I found them traumatizing. I never handled depictions of any kind of violence, including scary movies and other imagery, well. But anything related to antisemitism or the Holocaust triggered me at a whole other level. It made me feel conspicuously Jewish and thoroughly vulnerable. The first time I clearly remember feeling that was when our high school class took a field trip to see the film *Exodus*. Afterward, I had nightmares.

Curiously, later in high school and through college and into my adult years, I handled violence in other films with less stress and strain, but when I had children, I once again developed a low tolerance for seeing any kind of cruelty or brutality. A switch flipped.

Given my longstanding aversion to barbarism, researching and writing this book has been tough and has resulted in many a sleepless night. Bözsi's, Miklós's, and Ancsi's stories were the most difficult because their descriptions were the most graphic. Kati's telling me that living in the United States today feels like living in 1930s Europe has magnified my anxiety; the attacks on the press by the current regime and the rise in hate crimes has been triggering and has further inspired me to finish this book. At the same time, I am more open about being Jewish and more determined to raise concerns about antisemitism and fascism on social media.

While I never would have chosen to watch Holocaust-themed movies on my own, Miklós surprised me by his enthusiasm for them and asked me to watch a couple with him. The first was *Divided We Fall*, a thoughtful, nuanced look at relationships and ethics during World War II. We watched it twice. The other was *Life Is Beautiful*. Both Miklós and Kati had urged me to watch this heartbreaking movie because they said that the protagonist, Guido, reminded them so much of my father, both in his mannerisms and in his ability to make a game out of everything for the sake of his young son, so the boy wouldn't be so frightened in the concentration camp. The scene where Guido almost collapses under a load he is carrying reminded me of what Sanyi had said about my father's work carrying heavy cement sacks into a pit in forced labor.

Miklós then began to tell me details of his life in the Labor Battalion as a Munkaszolgálatos, or forced laborer. First, Miklós was in the Carpathian Mountains in Slovakia, clearing trees. While the local men would skid the lumber on sleds on the ice to the mills, Miklós was dismayed that his unit was ordered to remove the ice from the road, making pulling the heavily loaded sleds over the rough surface considerably more difficult.

The men were moved around the country, and the work was grueling. In Sárbogárd, in central Hungary, they built landing strips for the air force. In Szászrégen, in Transylvania (now Romania), they worked in a lumber mill. In Kőrösmező, Hungary (now Yasinga, Ukraine), they built roads in preparation for the German advance. In Deliatin (then in Poland, now in Ukraine), Miklós's unit loaded and unloaded freight trains. He was able to steal sugar off the trains, packing his pants with it after having tied off his cuff with string. Miklós's facial expression and bearing as he told me these stories reflected his pride in little triumphs of resistance such as this.

But in Deliatin, Miklós learned of a mass execution that happened on October 16, 1941, when security police shot 1,950 out of some 2,000 Jews. He also found out that other Jews were made to dig up the bodies, wash them, and then drink the water that the corpses had lain in before reburying them. He had already witnessed Jews marched to the banks of the river and shot into the water in several places, but nothing about that rivaled this particular cruelty.

In July 1942, Miklós was again in the Carpathian Mountains and had a bit of an adventure. The girlfriend of his lieutenant wanted a handbag made from viper skin. Miklós boasted that he was the official viper hunter. He first turned over rocks and located the snakes. Then, with a forked stick, he nailed down the reptiles. He would kill the snakes, skin them, and cure the skins with salt as they dried. The lieutenant, pleased with Miklós's success, gave him a two-week furlough. He promptly went home to visit his Gentile girlfriend, Böske Petö. He had such a good time with her that he failed to return to his unit on time. I've wondered whether he chose a Gentile woman as a rebuke to his mother for having sent him away from home when he was only four, but I never thought to ask. There weren't many ways an Orthodox young man could rebel against his parents.

When Miklós returned to his unit, having taken an extra week, he found there was a new commander, who had classified him as AWOL. He was put into a *büntetés század*, a unit of men who were to receive extra punishment, and they sent him toward the Russian Front.

Crossing from Romania into Ukraine, the men had to rebuild a bridge over the Prut River that the Russians had blown up. Although it was summer (1942), the water was icy cold as they carried large rocks to the footings of the bridge to make a stable base. Then three Jews were made to haul the same load of wooden planks as six of the Gentile Hungarians.

In Ukraine, as the local peasants drove their wagons past the workers, they took pleasure in whipping the Jews. Other peasants tied their horses to the back of their wagon and made a couple of Jewish men pull the cart to give their horses a break.

Conditions worsened as the men marched farther east to Pervomaysky in Russia on the Eastern Front. Here a commanding officer advised his subordinates that if they wanted to get home by Christmas to celebrate Jesus's birth with their families, "then you know what to do with these Jews."[1]

Miklós and his group marched several miles toward the Don River and then worked in the dark, digging trenches at night. Miklós was so cold, hungry, and desperate that he asked his friend to chop his fingers off, naively thinking he would be sent to a hospital. Fortunately, his friend refused and his buddies spurred him on when he felt disoriented and faint.

The men had to camouflage the trenches they dug. If there was a successful air attack on their position during the night, the Jewish laborers were held responsible—and the guards shot every tenth man. The bodies were thrown into an open ditch, and lime was thrown on top of them to keep the corpses from rotting quickly (and to keep the stench and infectious risk down).

All those who couldn't work, whether because they were freezing or ill or because their legs were too swollen from malnutrition, were shot to death and thrown into the same mass grave.

An especially barbaric punishment was to tie the victim up with a rope, hang him in an apple tree, hose him down with water, and let him freeze to death. "It was one of their favorite things." Miklós shook his head, staring down at the floor, as he recalled these nightmarish conditions.

The situation was so bad that Miklós volunteered to disconnect landmines. He stood in rough grasses and freezing rain, trying to feel the thin wires stringing the mines together. "Evidently, I was good at it because I wasn't blown up," he told me as he thought back to those miserable times.

On another afternoon, feeling delusional, Miklós stood with a shovel on his shoulder, exposing himself to the Russian sharpshooters, hoping he would get shot. He still believed that if he were hit, he would be taken to the hospital. But the bullets ricocheted off the shovel, and he felt sorry for himself for escaping injury.

One day Miklós found a dead Russian soldier lying in the field. Desperate for warm clothing, he tried to remove his sturdy boots—but the soldier's whole leg came off with the boot. Shocked, Miklós fled.

By mid-December 1942, there were only 26 of the 206 men who started together in Miklós's Munkaszolgálat unit. Eight of them, including Miklós, decided to try to escape. As they started to cross the Don River, Miklós heard the ice cracking, as it was not completely frozen. The men kept walking, and the guards sent up flares and then fired a volley of machine gun bullets, but none of the men were hit.

A voice called out from a bunker, "Stop! Where are you going?" Then they were taken into the shelter overnight. The following morning they started marching farther east, deeper into Russia. They got a lift in a truck, but when he got off, Miklós couldn't feel his legs, which were numb from the cold.

EARLY IN JANUARY 1943, Miklós ended up in a prisoner of war camp, Tambov, which also held POWs during WWI. The barracks were underground. Prisoners of many different nationalities were there—Romanian, Hungarian, German, Italian. From January until the end of March, the Russians imprisoned some thirty-seven thousand people there. Only seven thousand survived. Prisoners were so starved that if there was a kernel of grain in the latrine, someone picked it out and ate it.[2]

Every morning, Miklós and the other captives had to line up and carry their dead compatriots to be buried. One of the German soldiers was shocked to see lice crawling out of the bodies as they cooled, looking for a new host.

From there, Miklós was transferred to a camp closer to Moscow, an antifascist school, where the prisoners were lectured by some other prisoners who were Communists before the war. One teacher was Mátyás Rákosi (born Rosenfeld), who was appointed general secretary of the Hungarian Communist Party (MKP) in January 1945. The following year he became acting prime minister of Hungary. By 1948, Rákosi, self-described as " Stalin's best Hungarian disciple," became a dictator ruling Hungary.[3] Another teacher was Zoltán Vas (born Weinberger), who became secretary general of the Economic Council under Rákosi.

Among all the horrors Miklós described, I was amused and found relief in his occasional moments of black humor, like his hunting vipers to assuage a woman's narcissism.

While in Russia, Miklós was allowed to send a postcard home. A Hungarian who had remained in the USSR after World War I had become a political officer. Now in charge of the Hungarian POWs, this man asked Miklós to write on the card a special request. Miklós dutifully complied, writing, "Dear Father, Please send me some Szegedi paprika." Magdus later said this was the first word they had heard from Miklós since he was dispatched from the country.

From the POW retraining camp, Miklós was taken to Siberia in special railroad cars used for political dissidents. They were fitted with something like bunk beds, but you had to crawl in on your back or stomach and were unable to turn over. They also had a chain-link fence and a walkway for the guards. Under these miserable conditions, Miklós was transported to a hospital, where wounded Soviet soldiers were stationed. The Hungarian soldiers were put into a lily-white hospital room and dined with the Soviet officers.

After they recovered a bit in these relatively posh quarters, the Hungarians were taken to unload barges of lumber from the river and housed at night in a big barnlike building. Sleep was impossible because of the bed bugs and lice. Since the Russians couldn't get rid of the insects, they burned the place down. Mercifully, the men were not in the barn at the time. Many other Jewish labor servicemen died, deliberately trapped in torched buildings or shot as they tried to exit fiery deaths.

Miklós wound up in a camp outside Moscow. Later, he would speak with amazement of the fact that only a chain-link fence separated him from General Friedrich von Paulus, commander in chief of the German 6th Army at Stalingrad, whom Hitler refused to allow to surrender. A high-ranking Spanish general was also incarcerated there as a POW.

Finally, the Russians started to take the Hungarian soldiers back to Hungary. They were given some food for the trip, but much of it was stolen by other Russians transporting them in wagons to the railroads.

Their first stop in Hungary was at Nyíregyháza, and the women greeting the returning Russian-Hungarian units fed them *foghagymás bab leves*—bean soup with garlic—which caused terrible diarrhea in these malnourished men.

The men were stationed briefly in Debrecen and then transferred to Budapest to guard Rákosi and Vas, now prominent politicians. In March, they were offered a chance to either be in the army or serve as a political officer, or return to civilian life. Miklós quit immediately.

One of the memories seared into Miklós's consciousness was his first sight of the Danube upon his return to Budapest: Jewish corpses were still floating along the river banks. In the winter of 1944–45, the *nyilasok*, members of the brutal Arrow Cross (Hungarian Nazi) Party, executed twenty thousand Jews along the

Shoes on the Danube, 2008, Budapest

Danube. The Jews had to strip off their clothing and valuable shoes. Some were tied together in threes, and only the middle person was shot into the river, pulling the living ones in to drown in the icy water or be shot as target practice. It is said that the river ran red.

THE SHOES ON THE DANUBE PROMENADE is the most powerful Holocaust memorial I have ever visited. Breathtaking, it is an extensive display of iron shoes set into the concrete. It looks as if their owners had just stepped out of them. The shoes conjure up images of their owners, as some are work boots, some dress shoes, some worn down, some new. The most striking, however, are the little children's shoes, which cut to my core.

In 2007, when my mother's siblings came to see her, I was stunned to learn that after all they had survived, Kati and Miklós had not seen each other for more than twenty years after Kati immigrated to the United States in 1946. Separated by distance and too poor to travel, they had never told each other their stories. Even phone calls had been a rare luxury. In 1967, Magdus sent Kati fare to visit her sister and brother on the East Coast.

The stories told that night in my mother's house were not new to me—with one horrifying exception. I had stayed at the hospital on New Year's Day, but my daughter recorded my aunt and uncle's conversation. At one point, Miklós asked Kati if she knew what had happened to my mother's baby boy, who had been born in the ghetto and whom she had named József, after their older brother. Kati said she knew the baby had died in my mother's arms in the brickyard, while they were awaiting transport to Auschwitz.

"And then?" Miklós prompted.

Kati was silent.

"Magdus told me there were pigs in that camp," Miklós said heavily. "And the pigs ate the baby."

CHAPTER 27

Klari's War Years

Although I always felt the closest to Klari, I didn't learn her story until 2001. She, like her sisters and brother, never spoke of their wartime experiences. But she was ill at the time, and I was certain she wouldn't live much longer. I needed to hear her story.

That year, when I visited Klari at her home in Ann Arbor and we looked at pictures from the late 1940s, after liberation, I asked her why she was in none of the photos with her sisters. She simply replied, "Because I wasn't there." She looked pensive as she considered her response to my question: "Where were you?"

But that was well before I had heard others tell me their experiences, and I misinterpreted Klari's far-off expression as we spoke and looked at her old photos, including those of some of her old suitors. I thought she was thinking fondly about these handsome young men. Now that I know about her rape and more of the horrors she and her sisters endured, I realize her distant look was far from wistful.

One handsome young Romanian man, Tibi Jank, had a portrait of Klari made in which she looks dramatic, with dark, smoky eyes.

Tibi wanted to marry her and had even gone to his priest to ask that he convert her, falsely believing that it would protect her from Hitler. But Tibi was detained by the Russians in Pest and sent to Siberia. His brother was not arrested by the occupying Russians and, after the war, asked Klari to go with him to Arad, Romania, to await Tibi's release. Since Tibi had tried to save her life by marrying her, Klari agreed to go. She climbed onto a freight train, but when the train didn't move, she reconsidered and decided to go to Debrecen. She jumped off the train—a fortunate decision as one week later the border between Hungary and Romania was closed. She would have been trapped in Arad.

Later, as Klari and I looked through more of the old photos she kept in a small box, she told me about hiding in Budapest

Klari (about 24), 1944, Budapest

and starting on a death march to Austria. She confided that she "was used to being abused like a dog. But for somebody to have a kind word, that was too much to take." That is when Klari first told me the whole story.

Only this past year, Kati told me that she always thought that Klari was the most daring of all the sisters. "We just followed what they [the Nazis] told us. But at least she had guts," for having escaped from the death march.

Some years after my visit to Klari, when she told me about Lukács and where she was during the war, my mother and I were having a more serious spat than usual. She had always been jealous of how close I felt to Klari, and that day, in the midst of our quarrel, she blurted, "You think you and Klari were so close? I'll bet she didn't tell you about being raped."

WHEN KLARI FIRST SOUGHT vocational training, she lived at home and studied in Debrecen, as her older sisters had. She chose to apprentice as a seamstress under Etta néni, although her education was expensive for her father. Bözsi was already married and had

143

moved to Pest (eastern Budapest), living on Albas *tér* (place) in a tiny two-room apartment with her mother-in-law, Sári néni. When she finished her training, Klari moved in with Bözsi and Sári after Bözsi's husband, who was in forced labor on the Eastern Front, was murdered by someone who wanted his warm winter coat. Klari then had to stay in Pest, as by then, Jews were no longer allowed to travel. She thought that perhaps the move saved her life.

The Jews in Budapest were comparatively protected until near the end of the war. Randolph Braham, the definitive expert on the Holocaust in Hungary, explains the master plan for deportation and "dejewification." The priorities for "mopping up" the different territories were strategized:

Zone 1 (Kassa) included Carpatho-Ruthenia and northeastern Hungary. This was because both the authorities and local citizens "had less regard for the 'Galician,' Eastern, 'alien,' non-magyarized, and Yiddish-oriented masses than for the assimilated Jews." The plan was also sold as providing labor for the Germans, which found support among the right-wing groups.[1]

The priorities for deportation also started in the northeast, as that area was closest to the advancing Russian armies, and the Nazis were eager to complete the "Final Solution," ridding Europe of all Jews.

The Germans acted hurriedly in Hungary. They invaded the country on March 19, 1944. Jews in Carpatho-Ruthenia (the northeast) and Transylvania (areas appropriated by Hungary from Romania after World War I) were placed in ghettos or concentrated in towns with major rail centers beginning on April 16, and deportations to concentration camps for "extermination" began May 15 of that year. Budapest was spared from deportations until later because the Jews there were far more assimilated into mainstream Christian society, making it politically more challenging to kill them.

Referring to Hungarian Jews, Dr. Peter Hayes explains, "almost sixty percent of them, approximately 437,000 people, were deported in the space of only fifty-five days, between May 15 and July 9."

Ultimately, "between 500,000 and 565,000" Hungarian Jews were killed in the Holocaust, and the operation left virtually the only survivors in the Hungarian capital of Budapest.[2]

While not in ghettos until November 1944, before that time, many of the Budapest Jews were terrorized or killed by members of the Arrow Cross (the Hungarian version of the Nazis). That November and December, many were sent on forced marches toward Austria, including Klari.

Until 2001, all my generation of cousins believed that Klari was in Auschwitz with her sisters. When I finally asked the question, I learned that she was initially in forced labor near Budafok, on the western bank of the Danube River outside Pest. A large group of young Jewish women was walking in the mountains toward Vienna, trying to move away from the Russians coming from the east. They walked miles overnight, through the dark, and Klari's feet were blistered and raw from walking in boots with torn soles over gravel and branches. The women stopped for the night at a barn. It was so crowded that Klari and her friend Edit chose to sit outside in the drizzle. A friendly Hungarian soldier came over to them and offered them a ham sandwich and then took them to sleep in his tiny room in the guardhouse.

Sometime later, that guard, Lukács, told the young women that the soldiers had received orders that all the women should be shot and never reach Vienna. He told them that he would turn a blind eye and suggested that the women wander away in search of an escape. Most were too afraid to do so. Lukács offered to take Klari and Edit with him, but Edit stayed with the rest of the women as she was hoping to find her fiancé. Klari went with Lukács.

First he took her to a bar and told the two young women there to clean her up and give her some clothes. They then walked together in Budafok; when he saw a building with an Arrow Cross flag on it, Lukács said, "I'm going to leave you here because this is the safest place for you. I'm going to tell them that you are my sister who escaped from Debrecen." Lukács then went home to tell his wife and children that he had run into his sister from Debrecen and she would be staying with them for a while.

That night, he returned with a horse and carriage filled with a number of coworkers and took them all to Kápolnásnyék, his hometown in the Dunántúl (Transdanube), twenty-five miles southwest of Budapest. His family was dirt poor, with a dozen children. Klari worked under slavelike conditions there helping the mother with all her children.

After some time, more German soldiers were in the town, and when she slipped and spoke a few words of German to them, Klari caught their attention. It was clear that they didn't believe her made-up story. Lukács became aware that people were growing suspicious, so he took her back to Budafok, where she hid in a factory basement with twenty-seven others, including Lukács, who stayed with her and protected her from the German soldiers who wanted to rape her.

On Christmas morning, Klari ventured out in search of water and saw some strange-looking soldiers with big hats and bayonets—Russians! Now she had something new to fear. She had heard that the Russians were notorious for raping women. Once again, Lukács rescued her as well as two other young women, by hiding them at night in a hole under the furnace that was used for processing potatoes. They slept there every night for three months.

After the Germans completed their retreat from Pest, Klari was able to find her way back to the apartment she had shared with Bözsi and her mother-in-law, Sári. In that part of Pest, everything stayed intact in the homes of the Jews, and the doors were locked behind them when they left. On her return to Pest, Klari discovered the handbag she had left was still there, and she was able to retrieve the ID papers she had hidden in its lining "so she could remember who she was."

Soon Klari hitched trains back to Debrecen. She was also able to get more provisions from a friend in the black market before she once again returned to Debrecen.

Klari, circa 1942, in her parents' guest room, Sáránd

WELL BEFORE THE WAR, when Klari was in her teens, she was known for her fine needlework and spent hours embroidering intricate petit point. Even when I visited Sáránd in 2008, her childhood neighbor, Irén Bakó, recounted how Klari sat by the middle window working on an immense silk petit point of a painting by Hans Zatzka, *Abenzauber*, or *Magic Evening*. She had to sit by the window to work because she needed the light.

An older man, Dr. Kardos, from nearby Hajdúbagos, would ride over on his bicycle as he visited patients in surrounding villages. Short and potbellied, he would lean against the window on his elbow as Klari sat just inside, embroidering. Kardos wooed her, watching as Klari labored over the delicate needlepoint. Irén added that she knew the family was a bit upset with her for her flirtation with Kardos, but she was innocent.

Before the war, Klari gave him the intricate work, which had taken her two years to complete.

It's unclear to me exactly what their relationship was—I suspect there was a romantic interest, given the amount of work that went into her detailed reproduction. One of the sisters thinks she had offered to make him a needlepoint in exchange for his doing her

147

dental work, and he had brought her this canvas, which was far more complicated than she had bargained for.

In 1978, when my mother and I visited Hungary, with an address provided by Sanyi, we were able to contact Kardos and even visit his apartment, where Klari's needlepoint hung. Ma tried to buy the needlepoint from him, alienating him in the process. As I recall, she accused him of having "stolen" it from Klari. He refused to part with it.

My mother and her sisters did not like Kardos. When I returned to Debrecen in 2008, their old neighbor, Irén Bakó, told me how the family disapproved of his attention to young Klari, too, and were concerned that he would take advantage of her. It continued to bother my mother that Klari's precious needlepoint remained with this man whom she so disliked. Knowing how important getting that needlepoint back into the family had been to my mother, I was determined to try again to buy it. In 2008, when I returned to Debrecen after Ma's death, Kardos was also dead. I enlisted the help of a cousin, András's son, who was able to locate Kardos's children and negotiate with them for me to buy the needlepoint and return it to our family. Still having Ma's anger toward Kardos buried in me, I didn't want to deal with his children. I tried to gift the needlepoint to Kati, but she declined the remembrance of her sister.

AS I FINALLY LEARNED FROM MY MOTHER, Lukács, the Hungarian guard who Klari said saved her life by hiding her within his own family and later protected her from Russian soldiers, had actually raped and impregnated her. And Dr. Kardos, despite bemoaning the fact that she had refused to sleep with him, performed an abortion when Klari was already in her fourth or fifth month of pregnancy. Upon hearing the truth, I finally came to understand how and why Klari and I were so close: I had become the daughter Klari had lost.

CHAPTER 28

Klari and Magdus Search for Family

AFTER LIBERATION, people were scattered and disoriented, not knowing if their families were alive, how to find one another, or what they might discover when they headed home. But at least everyone was free to travel.

A number of survivors, like Kati, never wanted to set foot in Hungary again, let alone return to the homes they were torn from—not wanting to be surrounded by neighbors who had turned on them. Others returned in search of any surviving family members. People also searched for relatives in lists of survivors printed in newspapers or posted in train stations throughout the country. Connections were also made by word of mouth or chance encounters.

KLARI FOUND A TRAIN heading toward Debrecen. Not having any family there, she sought out her old classmate and close friend, Bözsi Losonczi. "Bözske," a fearless Catholic girl, had previously risked her life by offering to give the youngest surviving sister, Kati, her own identification card early in the war and had brought Magdus food when she was confined in the Debrecen ghetto. Bözske's family of twelve had hardly anything to eat themselves, but they unhesitatingly took Klari in and gave her food and a bed.

Where do you even begin to look for someone in a big city? Klari went to the *piac* (market) in front of the prominent yellow

Református Church, the focal point of the town, where the peasants brought vegetables and livestock to sell. She asked if anyone knew anything about her family, but nobody had heard any news.

One day Klari was sitting by the window at Bözskes. She looked up and saw a person walking by wearing a tattered Hungarian soldier's uniform and was stunned to recognize her brother Miklós! She was overjoyed at seeing her brother after years of separation in brutal conditions. She wondered if she was dreaming.

Later, the sister and brother talked about the incident. As it turned out, it wasn't entirely happenstance, as Miklós had gone to the *piac* with the same idea as Klari. One of the peasants selling wares told Miklós that Klari had been there and where she was staying.

The siblings decided to go back to Bözsi's apartment in Pest because it was still intact. There they had food—beans, peas, sugar, and flour—because Bözsi's brother-in-law, a policeman, excelled at stealing food and stockpiling it. One day the neighbor, who had a phone, summoned Klari over to take a call. It was her oldest brother, Pista, calling from the train station, asking her to come and pick him up! She ventured there on the streetcar and saw Pista "with a suitcase and his *hegedű* [violin] in the case, like he was coming home from vacation." In fact, Pista, his wife, and their young child were very lucky during the war, having been taken to a camp in Strasshof, Austria, where they had relatively decent food and housing while they worked. The sisters joked, with a tinge of bitterness, that Pista had been on vacation even more than Kati.

The siblings decided to return to Debrecen, hoping to find the others. Homeless and penniless, they found a bombed-out house to live in. They decided to venture out to see if Pista's home on Petöfi utca was habitable and if they might reclaim it. Klari recalled that one summer Sunday afternoon, she and Pista set out on a long walk up Piac utca, the major promenade, north to the Nagyerdö (literally, the "Big Forest"), a large city park where they previously had enjoyed picnics and swimming in the summer.

As they walked, a shadowy figure appeared from among the trees. Klari was shocked to see her older sister Magdus, emaciated and filthy, wearing a black-and-white polka-dot dress and a red *kötény* (apron), coming toward her. Magdus had aged almost beyond recognition and was out of her mind, with a vacant and disoriented look.

Magdus was covered with lice, so Klari took her oldest sister to be disinfected. Then they moved into a house that had no windows, no walls, and only a partial roof. They had no furniture except the box springs from under the mattress.

Klari was horrified to learn that Magdus used to sleep on the dish she still carried carefully, a *csajka* (tin pan), which she had been eating in by day and peeing in at night because she wasn't allowed out of the barracks after dark. This tin pan was her pillow and became her only possession, and she clung to it even after the war.

I, too, was horrified. I hadn't heard this story from anyone before, and it was very painful to hear more vivid details of what my mother had lived through and barely survived. She had suffered so much, and this was hidden from me until 2001, when Klari was dying. I was further impressed at her resourcefulness and resilience and felt bad about the additional pain I had caused her at times.

Klari said that when they walked down the street, every time Magdus saw a baby carriage, she would run into an entryway and begin crying. Klari thought she understood why seeing a carriage had such a devastating effect. She knew that her sister was pregnant when forced into the ghetto. After her suspicion that Magdus's baby had died was confirmed, Klari and her siblings always wondered, "Where was G-d then? What kind of sin could we have done that we had to suffer so much? It never ended."

I wondered the same, and while I, too, wanted my children to be raised with Jewish traditions and rituals, I haven't been able to believe in G-d. Klari reiterated her lack of belief to me when she showed me the quilts she was sewing for babies with AIDS and said how unjust and tragic their lot was as well.

At times, I wish I had a strong belief system and that I had been able to impart that to my children. I have seen so many patients who are suffering and dying yet are comforted by their belief that whatever is happening is G-d's will and they will be happy in their afterlife. I was not raised to believe in an afterlife. Rabbi Paskoff spoke of Jews' core belief on December 21, 2018:

> For Jews, it's not "so-and-so" is in a better place. For Jews, it's not that good people who die become angels. For us, we remember the good that people added to the world. We remember those acts of *tikkun olam*, those acts of helping to repair the world. Of taking a broken place, and in ways large and small, left their mark to make this world a little bit better, a little bit more decent, a little bit more whole.[1]

For those who are consoled by belief in a joyous afterlife, I am envious of their peace. But I find the idea incomprehensible.

FROM HERE, THE TIMELINE for the period immediately after reuniting is muddled, and I have not been able to clearly untangle the story, despite repeated interviews over the years. While frustrating, it shouldn't surprise me, as it reflects the chaos of the time, when dazed people wandered the city streets, grasping for glimpses of familiarity. Debrecen was heavily damaged by bombing; more than half the buildings in the city had been destroyed. My mother weighed only half of what she did before the war and was covered with lice.

Klari also returned to Sáránd with Miklós. Her brother had been ill with malaria when he was in Russia, and he suddenly relapsed while they were in Sáránd, becoming too sick to return to Debrecen. An old neighbor, Zsiga Kun, allowed them to stay with him while Miklós recovered.

Miklós recalled going back to Sáránd but not whether his house was there. Klari said that when she first went back, she was all alone and couldn't bear to go into the house. As she stood outside the fence, Mór's closest friend and neighbor, Tóth bácsi, who had risked his life by hiding Kati under his bed, came out of his home, glassy-eyed, as he was near death. He cried, "'I don't want to die yet. I want to wait until Apuka [Mór] comes home. All I ask of you is don't take that blanket away from me. I want to be buried with Kati's blanket." He died while Klari was home, and his last request—to be buried with Kati's blanket—was honored.

Magdus—Finding Klari

My mother recalled her reunion with Klari slightly differently than her sister had described.

Irén Szabo was home with her two children when Magdus unexpectedly arrived on her doorstep. She hadn't seen her childhood friend since the war began, but she unhesitatingly took in Magdus. Irén bathed Magdus, gave her food and clean clothes, and put her to bed. The next day, Magdus insisted on going for a walk to look for anyone familiar. Venturing out on the street close to the apartment, Magdus was shocked to see her brother and sister.

Shaking her head, she said, "They saw me. They were in civilian clothes, you know, the same as we were wearing before, and they looked normal! And I wasn't. I was 65 pounds and they were like I saw them before." Her voice breaking as she teared up, she added, "They thought I was a *szellem* [a ghost]—it's not me. Only my soul or something."

After a few days, Magdus went with Klari to look for a habitable place and they found a house that had a partial roof. They met a family friend who had lost his wife and five children, and this man offered to take Klari and Magdus to lunch. But Magdus saw a baby carriage on the street and began screaming with despair. She later said, "I had to go somewhere to disappear. I couldn't stand to see a child. It was so painful to see somebody [else's baby] alive, and mine wasn't. It was very painful."

She found a friend whose apartment she had shared in the ghetto. This man had been with Miki in Dachau and was confident he would have survived. Other people said she should assume her

Anna (39), Henduka (about 4), and Klari (about 11),
circa 1931, Sáránd

husband had been burned at Dachau by fleeing Nazis. Everything
was rife with rumor, making the time an emotional roller coaster.

Magdus decided to return to Sáránd with her brothers, and at
first wanted to try to reopen the family's business. The house was
there but they learned that neighbors had stripped their home of
the family's furniture and other belongings. The Germans had used
their home as a stable and, epitomizing their contempt for Jews
and viewing them as subhuman, did the unforgivable: trampling
the portrait of Anna, holding her youngest daughter, Henduka, into
the mud. It was the last sweet depiction of the two before they died
of typhoid.

The Germans put their horses in the bedrooms because it was a Jewish house. The Russians did the same because it was bourgeois. Somebody from the village had moved in.

As the siblings tried to reclaim their home and reopen their store, their reception was mixed. Many of the older people were helpful as the Ehrenfelds had been well-liked in the village. The farmers gave them milk to help them out. Some neighbors tried to pay their debts, saying they were hoping Mór's children would restart the business. Others returned objects they had taken from the Ehrenfelds.

Not so with the younger generation, many of whom were antisemites and unwelcoming.

After several months, the Ehrenfeld children concluded that the barriers they faced were insurmountable.

CHAPTER 29

Sanyi and Miki

WHILE MY MOTHER EVENTUALLY told me snippets about her romance with Miki during his military stints in the Munkaszolgálat (forced labor), I heard details about my father's concentration camp time and the immediate postwar period from my uncle Sanyi, who remarkably was able to be with his brother except for the final six weeks of their imprisonment. Sanyi first told me about this in 2003 when I visited him in Los Angeles. We revisited the topic on occasion as I learned more and pressed for exact dates and details.

Initially drafted in February 1939, my father was in an artillery unit before it was decided that Jews weren't wanted in the military. Miki was put in a forced labor unit in 1941, just three months after getting married.

The next year, his newly drafted brother joined him, and Sanyi and Miki worked together as forced laborers building roads and railroads throughout Hungary. The following year, they were shipped to Proscurov (Ukraine), then Brest-Litovsk, in White Russia, to clear minefields. Sanyi showed ingenuity here. He saw a hand-drawn colored picture and thought drawing would suit him better than dangerous labor. He managed to get paper and pencils and drew picture cards, which he gave to the Hungarian soldiers guarding the workers. The images were so popular that he spent his days drawing and writing while the others were out risking their lives. Fortunately, everyone in his unit survived.

156

Sanyi and Miki's Munkaszolgálat unit, December 20, 1943, Nagyszőllős. Sanyi is in the back row, farthest on the left; Miki is next to him.

At right are signatures and addresses of the men in the Munkaszolgálat unit

The laborers were transported by cattle car back to Budapest and then had to walk to the Austrian border, about 150 miles away. Then the Nazis again packed them into sealed cattle cars for their transport to Dachau, outside Munich, on November 9, 1944. On their arrival at the concentration camp, the SS stripped the prisoners of their clothes and personal items. The men were issued striped pajama uniforms with a Star of David and their prisoner number stitched on and given shoes with wooden soles. Unlike at Auschwitz, where prisoners' heads were shaved entirely, Dachau inmates' hair was cut so as to leave a two-inch stripe in the middle so that anyone attempting to escape could readily be identified.

In a satellite camp, Mühldorf, the brothers were rousted every morning at 3:00 a.m. and then stood for hours for roll call. At 6:00 a.m., they marched to their work site, where an underground factory to manufacture Messerschmitt-262 fighter airplanes was being built. Miki spent exhausting days hauling one-hundred-pound cement sacks into a hole. Sanyi collapsed under the weight and was allowed to spread wet concrete mix instead. This period in Dachau was the only time, Sanyi told me, that my father was down and worn out, no longer his fun-loving, vibrant brother.

MIKI AND SANYI WERE LUCKY to be together throughout forced labor and the camps until the last six weeks of the war. In March 1945, Sanyi was in the *Revier* (shorthand for *Krankenrevier*, or sick room) for weeks with an abscess in his calf, incurred when he injured himself climbing down wire mesh into a deep hole. Someone drained the abscess with a pocketknife and dressed it with the rough cloth from the cement bags. Sanyi was so miserable, he thought it would be better to die. When he had partially recovered, he was transported out of Mühldorf back toward Dachau. He was again taken in a closed cattle car, with no food or water, for six or seven days. On April 30, American soldiers freed the prisoners; Sanyi weighed about 70 pounds when he was liberated and was hospitalized.

Miki had to remain in the *Revier* as he suffered from Fleck typhus, as did many starving inmates. Typhus, caused by *Rickettsia prowazekii* and transmitted by lice, caused epidemics in the ghettos and camps, where crowding and poor sanitation made control difficult. Victims are wracked by high fevers, severe headaches and muscle aches, typical of rickettsial diseases, and a rash. Without antibiotics, about 40 percent die. The Germans were fanatic about periodic delousing campaigns in the camps, stripping and spraying inmates with chemicals and baking their clothes in ovens. Those liberated were sprayed by American soldiers with the pesticide DDT in an attempt to contain the epidemic.[1]

After his liberation, Sanyi was placed in a DP (displaced persons) camp in Feldafing. During his six weeks in this camp outside Munich, Sanyi had no idea whether his brother was alive or not. My mother said she learned much later that the two brothers had survived only because the German guards knew the American army was approaching and they were afraid to be caught burning the camp and the remaining prisoners.

Refugees wandering through the countryside were a major source of news of survivors. After Miki recovered, he learned that his brother was in Feldafing and managed to find his way there. When I asked Sanyi how he found his brother, he teared up and said he doesn't like to recall or describe this as it was too emotional, although filled with an "unbelievable joy."

I can understand Sanyi's reticence. I'm sure that my stirring up painful details about their horrible experiences and almost losing his brother to typhus at the end of their imprisonment was difficult for him. I wonder, at times, what details were too awful for him to share. His son and I sensed a wall beyond which we could not pass. While he spoke more openly to me than the Ehrenfelds did, it was not because he enjoyed doing so. My uncle felt that preserving history was important to future generations, so he graciously spent hours with me over the years, patiently answering my personal questions as best he could. But some secrets remain.

CHAPTER 30

Miki's Search for Magdus

KNOWING WHAT HAPPENED to the weak and the elderly in the camps and how they themselves had barely survived, the brothers were convinced that no other family members were alive. Then they heard that one transport out of Debrecen had gone to Strasshof, a "better" work camp in Austria, and that gave them some hope.

KATI WENT FROM STARVING and hiding in fields to living and working on an American air force base days after liberation.

The soldiers had taken over a nearby German air base, Fritzlar. When they saw how hostile the Germans were to the newly freed Jews, they offered the young women jobs at the air base.

Bözsi learned that Kati was at the air base, and after she was liberated at Grimma and recovered some strength, she joined her sister at the military facility.

Some of the two dozen women liberated with Kati had been friends or classmates in Debrecen and had remained together in Auschwitz and Allendorf. They were the lucky ones. One of them, Miri Klein, had attended the university with Sanyi. She heard Sanyi's name on the Swiss radio as a list of refugees in Feldafing was being read and wrote him a letter on July 17, 1945, saying she was with Kati. She relayed news of others she had heard were alive as well and, in turn, asked him to share the good reports of how and where people had been sighted. In her letter to Sanyi, she added, "I only heard your name and not Miki's, so for the time being I have not mentioned this to Kati."

When Sanyi received this astonishing letter from Miri, he immediately set off for Fritzlar, going alone on top of a cattle car that was full of coal, and was reunited with two of the Ehrenfeld girls, Kati and Bözsi, as well as with Miri and her sister, Ella. He was stunned to find the sisters alive, as he and Miki had assumed they had all perished.

While trying to reunite family members, Sanyi shuttled back and forth between Feldafing DP camp and the air base—surprising because it was no easy trek, almost three hundred miles atop freight trains. But after a few trips back and forth, Sanyi returned to Zennern, a village near the Fritzlar air base, and found a place to live. On one of these early trips, Sanyi proposed to Kati, whom he had known since she was about eleven, as he wanted to strengthen the bonds between the Glattstein and Ehrenfeld families.

THIS PART OF THE FAMILY, now together in Germany, assumed that Magdus had died, especially since she had been pregnant when put in the ghetto. Then Kati told them that because Magdus had milk leaking from her breast, she had been turned back from the selection for transport to Allendorf and presumably was killed.

In fact, Miki was so certain of his wife's death that he wanted to marry any of the other sisters, just as Sanyi had proposed to Kati only a short while before. The brothers were both determined to keep the two families united, having already been closely intertwined for ten years.

Despite his doubts, Miki decided to return to Hungary to look for any remaining family. First, he went to Budapest, to the apartment that Bözsi had shared with her mother-in-law, Sári néni, and Klari.

Miki was chatting with Sári and lamented the loss of his wife. Sári insistently said, "No, your wife isn't dead." Miki thought that Sári was crazed from the bombings or grief over her son's death and was imagining things.

On the other hand, Sári thought Miki was crazy, as she had been corresponding with Magdus. This back-and-forth continued for a while until finally, Sári néni got up and produced a letter from Magdus to counter his disbelief. Seeing his wife's handwriting, he finally believed her.

Stunned, Miki set off for Sáránd in search of his wife. Ever the jokester and echoing their early courtship, their private code, he knocked on the window of the old house and said, "Mr. Ehrenfeld, I'd like to buy some cigarettes." "You know, just to tease me," Magdus recalled. "But I knew his voice."

CHAPTER 31

Kati's Liberation

By LATE WINTER OF 1944–45, rumors were that the war was going poorly. The prisoners' hope was buoyed that their nightmare might soon be over.

In March, the Allendorf camp commandant summoned an assembly in the courtyard. I was astonished that Kati described him as a "very kind, older man," but reports by some other women also claim that SS-Hauptscharführer Arthur Wuttke had "a certain humanity."[1]

The commandant had orders to take the women on a death march from Allendorf to Buchenwald to be murdered in the gas chambers there. No witnesses to the Nazi atrocities were to be left alive. Instead, Wuttke told the prisoners that they could either follow him westward, away from the front, or disperse on their own—and he cautioned them to be careful. As the sounds of bombings and guns intensified, he told them that the Allies were closing in and they should be safest surrendering to the Americans.

The roads were filled with a caravan of carts that local citizens were pulling, filled with their possessions, as they also tried to escape the advancing armies.

Kati and her roommates decided to stay together and go a different direction from their captors. They took cover, sleeping in empty lofts or in haystacks. Some nights, they camped in an animal lean-to. They roamed the countryside, begging for food. Some people were kind, others not, but the women didn't consider the danger, given their hunger. It was early spring, so very few plants were growing in the fields yet. The women foraged and found an occasional turnip or potato that had been overlooked; they ate the new grass when there was nothing else. Kati helped the braver women steal eggs from henhouses at night, though she was reticent.

The women from Allendorf were still wearing their uniforms, with a piece cut out of the back and their prisoner number stitched over this to discourage escape.

After about ten days of wandering hungrily and warily in the countryside, Kati was liberated on April 1, 1945, her father's birthday. She and her bunkmates were huddled in a shed and saw American tanks coming toward them and several Americans in trucks on the nearby road. One of the women had a piece of white cloth, and she put it on a stick and waved it.

Some vehicles came toward them. The soldiers were shocked at the sight of these scraggly women, the first prisoners they had found. The women were emaciated, and many were yellow with jaundice and had oddly colored hair and purplish lips from their chemical exposure at Allendorf. They were filthy, wearing little more than their ragged dresses.

The Americans didn't know how to communicate with the women. Fortunately, one of the soldiers from the Bronx spoke Yiddish, as did one of the young women in the group.

The American soldiers, from the Army Air Corps, acted just like little children, excitedly showering the newly free women with treats like chocolate and chewing gum, which the women had never seen before. The women hopped into a truck and were taken to the nearest town.

The GIs commandeered a large house and placed the Jewish women there. They slept in clean beds and had comforts they hadn't experienced in more than a year—though it seemed like an eternity. The Germans who lived in the house were resentful both at being displaced to an outbuilding and at being told to feed the women, which they did only grudgingly.

One day, the homeowners were cooking small potatoes for their hogs in a huge iron dish. Kati and the others couldn't restrain themselves and gorged themselves. To this day, she says she never had anything that tasted so good and loves little boiled potatoes. However, a lot of the women got sick because they overate.

The Americans recognized that the Jews weren't very safe because there was a lot of hostility. Although they were not stationed in that town, somebody came to check on the women every day.

Becoming increasingly concerned for the women's safety, after a few days the soldiers trucked them to the nearby air base in Fritzlar and offered them jobs, food, and security.

CHAPTER 32

The Family Moves to Zennern

IN THE TURMOIL AFTER THE WAR, people did whatever they could to get by. All of my aunts and uncles spoke of some aspect of their struggle to find a way to get home again and look for family, beginning with my interviews with them and my mother in 2000.

After being liberated, Kati and the small group of women from Allendorf were taken to the nearby Fritzlar air base outside Zennern, Germany, so they would be safe. Zennern was a small village in the central Hesse region of the country, lying in lowlands. Before the Nazis made an air base for their fighter planes there, it was a historic village with records dating back to the 1200s. Even now, its population numbers less than eight hundred.[1]

After Sanyi learned that Kati was living and working at the American air base, he migrated to Zennern, the adjacent village. When Bözsi joined Kati at the facility, they shared a room.

When Miki returned to Hungary in late 1945, he found his wife and her brothers, Miklós and Pista. The two brothers were not having much luck restarting their little store in Sáránd.

After Miki's return, he and Magdus also tried to get their old apartment and business back and were unsuccessful. By the spring of 1946, they decided that they were unlikely to be able to reestablish their business in the postwar upheaval. Nor could they ever have a sense of security in a country that had so betrayed and mistreated its Jews.

All the Ehrenfelds who had returned to Hungary and tried to reestablish their lives in Sáránd and Debrecen resolved to leave the country and rejoin Sanyi, Kati, and Bözsi, who were in Zennern. They thought this move would give them the best chance to regroup and consider what their future options were, together as family, but the routes they took were circuitous. The trip especially frightened Magdus, as they had to cross the borders into Austria and Germany illegally.

Miki, Magdus, and Miklós caught trains toward Vienna, riding on top of the railcars when they could rather than being inside. They feared the Russian soldiers who were coming through the cars, looking for jewelry or watches. Watches were so new to these seemingly backward, primitive men that their arms were decorated with them up to their armpits.

Miklós recalled that if they couldn't take the ring off your finger, they cut your finger off to get at it. If you resisted, they threw you beneath the moving train. They failed to notice that Miklós was sitting with his rucksack tucked beneath him. And that is how a few remaining pieces of family jewelry, including my grandmother Anna's watch, were saved.

WHILE MY FAMILY MEMBERS were waiting for visas, they found it hard living among the Germans after the war. An additional frustration was that quotas for German Jews were higher than for Jews from Hungary.

In the American occupied zone, a number of homes were used to house refugees who had been imprisoned by the Nazis. Some survivors, my parents and Sanyi included, were given housing in German homes instead of DP camps. The owner had one room and shared the kitchen, and the Glattsteins had the rest of the house.

One daughter of the owner of the home where my parents stayed, Annaliese, became a babysitter for my brother and Klari's son, both born while their parents were waiting to emigrate. Sanyi had a long affair with another daughter. Both of the owner's sons had been killed in the war.

Miki, Magdus, and Klari, 1947, Zennern

BECAUSE THEY WERE NOT IN A DP CAMP, the family found themselves short on food. Magdus and Sanyi registered with the Air Force and a Jewish aid organization to get extra food and supply rations, above what they got from the Germans. She would regularly have to go from Eschwege to Kassel to get the extra food, changing trains en route.

On occasion, former enemies became friends. Sanyi, for example, was given a room with the Rausch family in Zennern. He soon realized that they were "very, very decent" and far from being Nazis. When I visited him in his California home, I was surprised to see he had a photo of five-year-old Roswitha Rausch in his office and later shared a picture of her in her middle age. They had continued to correspond throughout their lives.

Miki had access to a Mercedes and worked by driving black marketers from East Germany to West Germany. He removed the inside panel on a car door and hid jewelry or other valuables, mostly from Polish Jews, inside the now exposed compartment. He was arrested only once and was let go the next day because he was merely the driver carrying the contraband. While jailed, Miki

Sanyi and Miki, circa 1947, Zennern

dropped a line from his cell so Magdus could attach some cigarettes for him to pull up.

The Germans especially needed food, as everything was rationed and in short supply. Bartering was the coin of the realm and necessary for survival. Miki took canned food he received from the Americans and exchanged it for shoes or whatever else his family needed. There were no regular jobs in the village; the black market was the only place many could make a living. Magdus explained that "everything could be had for cigarettes or chocolate."

Miki often worked with one German woman on the black market as he spoke little German. Soon, they were brazen about their affair; as he brought her to his home and they talked openly in front of Magdus, Bözsi, and Kati about going camping together while doing their black market runs. Kati describes the woman as "no beauty"— rather a nondescript, thin, average-looking brunette who was "not a spring chicken." She, too, was married and was introduced as Frau X.

I'm not sure how long this affair—or any of Miki's other affairs— lasted. Kati believes it started soon after Miki arrived in Germany and continued while he worked with this woman throughout his time there.

I've no doubt that my mother remained profoundly depressed and scarred by the loss of her baby and her experiences in the camps. Given that my father was always reportedly a fun-loving, happy-go-lucky kind of person (unlike the rest of the family), I can envision a scenario where he might have "cut his losses" and looked for a less damaged partner. I'm moved by the depth of Miki's loyalty, love, and caring for Magdus despite her mental state and that they decided to start another family. He even gave her a beautiful gold bracelet with roses painted on each segment when she delivered my brother.

I can understand his seeking fun and sex elsewhere, though I still find it disturbing, given how devoted she was to him. What was she going to do? Magdus was tied to him, dependent on and lost without him, and deeply in love with him. Besides, everyone in the family accepted his sexual forays as "just his nature." Despite my disappointment, I also respect and admire him more for having stayed with her and trying to make her whole again.

And I recognize, too, that Miki's philandering soon saved my brother's life.

CHAPTER 33

Klari and Imre

ONE OF THE THINGS I FOUND SURPRISING was the quick romances and marriages after the war and how Miklós and the sisters settled into relationships with people they barely knew. Perhaps I shouldn't have been surprised—it is natural that people who survived such trauma would grasp at any joy and signs of life and a future, but the speed of their bondings caught me off guard. They were especially quick to marry others they had known of before the war who had shared experiences and who were familiar faces that represented memories of happier times.

Klari's story is the most colorful.

The Proposal

When she first returned to Sáránd with her brother after liberation, Miklós became ill with malaria and needed medicine. There was no pharmacy in Sáránd, nor was there public transportation to the big city, Debrecen. Klari set off, walking nine miles across the Great Hungarian Plain in the intense summer heat. She had enough money for the medicine Dr. Kardos had prescribed but nothing extra for food or drink. Knowing that the *cukrászda* (sweets shop) usually gave patrons a glass of cold water while they were deciding what to order, she ventured in and sat down to cool off and recover. At the next table, an older man was haggling with a Russian soldier, exchanging bills.

The civilian, Simon Pollack, walked up to Klari and asked if she was the young Ehrenfeld girl from Sáránd. He said he had recognized her from her childhood when he bought grain for his business from the family's store.

Klari returned to Sáránd with the medicine. As soon as Miklós was better, Klari and her brothers left Sáránd and moved to an empty apartment in Debrecen. Simon promptly showed up.

Within a few days, this man in his sixties, who had lost his wife and five children in Auschwitz, wanted to court Klari. She had no interest in marrying someone more than thirty years her senior, but they struck a deal.

Simon was living with a group of five men, and Klari, in need of funds, agreed to do their shopping, cooking, and housekeeping. Since the Russians occupied Debrecen and it was not safe for a woman to walk alone on the street, each evening one of the men would walk her home.

In the meantime, Pista and Miklós decided they were going to return to Sáránd and try to reopen their store. They asked Klari to join them, and Klari informed her employer that she would be leaving Debrecen to go with her brothers. As Klari told me how this led to her betrothal, her eyes crinkled and her mouth broke into a broad grin:

> One night it was Imre Goldstein's turn to walk me home. I know what happened. The men had been sitting together, and they decided somebody has to marry this woman because we can't afford to lose her! They flipped a coin, and Imre lost. So we're walking home, and Imre says, "Okay, I give you a choice. You either go to Sáránd and keep house for your brothers or marry me." I said, "Let me think about it."

Klari went home and told Magdus the story. "Well, what do I have to lose?" Klari said to my mother. "A Jewish guy and he wants to marry. And probably he can make a living. Why not?"

Imre, 1947, Zennern

Magdus said she wasn't sure. "Do you know anything about him? I don't know." Magdus knew Imre only casually, from his coming to the shop to have something sewn.

Miklós's opinion was different. Miklós teased his sister about the need to maintain proper appearances: "If you ever tell anybody that you spent one night [alone] under the same roof with this guy, you blew your chances" of marriage. Imre had been a friend of Miki's and, feeling stifled in their Orthodox homes, they had often skipped school together. They also were mischievous and both were pranksters. They enjoyed rebelling by going to the park and cooking bacon for a forbidden treat. Both men preferred playing the role of *szoknyavadászok* (literally, skirt hunters) to studying.

Klari showed me a photo of the handsome young Imre. "We didn't have running water where we lived. I remember he used to wash himself outside in a *lavor* [basin], *félmesztelen* [half-naked], with his broad shoulders and very small waist." Klari said, "He was okay, but then I made him fat with my cooking for him." She pointed at the photo, "See, this is the guy that I married and not this big, fat, old man" whom I knew. The nightly midnight snacks of hot corned beef or pastrami sandwiches had taken their toll.

After the War and in America

Klari and Imre wed in November 1945. By the spring of 1946, all the Ehrenfelds who had returned to Hungary and tried to reestablish their lives in Sáránd and Debrecen—Klari, Magdus,

Pista, and Miklós—and their spouses gave up and decided to leave their country. The Hungarian border was not open, so they had to escape illegally. Many Eastern European Jews wanted to go to areas of Germany that were then occupied by the British or Americans, seeking safer havens.[1]

Klari and Pista's wife, Aranka, were pregnant, so they felt some urgency. The couples left by different paths.

Klari and Pista found some men who wanted them to go to Palestine. They smuggled the couples into Austria, but that came at a high personal cost to Klari. Since the couples had to discard every paper that gave a clue to their citizenship or identity, Klari had to leave her father's last letter, which she had treasured and carried with her throughout the war.[2]

Knowing that Kati and Sanyi were in Zennern, Miklós, Magdus, and Miki decided to join their family in Germany rather than settle in Austria.

After some time in Austria, Klari and Imre joined the rest of the family not far from Zennern, and their first son, Peter, was born in Ziegenhein in the fall of 1946, a large (two-thousand-person) DP camp at the site of a former Nazi POW camp.[3]

Although they were fed, life in the DP camps was still challenging. Both Pista's and Klari's first children were born in DP camps, where deliveries were generally being assisted by other women. Since there was no mohel in his camp, Imre engaged the services of someone whose training was making gutters. This man, Rostás, performed the ritual circumcision for Peter with tin snips. Klari helped other women in the camp by serving as a wet nurse for their babies and found that job very fulfilling.

After the Ziegenhein DP camp, Klari and Imre were able to share a house in Zennern with a German family, just as my parents did. Imre soon got a job as a driver at the Fritzlar air base.

Klari and Imre's eldest son, Peter, filled in details of their immigration and early life in the States.[4]

Kati was the first of the sisters to immigrate to America. While at Fritzlar, she fell in love with an American serviceman, Pete Peters, and he brought her to Iowa with him in 1947. Once settled on their farm in Iowa, Kati and Pete sponsored Klari's family's immigration to the United States with the help of Paul Porter, a neighbor, who promised Imre a job.

The Goldsteins were granted a visa in May 1949 and embarked from Bremenhaven to Boston on June 16, 1949, with seventeen hundred other refugees on the army transport ship *General Muir.* Their destination on the passenger list was "Route 2 Council Bluffs, Iowa," Kati's home. Men were separated from the women and young children for the eight-day journey. Imre was given a job on board, making coffee for the thousands of refugees and crew. He grew to detest the smell so much that he never again drank coffee.

The family arrived in Boston and immediately went to New Yori City, where my parents were living at the time. After a week they traveled by train to Omaha via Union Station in Chicago. Traveling was confusing and frightening since they didn't speak the language. A soldier who happened to have learned a bit of German while overseas helped them find the correct platform.

With a toddler in tow—and, inexplicably, a dozen boxes of detergent—the Goldsteins arrived in Omaha and were taken directly to the Porter farm on Star Route, near Pete's farm in Neola, Iowa.

Imre worked as a farm hand, earning $135 per month and was provided housing, a garden plot for vegetables, chickens, a pig, and a cow, which Klari promptly named Rozi. Their small farmhouse had a parlor and kitchen downstairs and one bedroom upstairs in the partially finished attic. As in Sáránd, a wood stove downstairs provided heat and a cooking surface, and the family read and worked in the evenings by the light from a kerosene lamp. Here, too, there was no indoor plumbing, though the outhouse was closer than in Sáránd. They also had a well with a hand pump and another, open well with a bucket that could be lowered on a rope to draw up water. Once again, Klari would lower a container of meat down the well to keep it cool since they had no refrigeration.

Imre, Klari and son Peter, and Kati and son Mike, 1949, Neola, Iowa

Neither Klari nor Imre spoke English, so they relied on gestures to communicate with others and their experience to run the farm. Imre was raised on a two-thousand-acre farm in Haláp, east of Debrecen, so he certainly needed no instruction in farming, though Porter was unaware of that. Imre also had a six-year-long apprenticeship as an auto mechanic in Hungary, and he put those skills to use repairing and improving the farm equipment.

Klari adapted her dressmaking skills to clothing her family and making furniture covers, curtains, and quilts. She also knit warm sweaters for her family to help them through the cold Iowa winters. Klari was always working—milking the cow, collecting eggs from the chickens, tending the garden or her son, splitting firewood with an ax, and preparing meals.

In her spare time, Klari taught herself English, reading the dictionary cover to cover. She also wrote letters to both her siblings and Imre's relatives, now scattered across the United States, Hungary, and Israel.

That winter of 1949, the outhouse was blown over during a storm, so Porter allowed the family to move into another small farmhouse that had indoor plumbing and electricity.

Although the Porters were very kind to Imre and Klari and sympathetic to their plight, Pete insisted that the community not know that Kati was Jewish nor a Holocaust survivor. Just as he had asked Kati to hide her identity, so he did with Klari and Imre, who later changed their name from Goldstein, which was too obviously Jewish, to Gray. According to Kati, neither Klari nor Imre liked being in Iowa and having to hide who they were. They wanted to live in a Jewish community and not live a lie.[5]

In the spring of 1950, Pete took Imre to Council Bluffs, where he bought his first car, a 1936 Ford business coupe.

THAT SUMMER, the Goldstein family moved to Detroit, Michigan, to join Imre's relatives. Imre's cousin Andrew Berger had immigrated in the 1920s and was a chassis engineer at Chrysler. He sent vague assurances as to a job for Imre there, should he want it.

Simon Pollack, Imre's brother-in-law, who had once hired Klari to be the housekeeper for a group of men in Debrecen after the war, also was living in Detroit and working at Packard Motor Company. He, too, urged Imre to move there.

Either the American Jewish Joint Distribution Committee or HIAS (Hebrew Immigrant Aid Society) helped Klari by making the arrangements for housing.

Little details didn't faze Imre. No driver's license? No problem. No backseat? Their toddler slept on the shelf under the rear window. No money to stop en route? They drove seven hundred miles straight through to their new home—a room in a two-family flat with a shared kitchen and bathroom. Unsurprisingly, Imre found no job waiting.

Despite hardly speaking any English, Imre found work at a warehouse where the foreman spoke German, and he spent the next year loading crates of whiskey onto trucks.

After that, Imre worked at a series of gas stations and auto repair shops.[6] Klari was not able to work outside the home nor get involved in the community; Imre wanted a traditional homemaker wife.

Their son told me the family's name change occurred in Detroit when Imre was working for an antisemitic man. As part of the naturalization process, the judge asked Imre if he knew he could change his name. Imre replied that he would like "Garay," a name he had used in Hungary. Not understanding, the judge wrote down "Gray" and changed "Imre" to "Emery," the name he used for the rest of his life.[7]

The couple raised two sons in Detroit. Klari provided her children with a Jewish education, wanting them at least to know their roots and have some belief system if they so chose. The war had shattered her own beliefs.

Imre died in 1987, Klari in 2001. Although Halachah (Jewish law) and tradition mandate burial, Klari chose to be cremated, "to be with her father" once again.

CHAPTER 34

Miklós and Ella

MIKLÓS'S FINDING A MATCH after the war was far more straightforward than his sister Klari's.

After being unsuccessful in resuming the family business in Sáránd, Miklós decided that he would leave Hungary. He joined Miki and Magdus in going to Zennern, Germany, a village near the air base where Kati and Bözsi were working. Soon he started working in the motor pool at Fritzlar.

There Miklós met two sisters, Ella Klein and her sister, Miri, who had been classmates of Klari and Sanyi, respectively. Later, Ella and Miri were in the same barracks with Magdus and Kati in Auschwitz. They had helped care for Magdus as she was recovering from her baby's death and after she had been severely beaten in the camp. They were lucky, being transferred with Kati to Allendorf, a less horrific work camp.

Miklós's daughter, Linda, shared the details of her parents' romance and early life together. At Fritzlar, Miklós became smitten with Ella. He told her that he was first attracted to her because he liked the way she walked. Despite the fact that Bözsi told Ella not to date Miklós "because he would never amount to anything," the two soon became engaged.[1] They immigrated to the United States in 1946 having been sponsored, along with Miri, by Ella's uncle, who had immigrated there after World War I.

The couple settled in New York City. Miklós would have liked to become a detective, like the father of his first childhood crush at age

Ella and Miklós's wedding, 1946, Scranton

eleven, Anna Dobos.[2] Ella asked a Jewish organization if it would sponsor his higher education, but she was turned down, alienating her from groups like B'nai Brith for the rest of her life.

Miklós then had a succession of jobs, first working in an auto repair shop, where he learned English from Trinidadian workers. After having an unsuccessful milk route, he became a New York taxi driver and put in long hours as a cabbie for the rest of his working life. His unflappable temperament served him well in that career. When not working, he enjoyed tending a small beehive in his yard, as his brother Pista had done in Sáránd in the 1930s, and reading. He read three newspapers every day throughout his life: the *New York Times*, the *Daily News*, and the *New York Post*.

Ella was a Comptometer (mechanical calculator) operator at Sears; then she owned a dress shop with a friend from the war. Ella later focused on raising their one daughter and spending time with her sister, Miri, who lived with them. Ella was renowned among the sisters for baking the best *túrós béles*: little square pockets of strudel dough, paper thin, crisp, buttery layers, filled with farmer's cheese—like a cheese danish, except far tastier and more delicate, requiring considerable skill to work with such thin dough. (I later learned that her "secret" was cheating, having switched to Pepperidge Farms puff pastry, as it was so much easier than making the dough from scratch.) She also added a hint of lemon zest, which lent a refreshing taste and scent.

GATHERINGS AT THE SISTERS' AND MIKLÓS'S HOUSES were all centered around food.

Miklós and Ella's small neat row house in Queens, up a steep flight of stairs, was always impeccably clean. The formal dining room formed an L with the living room, with its soft sofa and easy chair, and the far wall was covered with innocent photos of their child and a jarring painting of one creepy-looking old lady ancestor. The small kitchen filled out the rest of the L. I don't know how Ella made such abundant meals in that cramped, rather claustrophobic kitchen.

I remember visiting once when I was a kid and she had put out a plate of cold cuts. One that I found particularly tasty was unfamiliar to me, rectangular with rounded corners on the narrower end. She half-smiled and later told me that it was tongue, which totally disgusted me.

Meals and noshing at Miklós and Ella's were a much more formal affair than at the sisters'. Ella always covered the table with a crisp white tablecloth ("How did they get the stains out?" I wondered) and then elegantly set with grayish white china with a thin silver rim and shiny silverware, neatly arranged. Ella used nice glasses, too, not the random plasticware and mismatched things we hauled out while my mother's good china and glasses—the rainbow-colored frosted tea glasses with teak wood held by gold bands encircling the middle or the Colorado centennial set—were still unused in the hutch, too pretty and expensive to risk being harmed.

Ella often served chicken soup with matzoh balls. I liked watching the steam rise from the surface, where mounds of the matzoh balls, like small hills pocked with craters, floated amid small circles of oil drifting around. Bright orange chunks of carrots lent a jagged sharpness to the broth. The main meal was often brisket surrounded by vegetables, or a roast chicken.

The highlight was, of course, dessert, especially Ella's acclaimed *túrós béles*.

WHILE NEITHER MIKLÓS NOR ELLA WAS CHATTY, the two were comfortable to spend time with—so much so that I asked Miklós to escort me down the aisle at my wedding.

George, Judy, Miklós, and Mark, June 17, 1984, Cumberland

CHAPTER 35

Gatherings at Anyu's

WE DIDN'T HAVE BUSTLING GET-TOGETHERS often, but when we did, they were usually at Miklós and Ella's apartment in New York or at my mother's house in Silver Spring. Ma's were much more informal, sprawling affairs. Our ranch house was run down, and Ma was afraid to get it fixed up as George viewed improving the aesthetics as "unnecessary" and not the best use of her resources. The place had a dingy, worn, yellowish-brown wall-to-wall carpet. At the edges, around the baseboard, you could see it once was a nicer gold color and had a nubbly texture.

The dining room, which you actually entered from the outside, was furnished with a shiny walnut table, sideboard, and hutch. The chairs were modern with thin, curved rim topping the slatted backs. I refinished the seats when I was in high school, covering them with an orangey linen-like fabric to brighten the dark furniture. My father had made a top for the table, so it wouldn't get scarred from use, with a thin piece of plywood covered with white batting and a brown Naugahyde-type material. I don't think I ever saw the lovely wood except when we would take off the cover to pull out the leaves when we had company. My mother cared for that furniture a lot. It was probably one of her first big purchases in this country, bought around 1959, and pretty much unmarred until her death in 2008.

The interior walls of the house were always a very pale yellow and were decorated with artwork that I had made from kits—a king and queen above the sideboard and a Buddha and Indian deity on either end of the sofa in the living room. I must have made those when I was eleven or twelve, as I remember my father indulging me with the kits—though perhaps that is just my imagination. The more open walls bore wooden plaques from Israel of dancing figures. I can't find them now, though I recently tried going through boxes and purging some items that my brother and I had no special emotional attachment to, like those tea glasses, reminders of so many things that were too pretty to be used and how I am becoming my mother in many ways.

When we gathered round the table, we ate and gossiped and laughed loudly, while a stream of food appeared from the too-small kitchen. Ma usually made *töltött káposzta*, stuffed cabbage. That was so much work! Blanching the cabbage leaves to soften and separate them, filling each leaf with a mixture of ground beef and rice, and then tucking in the ends of the leaves, forming a pocket. I never got the hang of it, not that I tried more than once or twice. It was too much work, and I didn't master the art of wrapping and tucking so that the meat remained in the cabbage. The cabbage rolls were cooked in a sort of stew of tomato, sauerkraut, and paprika until soft. The spicy sauerkraut and cabbage scent greeted people when they walked into the house.

Other times, she would serve *csirkepaprikás*, an aromatic chicken stew with onions, tomato, and lots of paprika. (Traditionally, the dish was made with green pepper, too, but we didn't like that as much.) She would also make *nokedli*, egg dumplings. She would hold the runny dough over a pot of boiling water and then pinch off pieces with one of her big leaden spoons she had brought from Germany and drop them into the water, sometimes splashing herself with the scalding water. I would always beg for her to leave a little of the raw dough for me to scrape out of the sauce pan she mixed it in. I recently found those spoons, which had been tucked away for safekeeping. They and her kitchen table, with its white enamel top decorated with red flowers and trim, are some of our favorite and most meaningful inheritances because of the memories they rekindle.

Ma often served the chicken with *uborkasaláta*, paper-thin slices of cucumber, salted and rinsed, in a tangy vinegar dressing with small bits of onion and, of course, sprinkled with paprika.

Ma often made *cholent* as well, a favorite of mine and Miklós's especially. *Cholent* is a traditional baked bean dish with barley and small bits of beef, generally served on the Sabbath, when there is a prohibition against cooking or working. The meal was prepared on Friday afternoon and then sealed and tucked into a low heat oven until the next day. Miklós suggested adding a bit of smoked turkey to it for flavor; my mother, the previously Orthodox Jew, insisted that a ham hock gave the best flavor.

Our home was run down, and the dining table, while covered with a tablecloth, was set with mismatched pieces. Ma had some cheap china, white with a grayish-green border, I think, but mostly we used melamine dishes, white with a spray of small orange and brown autumn leaves on them. The coffee cups were small, not the big mugs we are used to now. Drinking coffee from them was not very satisfying.

While not the best cook among the sisters, Anyu was arguably the best baker. She always served *dobos torte*, a seven-layer chocolate cake; *diós* and *mákos*, walnut and poppy seed rolls, respectively; and her chocolate mint cake—not Hungarian but refreshing, cold brownie-like squares. The mint cake was easy to make, so we didn't have to ration it as carefully as the *dobos*.

Besides the diós, *gerbeaud* was my favorite. Gerbeaud was three layers of buttery pastry with layers of jam and chopped walnuts in between. Ma always used Polaner raspberry jam for the one layer and apricot jam for the other, not only because the flavors of the two fruits complemented each other with their contrasting sweetness and tang but because she found the different colors pleasing. She usually cut the pastry into rectangles, but when she wanted to be especially fancy, she would make diamonds. She liked to top the gerbeaud with a layer of dark chocolate frosting; I preferred mine plain, as the chocolate overpowered the fruit and butter flavors. I have Ma's sheet pans. They are burned and discolored in the corners and slightly warped, and the bottoms are crisscrossed with knife marks from her decades of baking. I've made gerbeaud and diós on rare occasion, but my efforts always feel an inadequate homage to her skills. I also feel guilt, too, in confessing that our freezer still contains remnants of her pastry, more than ten years after her death. No one can bear to eat them, nor does anyone want to discard the loaves of pastry, carefully wrapped in foil and labeled with her shaky writing. I've suggested that my husband feed them to the compost pile: ashes to ashes, dust to dust. She would be happy having them nourish the peonies and azaleas we planted.

What I found so difficult when Ma tried to teach me to bake was that recipes are not precise and that how the dough behaves varies with the humidity (or other mysterious factors) and getting it right must be learned by touch and practice, not by meticulously measuring out each ingredient. That's a very meditative concept to try to explain to someone young and inexperienced—that baking is an inexact art rather than a precisely reproducible lab experiment. Each moment is unique and requires an awareness of that moment's differing conditions. Therein lies the art I never learned.

I find myself wondering, too, how on earth the sisters baked these delicacies in a wood-fired oven in Sáránd. They had no electricity, no lights, no running water. And how did they make enough stuffed cabbage to feed their large family and their family's workers? Preparing such meals is such backbreaking work even with our modern conveniences, so I have only rarely even attempted to recreate them. The sisters were much stronger than I.

CHAPTER 36

The Twins: Pista and Józsi

OF MY AUNTS AND UNCLES in the Ehrenfeld-Glattstein dynasty, as I jokingly call them, I know the least about the twins, Józsi and Pista.

They were identical twins born to my grandfather Mór and his first wife in 1907.

While their looks were identical, their personalities were not, and the family could tell them apart. Others often mixed up the two. In fact, one day even Pista's fiancée didn't recognize that Józsi was visiting her, not Pista.[1]

Pista was much more reserved than his brother. Józsi was very outgoing and loved by everyone.[2] Both played the violin, often regaling the family with Gypsy melodies in the evening.

THE SISTERS ADORED JÓZSI and said he was always kind to them and helpful, with a much sunnier disposition than most of the family. He was especially tender toward Kati after she lost her mother when she was seven. He was seventeen years older than she and gave her extra attention. One of Kati's early memories is that of Józsi teaching her how to dry herself after bathing by wrapping a towel around her and showing her how to move it back and forth.

Being outgoing, Józsi went off to Budapest, where he worked in a large grocery store. He came home full of ideas to help his father. Kati always listened in, as she was nosy.[3] For one, he boosted sales in the family's store by building a creative display for the prepared food products and shoes on the window facing the street. Similarly, he built a bowling lane in the back of their yard, with carved wooden pins, to entertain the men who came to the tavern.

Józsi spoiled Kati, and she dreamed of running into him when she was going to school if he was home from the city. Debrecen was very modern with paved streets; Sáránd felt comparatively backward to Kati with only rutted dirt lanes. On the side of the road were temporary stalls—like an outdoor market—that included ice cream stands in the summer. In the winter, some stands sold baked squash and pumpkin by the piece. It was delicious and warming, but Kati didn't have money for treats like those.

Kati remembers walking on the street, thinking, "'If only Józsi would come'—it was always Józsi. I kept daydreaming, walking on the street. If I would meet him, he would be coming on the opposite side, and I would see him, and the first thing he would do was buy me an ice cream cone. That was my dream."

Although the sisters adored the twins, they still fought with them. One day Magdus clawed Józsi's face.[4] However, he never told anyone that she was the culprit, blaming the cat for the deep scratches instead.

Even haughty Bözsi only had kind words about her half-brother, noting that he would run after them as they walked to the train station to give them chocolate and nuts so they wouldn't get hungry on their long school days.

When Kati was about ten, Józsi took her to the photographer in Debrecen for her identification photo for the train to school and then bought her an ice cream cone. Around the same time, Józsi also gave her a gold ring engraved "Kato." It's one of the few pieces of jewelry not stolen from her house a few years ago.

Józsi was drafted into a forced labor battalion unit, the 101.4th *táb. Mu. Szd.* He was killed by a landmine on September 23, 1942, in Belogorye and is buried in Szirovka.[5] He is the only close family member for whom there are no photos, a source of great pain for all.

Kati and the other sisters describe Józsi simply as "a good human being."

BEFORE PISTA BECAME ILL with tuberculosis, he worked as an *asztalos* (furniture maker) in Pest. He later worked as a beekeeper on a large estate near Sáránd, riding his bicycle there every day from Debrecen when Jews could no longer ride the train.[6] He was in a sanitarium in Debrecen for a long time after having part of his lung removed to help control his tuberculosis. (There were no antibiotics at that time.) After he recovered, Mór opened a general store for Pista on the other side of Sáránd from his own. Mór had initially bought the building as a home for Anna's siblings when they were ill with TB. After they died, he converted this house into a satellite store for his son.

After marrying, Pista and his wife lived in Debrecen. They were in the ghetto with Magdus, and her old friend Bandi Egri brought them food to help keep them from starving. When the Jews were deported, Pista and his wife were lucky enough to be on the first train, which went to Strasshof, Austria. The other trains transported most of Debrecen's Jews to the killing machine, Auschwitz. Strasshof was a much less brutal concentration camp, and Pista even came back with his violin intact.

After the war, Pista returned to Debrecen and, with Magdus and Miklós, tried to reestablish his father's store in Sáránd, as well as to make soap. When those efforts failed, he and his wife decided to leave with Klari and Imre. The two couples went to Austria and then parted ways. Pista and his wife stayed in a DP camp in Admont for two years.

The small town of Admont, Styria, is nestled in the Gesäuse Mountains in central Austria, surrounded by majestic peaks. A Benedictine monastery was founded there in 1074 and now is home to a vast library in addition to its neo-Gothic cathedral. During the war, the Brandenburg 802 Panzer division was stationed there. This was a specialized operations unit that used camouflage (e.g., wearing Soviet rather than German uniforms) and was focused on sabotage.[7] After the war, Admont was part of the British occupation zone, and the Nazi military camp was converted to a DP camp for two thousand Jews.[8]

Pista, circa 1960

Looking at photos of Admont and the surrounding valley, I can well understand why Aranka, Pista's wife, wanted to stay there. I likely would have wanted to as well.

While Pista and Aranka lived at the Admont DP camp, their daughter, Mari, was born. Pista worked as a furniture maker, as he had in Hungary. The family did not make it to the Zennern area until 1948, well after Miklós left in May 1946 and Kati left in May 1947, so they never saw each other after the war.

Once in Germany, they lived as DPs in barracks divided into separate family living units. Pista continued to work making furniture in Zennern for at least the next year. My mother wanted Pista to come to America and blames Bözsi for having been unwilling to sponsor her brother. Pista's daughter says he would have been denied entry into the United States because of having had TB and that he wanted to go to Palestine anyway.[9]

In December 1948, Pista and his family embarked on a boat to Israel. It was a difficult passage in the winter, and the ship almost sank from the weight of so many people. After landing, Pista's family was placed in a tent city in the desert in Ra'anana, north of Tel Aviv.[10] After several months, they resettled in Haifa in a small one-and-a-half room house with a larger yard. Pista planted a garden and apple, orange, and mandarin trees there. He died in 1967.

CHAPTER 37

Mari and Jakus

I HAVE ALWAYS BEEN VERY CLOSE to two survivors in my extended family whose unusual stories belong in this saga—my great-uncle Jakus Grünberger, who helped raise Miki, Sanyi, and Jenö after their father died, and his daughter, Mari.

Jakus and his older sister, Ilonka, helped their sister Ella bring up the boys and adopted another orphaned nephew, Jancsi.

Ilonka, who was twelve years older than Ella and Jakus, had married Albert Lovenheim and immigrated to Amsterdam, New York, in about 1899, where they became American citizens. They had a daughter, Hella, in 1904, and a son, Jerome, born in 1906 in New York.

When Albert's mother became ill, the family moved back to Debrecen in 1910, and Albert started a grocery business. He died of pneumonia five years later. Mari told me it was attributed to his having become soaked when he refused to violate the Sabbath by carrying an umbrella, despite the rain.

The three Grünburger siblings, Jakus, and his two widowed sisters, Ella and Ilonka, banded together in one apartment building in Debrecen, raising the family's children. Ilonka also took in as boarders students who wanted to attend the Debrecen Jewish high school.

Hella studied to become a milliner and opened her own salon after finishing school. Jerome decided he'd have a better future in

America, so he returned to New York and, after a brief stint in New York City, joined his uncle Ignatz in Little Falls.

In a surprise turning point, in 1937, Jakus, then forty-seven years old, married his niece, Hella, age thirty-three. A year and a half later, they had a daughter, Mari, who was born in Debrecen. Because Hella had been born in the United States and was thus a US citizen, Mari inherited her mother's American citizenship. Showing foresight, Hella registered her baby's birth with the US consulate. Ilonka was also a US citizen but had lost her papers and could not prove her citizenship.

Mari describes a normal childhood, attending a Jewish nursery/ day school. After the Germans invaded Debrecen, she and her family moved into a friend's apartment in the ghetto. On June 21, 1944, the Jews were forced to go to the Serly brickyard, where they lived, fully exposed to the elements, with more than thirteen thousand others, including my mother and her newborn. Mari was only five years old.

In late June 1944, when the Jews of Debrecen were being deported, Mari believes she, her parents, and her grandmother were on the second train, which was rerouted to the Strasshof concentration camp,[1] after the rail line they were on, going toward Auschwitz, was bombed and became impassable.

Stunningly, Mari, Hella, and Ilonka were all US citizens at the time they were imprisoned.

Mari says the family was split up on their arrival to Strasshof after an examination. Jakus was sent to another camp, Traiskirchen, twenty miles south of Vienna, where all the men with advanced degrees were put to work digging ditches and doing other hard labor. There, a guard struck him with a shovel and he developed an infected leg.

Mari, her mother, and her grandmother were sent to a camp in Lobau, on the east side of Vienna, where there were oil refineries. They lived in barracks and Hella worked cleaning bricks while Ilonka cleaned officers' quarters. Ilonka occasionally found potato peelings, which supplemented their meager diet of a mash left over from processing sugar beets. The children were given about a half cup of milk each day from the camp commander, who was not as cruel as many others. In fact, Hella was even able to persuade him to have Jakus transferred back to join his family. An astute woman from Debrecen tried to teach the children a bit of German so they would be able to speak with their captors and communicate who they were and where they were from if they became separated from family.

Because of the presence of refineries, the camp was bombed day and night, and the prisoners would run to the forest and hide in foxholes. Mari was not able to run quickly and remembered her father running with her, carrying her on his shoulders. When they couldn't make it all the way to protection, they lay on the ground as the bombs dropped around them.

When the bombing intensified, the prisoners were transferred briefly to Solino, on the other side of Vienna. Mari was excited to have the novel experience of living in a small trailer with another family.

In March or April 1945 the family was sent back to Strasshof for several weeks. They were loaded back into cattle cars. Rumors were that the train was taking them to Bergen-Belsen, a camp in Germany. An Allied air raid struck the train, killing all the people in the wagon two cars ahead of the family. Mari recounted tearfully that her grandmother said, "Let's pray. G-d listens to the prayers of children."[2] And they prayed, "Ana Hashem hoshea na. Ana Hashem hatzlicha na" (Please G-d, save me.[3] Please G-d, make me successful).

Mari and her branch of the family continued to be devout throughout their lives, observing Orthodox Judaism and attending services religiously. Only in the 1990s did she recognize that these prayers, which are psalms in the special holiday Hallel prayers that she had been reciting for years, were the same prayers she had said some fifty years earlier when she was a terrified child. She became shaken and cried when this flashback hit her.

AFTER THE RAILROAD BOMBING, they returned to their barracks. Two days later, the Russians came and they were liberated. Hella rubbed soot on her face to appear unattractive to the Russian soldiers.

Jakus managed to find a wagon in disrepair, and his friend found a lame horse, so the two men teamed up to return to Hungary. They had made it only fifty miles when the horse died and they were stuck in Bratislava, a fraction of their way home. A kind farmer's wife let them stay in her barn and gave Mari coffee and bread with butter.

On May 8, 1945, V-E Day and Ilonka's birthday, the family arrived in Budapest. Jakus went to the Red Cross, which contacted Ilonka's son, Jerome, in New York, and he was able to send them money.

They returned to Debrecen and found their apartment had been appropriated, so they stayed with Manci Weisz, who had shared her apartment in the ghetto with them the previous year.

Mari was sitting by the window, having her hair brushed by her mother, when she glanced out the window and cried, "Look! There's Magdus!" Hella ran after my mother and brought her back to the apartment for their reunion. As the women chatted, Mari overheard my mother talking about the gas chambers and other horrors of Auschwitz. Mari told me she was afraid to go to friends' homes that had gas stoves for years afterward.

Later that summer, after Miki and Magdus had reunited and were planning to join Kati, Klari, and Bözsi in Zennern, Miki begged his uncle to bring his family as well. He hoped they would all be able to immigrate to the United States and remain together. Jakus, however, was always very strict and law-abiding. He thought they would be able to leave Hungary for the United States legally if they waited only a few months, so he wouldn't agree to crossing the border into Austria illegally. He should have reconsidered.

IN SEPTEMBER 1945, Hella went to the US consulate to try to obtain visas to return to her family in the United States. She was told the staff were busy and she should come back in December.

Jakus, Hella, Mari (about age 7), and Ilonka, circa 1947, Debrecen

After the war, voting became mandatory in Hungary with severe penalties for those who didn't meet their obligation. By following the new mandatory regulation Hella unwittingly lost her American citizenship on this technicality and was unable to return to the United States.

Meanwhile, Ilonka had lost her citizenship papers and the authorities were unable to verify her status as a US citizen, so she and the whole family were stranded in Hungary.

In 1945–47, with Hungary under Soviet rule after the war, travel visas were not being issued.

In 1949, Ilonka, then seventy, was granted a Hungarian passport, which was then being allowed for elderly. She and Mari flew to London, which was a bit frightening for the nine-year-old girl, especially as it was foggy so the flight was delayed, arriving at two o'clock in the morning, and no one was there to meet them. As an American citizen, Mari was allowed to take $100 out of Hungary; her grandmother was allowed only $10. The next morning, October 28, 1949, they sailed from Southampton on the SS *Washington*.[4] Mari didn't speak any English, so she wasn't able to chat with the other children on the ship. However, her grandmother treated her to her first box of crayons—eight bright colors to entertain her on the long voyage.

They arrived in New York City on November 4, 1949, and were met by Jerome, my parents, and Sanyi. They stayed with my parents in their apartment on East Seventh Street for a few days. The next week, they joined Jerome in Little Falls, and Mari grew up there.

With all of the Catch-22s faced by her family in Hungary, Mari was unable to see her parents again until 1958. They had to apply to immigrate as Hungarian Jewish refugees, and by the time they did so, the wait was almost a decade.

Mari thus grew up with her grandmother and uncle. She was held back in school because of not speaking English. After high school, she went to nursing school in New York City and practiced primarily as a school nurse.[5]

Another injustice was that Jakus, who was a lawyer in Hungary, could get only largely menial jobs as a night watchman or as a delivery boy in New York. At age sixty-eight, he willingly accepted such jobs to support his family. He retired at eighty-one.

My father was thrilled again to be able to visit Jakus, his surrogate father, and we regularly went to see him in New York. Our New York relatives didn't often visit us, in part because they remained very observant and our home wasn't kept kosher. We stayed close, however, and I continued to visit them after my father died.

CHAPTER 38

Ancsi

AFTER MY FATHER DIED, I periodically visited relatives to take a break from life with my mother. In my early teens, two of the people who were most comforting were my father's first cousin Ancsi Glattstein and his wife, Gloria. At the time, I almost took it for granted that they would adopt me for short periods. After having children of my own, I began to understand what a burden having me stay with them must have been on top of caring for their own children.

When my daughter, Heather, was preparing for her bat mitzvah, she did an oral history interview with Ancsi.[1] Her project helped fuel my videotaping of many other family stories.

Ancsi's father, Ferenc, was a brother of Miki's father, Zsigmond, who died when his sons were all less than eight years old. Feri helped by trying to mentor the young boys, and the families remained close.

Gloria and Andor "Ancsi" Glattstein, 1993, Seattle

Rachel Leah Horowitz Glattstein,
circa 1900, Tiszadorogma

Ancsi grew up in Edelény, where some of the Glattstein brothers—Herman, Samu, and Feri—moved to work in the offices of the Edelényi Kőszénbánya coal mine, owned by the Regina Horowitz-Margareten family.

The boys' mother, Rachel Leah, was part of the Horowitz-Margareten clan. She was my step great-grandmother, a striking woman. I was always intrigued by her elegant attire and that Samu's daughter, Clara, looked identical to her.

Regina (aka Rebus néni) later helped two of the Glattstein children, my great-aunt Etél and great-uncle Samu, emigrate, Etél in 1928 and Samu, who lost his first wife, Bella Berkovits, and six children in the camps around 1951. Feri was a salesman for the mining company, and his travels often took him to Debrecen, where he enjoyed visiting his nephews Miki and Sanyi.

Ancsi attended a one-room secular school in the mornings and cheder (religious school) in the afternoons. Despite (or perhaps because of) this humble but rigorous education, complete with corporal punishment, Ancsi went on to later achieve honors in his postgraduate studies. After elementary school, he had to move to nearby Miskolc and live with his aunt to continue his education.

Soon after Germany invaded Hungary, all able-bodied men age fifteen and older were conscripted to work in forced labor units. The Nazis deported all the women, children, elderly, and infirm to Auschwitz, a death camp, where those unable to work were murdered on arrival.[2] Ancsi's mother, grandparents, and two younger siblings were among those killed. Before being sent to the

Ancsi and his sister, Edith (Szuri), circa 1935, Edelény. (She and the rest of his family were killed.)

gas chambers, his uncle was forced to write a postcard saying he was being treated well, postmarked "Waldsee," Germany—except this was a fictitious town.[3]

By October 1944, Ancsi and his father were brought to Budapest. Feri managed to get them into a "safe house" under Swedish and papal protection. After about ten days, the Arrow Cross tipped off the Nazis, who raided the safe house. The Nazis rounded up men hidden in the safe houses in Budapest and sent the 1,700 Jewish men to Engerau (Petžnalka), just across the Danube from Bratislava (now the capital of Slovakia) to build tank traps against the Russians.[4]

Conditions were dismal. They lived on the roofs of some of the factory buildings, on bare concrete with no heat. Food was almost nonexistent. Each prisoner got one slice of bread and weak soup during the day. By spring, only about 1,400 were still alive, the rest having perished from exposure, starvation, or infection over the winter.[5]

The Russians continued their advance, undeterred by the tank traps along the German defensive line known as the Southeast Wall (Südostwall or Reichsschutzstellung), killing at least 15,000 Russian troops in the process.

On March 30, 1945, Good Friday, guards killed many of the inmates. The remainder began a death march to Bad Deutsch-Altenburg, farther toward Austria, then to Weinerneustadt.

Ancsi, then fifteen, now believes that his father gave him his own rations to try to save him. Feri became very weak and swollen from starvation. He also became very depressed, saying that he knew he would be "liberated" by the time of his own father's Yahrzeit on the upcoming Pesach. Feri could not continue, even with two people trying to support him. He sat down, exhausted, and the German guards shot him in front of his son. Ancsi tried to stay with him, but the guards drove him away with their rifle butts, knocking out his teeth in the process.

Dazed and delirious, Ancsi continued on the march to Weinerneustadt on the Leitha River, a tributary of the Danube. Once there, the men were packed into freight boats that were usually used to ferry hops. They were given no food or drink. Many jumped into the river, trying to escape their torture, and were shot by the guards.

After five days on the boats, they reached Linz and then were marched to Mauthausen, a concentration camp high on top of a hill. When they arrived at the site, the men had to climb 186 stairs during the night, egged on by the SS with their vicious dogs and whips. They then were herded into tents. By that time, early in April, the Germans knew the war was lost, and the prisoners were not forced to work in the quarry. The camp was bombed once while Ancsi was there, so the men were driven in the rain to another horrible camp, Gunskirchen, where their ordeal continued.

Ancsi was liberated on Friday, May 4, 1945. The guards had apparently been given orders to destroy all trace of the camp and its inmates before the liberation. The inmate leadership of the camp persuaded the guards that if they spared the prisoners' lives, they, too, would be shown mercy when the liberators came. The German guards ran away under cover of night, leaving the prisoners free.

With their new freedom, chaos ensued among the starved and crazed men. Some of them broke into the food storage areas and couldn't control themselves, gorging themselves to death there.

Ancsi estimates he weighed about seventy-nine pounds. He and some friends and distant cousins decided to go home together. The stronger ones were able to find and steal a couple of horses and a wagon. They took all the loot they could find and packed it up. Ancsi and the others started walking Saturday morning alongside the overloaded cart. By that afternoon, he felt sick and feverish and begged the others to leave him.

They stopped in Steinmunchen, a town on the outskirts of Linz. The young men took Ancsi to the house of an Austrian woman, asking her to take him to the hospital of the Sisters of Mercy. She did, and they found he had typhoid. Ancsi was so ill that he remained in the hospital for more than a month. While some details are hazy to him, Ancsi remembers being very angry with his doctor because she would not permit him to eat anything more than a thin soup and a few crackers. She was trying to prevent him from dying from rapid refeeding (which causes severe electrolyte/ chemical imbalances and can result in cardiac arrhythmias, among other problems).[6] In the meantime three of the nine or ten young men he was with died overeating.

After the hospital released Ancsi, a refugee organization felt he was still too weak to repatriate to Hungary, so it kept him in Linz to recuperate. He finally returned to Edelény in August and stayed there or in Miskolc until December. While he found some of his cousins, Ancsi learned that he was the sole survivor in his immediate family and he could not adjust to staying there.

ANCSI, NOW ORPHANED AND LOST, joined a group of homeless children in Budapest who were being trained for a new life and future in Palestine by the Bnei Akiva youth group from Hapoel HaMizrachi, a resettlement group organizing Aliyah Bet, the immigration of

Ancsi Glattstein, 1946, Leipheim

Jews to Palestine outlawed by the British mandate government organization.[7]

With their leaders having bribed the guards, Ancsi and twenty-five others crossed illegally into Salzburg on a train in December 1945. Though they were shabbily dressed, their determination propelled them to hike through deep snow in the forest to cross into Germany.[8]

The border to Palestine was closed in the interim, and the boys were forced to stay in a DP camp in Leipheim, Germany. While discouraged, they tried to focus on learning trades and skills that might be useful in Palestine, their goal. On August 31, 1946, two trucks abruptly appeared, and the boys were taken to Marseilles.

To smuggle them into Palestine, an 1870 cargo ship, the *San Dimitrio*, originally holding sixty-five passengers, was refitted with narrow shelves to hold thirteen hundred *ma'apalim*. These illegal refugees seeking to settle in Palestine were packed in layers, like sardines. The vessel was renamed *Latrun* after a fortress where Jewish leaders of illegal settlements were imprisoned.[9]

The young people descended into the dark belly of the vessel and then climbed into their slot for the voyage. Ancsi had been trained as a group leader, assigned to distribute the meager portions of food and water during the journey.

Soon after embarking, the ship hit a rock and began to leak. The captain wanted to return to France, but the passengers refused and worked in shifts day and night to pump out the incoming water. As it used up its supply of coal as fuel, the ship also began to list, and people had to quickly shift from side to side to keep the boat from upending.

After eight hellish days, as the *Latrun* neared the shore of Palestine, British Coast Guard planes spotted it, and two battleships intercepted the vessel. The British towed the listing boat to Haifa, transferred the passengers to the destroyer *Ocean Vigor*, and took them to detention centers on Cyprus. They first lived in tents in Larnaca and later in Quonset huts in Famagusta.

Having survived the war and this perilous voyage—losing his family, homeland, and all possessions—on November 3, 1946, Ancsi found himself on Cyprus, once again imprisoned behind barbed wire.[10]

IN AUGUST 1947, Ancsi was allowed to enter Palestine legally. He describes reaching Haifa at sundown, with the "graceful city glowing in the sunset . . . and the harbor whose quiet waters were caressed by the last rays" of the setting sun.[11]

Not wanting to go to another group settlement, Ancsi reached out to a cousin of his mother's, who took him in and taught him weaving. On November 29, 1947, the United Nations voted for the partition of Palestine, marking the start of the war with the Arabs. Ancsi soon received a note to report for military duty. While Ancsi could have been exempted from military service, being the sole survivor in his family, he chose not to do this.

Sadly, the Holocaust survivors, or *gahal*—who made up 40 to 50 percent of the recruits from abroad in the security forces and perhaps a third of the fatalities—were again often treated like second-class citizens rather than being considered more respected volunteers, or *mahal*.[12]

Ancsi served in the Palmach (elite commando unit akin to the Green Berets) in the war for liberation. He went to Kibbutz

S'de Eliyahu for training and preparation, working in the vegetable gardens and training in weaponry. After basic training, he moved to a military base in Rosh Pina, the headquarters of the First Battalion. This unit was commanded by Yigal Allon, military leader and future Israeli politician.

Ancsi's unit included recent *olim* (immigrants making Aliyah, returning to Palestine, which they considered the Jewish homeland), young women, and some local youth. They all fought together and became a close family of their own. They joined battles in Nabi Yusha and Mishmar HaEmek, among others.[13]

Ancsi was injured by shrapnel and given two weeks to recover. Instead of being allowed to lie idly, he was trained as a field medic, a role he continued in when he returned to active duty.

In early June 1948, Ancsi was about to go on a much-needed week-long leave. Instead, he was told of an urgent assignment to go up the makeshift "Burma Road."[14] This was a shepherd's path between Kibbutz Hulda and Jerusalem, initially passable only on foot and by mule, given its steepness and unevenness. Jerusalem was under siege by Arabs, who had cut off almost all supplies and had a stranglehold on the city. Ancsi and his mule walked the entire night, ferrying ammunition up this steep road, trying to help break the siege, and then evacuating the wounded on their return down the hill.

Soon, the Haganah (precursor to the Israeli Defense Forces) was able to improve the road enough to make it passable to four-wheel-drive vehicles and small trucks, and it broke the siege of Jerusalem.

Having successfully completed this mission, Ancsi had a brief leave and then was immediately sent to one of the Battles of Latrun.[15] The fortress at Latrun was a critical site as it overlooked the road between Tel Aviv and Jerusalem and became the site of several major battles.[16]

Two of the soldiers at Latrun went on to become prime minister—Yitzhak Rabin and Ariel Sharon, who was severely wounded in the May 24 attack on the fortress, which ended in a slaughter of Haganah.[17] A second battle occurred on June 1 and a third on June 8–9, Operation Yoram, commanded by Yigal Allon, in which Ancsi's unit fought. Based on the timing of events mentioned in Ancsi's memoirs, I believe that he fought in this third Battle of Latrun. Only three people in Ancsi's unit (of seventeen close friends) survived the battle. After all that he had survived, Ancsi's spirit was broken.

The "Promised Land" of milk and honey had proven to be anything but.

GLORIA AND ANCSI'S CHILDREN graciously provided documents and photos and answered my questions to fill in the blanks in Ancsi's story.

After his discharge from the army in 1950, Ancsi was again nurtured by cousins in Tel Aviv, Israel, and his interest in weaving was rekindled. He met Larry Karlin, a student from the Philadelphia Textile School, who was then studying in Israel, who fueled that interest. Ancsi began studying English, physics, and math, wanting to attend the same school. When he was accepted, Ancsi immigrated by boat to the United States in 1951, arriving at Ellis Island. He was met there by cousin Florence Radkowsky, who also eased my parents' adjustment when they arrived in New York. Larry and his family welcomed Ancsi to Philadelphia and to the school, and the men became fast friends. Ancsi excelled at the school. While studying in Philadelphia, he often visited Magdus and Miki in Washington, a short train ride away. I suspect that since he had lost both of his parents at such a young age, my parents became surrogates for him. I know he called Magdus *édesanyám*, "dear mother." During his vacations, my father even employed Ancsi to help cut pieces of leather or materials for the orthopedic appliances in his shop.

Larry became like a brother to Ancsi and took him to a friend's home in Long Island for his first Thanksgiving in America. The friend's father, Mr. Honig, was so taken with Ancsi that he offered him a scholarship for the remainder of his schooling and a summer job in his textile factory (likely Anglo Fabrics) in Webster,

Massachusetts. After graduating in 1955, Ancsi worked at the factory as a textile engineer, designing fabrics.

Ancsi moved to New York to become a partner in Yuma Woolen Mills in 1959. Such textile companies, which specialized in fine woolen fabrics for women, fell on hard times as the textile industry changed, with the move toward synthetics; Yuma closed in the mid-1970s.

Ancsi was well ahead of the changes in textile manufacturing with a backup plan—by the late 1960s, he had been working with a maternal (Salamonovits) uncle who had a nursing home in Greenwich Village. Ancsi liked the work and atmosphere, so he went back to school and obtained a master's in nursing home administration, a career he thrived in. Because of his upbringing and earlier traumatic experiences, he accepted and respected people who were looked down on by others because of age, poverty, language, or other differences. He was very concerned about the well-being of both his staff and the elderly residents, and his empathy toward them earned him respect.

Ancsi also was quietly generous in supporting charities and less well-off family members and taught us to pay it forward and help others in greatest need.

As I saw Ancsi over the years, one of the things that stood out was his calmness and even keel. I would flit in and out of his life, and he was always there when I returned, never chastising me for my lapses or being as moody as the Ehrenfeld sisters were.

But Ancsi had lingering fallout from his earlier ordeals that were not visible to me. Until the 1980s, he never spoke about his wartime experiences and losses and shielded his children from this history as well. But he would be haunted during the night.

In the early 1980s, Ancsi was asked to speak at a small Kristallnacht remembrance. From then on, he opened up and talked with school groups annually to educate them. He similarly became very involved in his synagogue.

I never understood how someone who suffered such traumas could remain devout nor how he was able to regain a sense of normalcy. To me, Ancsi seemed to be one of the calmest and most stable of the colorful personalities in the clan.

One of the life lessons he shared with my daughter as she prepared for her bat mitzvah was one passed on from his own father, which he learned in the coal mines—to remember that there are many types of people with different backgrounds and ways of life. He said, "If you treat them like people, they may act like people. If you treat them like dogs, they won't act like people."

In her eulogy to her father, his daughter recalled, "He would say that he only survived because every once in a while there was a kind guard or person that would give him some food."[18] Ancsi's firm commitment to recalling (and bestowing) kindness and gratitude no doubt helped him live such a fulfilling life after the many hardships he endured.

CHAPTER 39

Sanyi and Kati's Romance

AFTER KATI AND HER FRIENDS from Allendorf were liberated, the American soldiers, seeing that young women were not safe on their own in the German countryside, offered them jobs at the air base, as the base needed help and the men weren't supposed to hire or fraternize with the local Germans. The two dozen young Hungarian Jewish women were given lodging in a building at the base, allowing them all to stay together. Each basked in the luxury of having her own room.

Kati worked in the restaurant as a waitress and then in the mess hall. Some of the women cooked in the kitchen or washed dishes, and some cleaned the officers' barracks. Kati had taken a correspondence course in English through a Budapest newspaper and could count to ten in English. This, she later joked, was her qualification to work at the PBX (the air base's telephone exchange) as a telephone operator.

KATI'S CRUSHES NATURALLY CONTINUED after the war. It was her nature to flirt, and soon Americans began to pop up in her love life. In Fritzlar, her first American boyfriend was Johnny Spirenza, from the Bronx, who wanted to marry her.

Kati's youthful infatuation with a succession of men was a running joke among the sisters, and Kati herself recounts these tales with a certain self-deprecating humor and almost embarrassment about her naiveté. I had similar tendencies of too easily developing crushes on men, though less often than Kati. When she told me her stories, I actually felt closer to her, and we still giggle about them like schoolgirls rather than like the older women we have both become.

At twenty, Kati was ripe for something more serious, and she had actual suitors, one of whom was my father's brother Sanyi, whom she had known since she was eleven and he nineteen.

The Glattstein boys and the Ehrenfeld girls seemed to enjoy flirting with each other, particularly with Klari and Kati, the youngest two. Klari laughingly told me that my father, Miki, had told her, "If it wouldn't be Magdus, I would marry you!" When Klari confided that to Kati, who was then fourteen, Kati exclaimed, "Miki said the same thing to me!" But Kati took Sanyi's overtures more to heart and became deeply infatuated with him.

INTERTWINED WITH THESE YOUTHFUL ROMANTIC FORAYS is a less happy, complicated story of broken hearts between the Glattstein boys and the Ehrenfeld girls that is told differently by each of the sisters. After liberation, Sanyi found Kati at Fritzlar, and they got engaged. She even had a wedding dress made for her, sewn from sheets. But then Sanyi left the air base in search of the other sisters.

In the meantime, Kati met Clarence "Pete" Peters, an American bomber pilot, who became a serious suitor. Pete was handsome in a Waspish manner, with a thin nose and mouth and a slightly knowing, cocky demeanor, and was exotic.

When Sanyi returned to Fritzlar, Bözsi had already found her way to the air base. Kati unexpectedly broke off her engagement to Sanyi. Kati's version of the story is that she decided she didn't want to marry him because, at home, he had hidden their "secret" flirtation when she was a young teen, and she felt he was ashamed of her.

When I visited Sanyi in 2003, I told him that Bözsi, who seemed the coldest and most calculating of the sisters, also threw a wrench in the engagement by asking Kati, "Why would you want to marry Sanyi when we can each find an American soldier to take us to

Kati (22) and Pete (23), circa December 1946, Zennern

the US?" Bözsi could also be biting and added that the only reason Sanyi wanted to marry Kati is that he feels sorry for her because she was "a little Jewish girl alone, a *kis falusi liba* [little village goose]." Klari had told me this story, adding sarcastically about her older sister Bözsi, "She was always a kind soul."

Sanyi then shared with me that he was in love with Kati and wanted to marry her, but she said she was an "idealist" and wanted to wait for someone to fall in love with. He added that he would never have tried to talk her into marriage after that.

I personally subscribe to the plausible explanation given by the pragmatist Klari, who was all too familiar with her sisters' personalities. While Sanyi was very much interested in Kati, Bözsi's withering comment about Sanyi's motives helped tip the scale toward Pete. Besides, Pete was an American flyer and more exciting than Sanyi, whom Kati had known since childhood. Further, Kati did not want to return to Hungary, and Pete was her ticket to a new life outside Europe.

Kati's job as an operator ended because of Pete: she left her desk at the switchboard one day to go out and meet with Pete, so she was fired. He rented a room for her in Fritzlar, and she stayed there with Bözsi.

Kati's daughter recounted to my mother and me when we visited Klari in 2001 how the US military tried to prevent Kati and Pete's marriage. First, he was unexpectedly discharged and sent back to the States, as his superiors didn't want the American soldiers fraternizing with Jewish girls. (The officers turned a blind eye to fraternizing with German girls per unofficial policy.) Kati was stranded in Germany as a stateless person. Then the air force doctor falsely claimed that Kati had syphilis and could not emigrate. Pete and his family were persistent, and after they enlisted help from an Iowa senator, Kati was finally allowed to begin her journey to America.

Kati left Frankfurt for America on May 11, 1947. She married Pete a few days later and embarked on this new chapter of her life, which she later described as leading to her "second Holocaust."

CHAPTER 40

Kati and Pete

IMMEDIATELY AFTER KATI AND PETE got married in Elkton, Maryland, the "quickie wedding capital of the East Coast," the couple embarked on a train ride across the country to Iowa, Pete's home. Kati's first surprise in America happened on this train when Pete asked her to promise never to tell anyone that she was Jewish nor that she had been in concentration camps. She said Pete told her, "My family would not accept you; I want you to be treated like everybody else." Always having a compliant nature, Kati obeyed her husband. While this makes me angry at Pete and sad for her, I can see that she would have felt she had little choice. She was still unworldly and would have been alone and destitute in an alien country.

So for decades, Kati hid her past, becoming more and more isolated on a farm in Council Bluffs, Iowa, where they raised cattle for milk and meat, as well as seven hundred chickens. She sold eggs to hatcheries and slaughtered and dressed many of the chickens for food. To help make ends meet, she found a job as a clerk at Safeway, but it was a difficult commute on the streetcar. Pete was mortified that his wife would work in a grocery store. Kati earned $39.50 for a forty-eight-hour or longer workweek, but it was enough so that she and Pete could buy a car. Kati's first job in the United States lasted only a year, as she was let go when the serviceman she had replaced returned from his assignments and resumed his job.

Soon Kati had three children, the first just a year after marrying. Kati described Pete as a philanderer and an alcoholic and very conservative politically. After Pete's grandmother died, his grandfather Jake, a prominent attorney, moved in with them. He had dementia by then and required considerable care. Pete's cousins had become lawyers and assumed their grandfather's thriving law practice. They did not want the burden of caring for Jake.

Pete was an ugly alcoholic and blamed Kati for many of his woes, bemoaning how different his life would have been had he married an American woman. Pete became abusive, beating her and his grandfather. I was quite surprised when she explained that she had thought this was normal. Kati remained very isolated on the farm and didn't have friends for a long time.

After Pete's grandfather died, Pete discovered his grandfather had not left him the family farm as an inheritance, as he and Kati had expected would happen. Pete started drinking more heavily and became more physically abusive.

Pete abandoned Kati and the children when the youngest was two, and she struggled as a single parent. She and the three children ended up living in a converted but uninsulated chicken coop, which was a nightmare, especially when her baby was sick in a winter storm.

Kati knew she needed to get a better job than clerking at the Safeway and—with an active toddler in tow—she applied at a bank in 1959. She begged the interviewer to hire her, and he did—and she promised never to bring her child to work.

Even after Pete left her, Kati hid her past from everyone, including her children. They attended a Lutheran Sunday school because Kati felt she "had to keep up the charade." She, like the other sisters, also wanted her children to be raised with religious beliefs, even though hers had gone up in smoke.

Kati worked for years as a bank teller, but juggling her responsibilities as a mother and her work was difficult. Her eldest son, Mike, helped as best he could but committed suicide when he was nineteen, reportedly saying he didn't want to be like his father. To this day, Kati blames herself for not having been attentive enough to Mike and describes his death as her second Holocaust. Her other children did well in school, earning scholarships to college, and eventually left Iowa. Kati's daughter, shaped by her mother's stories about people who have been subject to intolerance or prejudice, became a legal aid defense attorney, wanting to defend such people and reach out to them.

Kati underwent considerable therapy after her son's death. After returning to work, she became successful in banking and eventually was named vice president of the bank. She attributed her success to her hard work and her deep loyalty to the company. Professionally, she fulfilled the American Dream.

In another sad footnote, Kati initially tried to hide her marital problems from Bözsi, and she didn't tell Magdus about them even after Pete moved out. Phone calls were a luxury in the 1950s and trips were even more rare. Apparently, in the late 1950s, Sanyi asked Magdus if she thought Kati's marriage to Pete was going to last because he was still in love with her. Magdus discouraged him from pursuing the matter, not knowing Kati's marriage was by that point doomed.

Hearing this made me so sad, as I thought about how much happier both Kati and Sanyi's lives might have been. Sanyi married a Hungarian Holocaust survivor and divorcée in 1958. She had a nine-year-old son and they soon had another son together. Zsuzsi was aptly nicknamed the "Ice Queen" by her brother, but they remained together until Sanyi's death in 2010.

Fortunately, after two decades alone, Kati met a man who was kind and loving to her, Bill Williams, and they were happily married for thirty-six years. After hiding that she was Jewish for decades, Kati "came out" quietly with Bill's encouragement. He thought she should be proud of her background and would introduce her as a survivor. Still, she began sharing her story publicly only in 2008, after a story on World War II vets and liberators came out in the *Omaha World-Herald*.

CHAPTER 41

Bözsi and Jack

AT THE AIR FORCE BASE in Fritzlar, Bözsi also worked as a telephone operator. A captain came in to call his family, and it became another "boy meets girl" story. By three to four months after liberation, Bözsi was once again a showstopper, with her wavy black hair and fine figure.

The captain was handsome in his uniform, tall with broad shoulders and an angular jaw. His high forehead set off his bushy eyebrows and thin hair, already graying at the temples. Jack Kasik, or "János" as he was nicknamed by the sisters, went home on leave but soon returned and proposed. Bözsi converted to Catholicism and had none of the troubles emigrating that Kati did. The couple wed in Eschwege, Germany, in 1948.

Bözsi soon became pregnant, and Jack sent her to the States alone, having heard that the United States was going to restrict the entry of war brides on January 1, 1949. She flew to New York City, arriving on Christmas Day. But instead of "America the Beautiful," Bözsi found filth and debris on the streets, noting that while you could say many bad things about Germans, at least they were clean.

Bözsi spent two months with Miklós and his new wife, Ella, and then went to Iowa in February to stay with Kati and have her firstborn there. Tensions grew between the two sisters, as Pete and Kati lived in a small farmhouse and had a baby of their own by then. Kati was surprised that even though Bözsi was "very pregnant," she acted provocatively toward Pete; she was still attracted to "anybody in pants." Her lack of modesty and joy in sunbathing later troubled her brother Miklós as well.

Before leaving Germany, Jack sent both Miklós and Kati a beautiful set of dishes to thank them for allowing Bözsi to live with them during her pregnancy. Both of her siblings had the china displayed in their living rooms throughout their lives here.

Jack Kasik, circa 1946, Zennern

Jack and Bözsi's son, David, kindly provided more details about his parents. When Jack returned from Germany in the fall of 1949, he was stationed in San Antonio, Texas, so Bözsi moved there. While she hated living in Texas, she continued growing her family, and her second child was born in San Antonio. Jack's work entailed driving from base to base assessing PXs in Texas and New Mexico.

After leaving the service, Jack was hired by a Denver oilman to buy and sell oil leases in the Dakotas and Montana. The year after he was hired, he went to the Dakotas and Montana for a while, still looking to make his fortune. Bözsi went with him on one trip, leaving her younger child in Houston with Jack's relatives. The baby became ill, and Bözsi, still fiercely strong and independent, drove alone from the Dakotas all the way back to Houston with their toddler son in tow.

Soon, the oilman boss asked Jack to relocate to Denver. Bözsi insisted that she would move only if one of her sisters did as well, so my parents moved west. Bözsi, by far the most confident of the sisters, could also be very persuasive.

Once settled in Denver, with her children in school, Bözsi resumed making orthopedic corsets. She initially worked with Miki and Magdus at Gaines Orthopedic Appliances.

Later, Bözsi set up her own shop with Jack. She also trained to become a prosthetist. She specialized in devices for mastectomy patients and a sex-change practice. During the Vietnam era, she had a government contract to make corsets and braces for injured servicemen who were hospitalized at Fitzsimons Army Hospital.

She and Jack had three children, who were raised as devout Catholics. The parents were strict disciplinarians. Corporal punishment was more common in the 1950s, and Jack would brandish a belt; Bözsi preferred to use a wooden spoon. Despite that, her son remembers a warm, loving home and the respect and caring his father showed toward his wife. I remember her referring to her husband as *vén troger*, or "decrepit old good-for-nothing," perhaps because he had failed in his ambition to become a millionaire. Her son recalls her affectionately calling Jack an "old goat."

When Jack failed to realize his dream of becoming a millionaire with the oil boom, he had various jobs, including working as a janitor (as had my father) and helping with his wife's custom corset business.

I remember being afraid of both Jack and Bözsi when I was a child and being stunned and hurt by Bözsi's coldness and lack of sympathy toward me when my father died. I interpreted her response as "get over it." Had she inherited her own mother's coldness and hardness? Kati thinks so.

Even before the war, Bözsi always seemed tougher and more adventurous than the other sisters, a tomboy who enjoyed riding horses bareback across the wheat fields of the Great Hungarian Plain. Certainly her months of working in Kanada, forced to search through the belongings and clothes of murdered Jews for valuables and items that might be of use to the Third Reich, hardened her more. Whatever caused her coldness, both my mother and I were stung by Bözsi's lack of support.

Even though my mother and Bözsi had moments of closeness, having both survived Auschwitz and then living near each other in Denver, Bözsi refused to stay with her newly widowed sister for more than a week, deepening Ma's hurt and sense of loss. Was she overwhelmed by our raw emotion or just so hardened by her time in Kanada that she lost any sense of compassion and humanity?

As an adult, I developed a better appreciation of Jack and his dry humor. We shared one fun evening at the wedding of a cousin. It was held at a fancy country club, and we were all feeling very out of place. The table for the Ehrenfeld family was tucked back next to the kitchen door, immediately making us feel like second-class citizens. I had brought along my beloved companion Keets, a husky mix, and he stayed in the car. I went out to take him food scraps and walk him periodically. Jack enjoyed coming with me and derived particular pleasure at Keets's leaving a smelly dog pile on the manicured golf course that night.

IN THE MID-1950S, the Germans began authorizing reparations to victims of the Holocaust. A lengthy and grueling evaluation was conducted to determine if an applicant was worthy. Bözsi reportedly was brassy and argumentative rather than deferent when she was interviewed. Although Bözsi arguably had the most traumatic experience and stories from Auschwitz and was there the longest, the first physician evaluating her (Dr. Weiker) said she was "sane" and reparations were denied. She appealed and subsequently received a very small subsidy.

WHILE BÖZSI'S SON also recognized her as "disillusioned and toughened" by her prolonged stay in Kanada and the four-month death march, David spoke of a tender side that I never saw.

He shared a letter Jack wrote to his sister about Bözsi in 1948, introducing her to the family, three years after meeting her: "She is a lady, kind, gentle and trusting; she loves me very much and has from the start. It has taken me long enough to find out that I love her, too. So we will be married."

David also recalled a story shared by a young woman who began visiting Bözsi as a high school community service project. This blossomed into daily visits and her becoming Bözsi's "youngest best friend" and a growing love between them.

JACK DIED IN 1988 and was buried in his family's plot in Massachusetts. His death resulted in two changes in Bözsi's behavior. One is that her "Queen Elisabeth" persona became more vocal and demanding. The second, more surprising change was that she stopped going to church and resumed Jewish observances, like attending Shabbat services and honoring holiday rituals like Passover. Later, she even wanted a Jewish funeral, though she chose to be cremated and have her ashes spread in her beloved mountains.

When Bözsi had her mitral heart valve replaced in 1994, she had a German cardiologist, Dr. Dieter Schneider, who selected the surgeon. Bözsi asked, "He's the best for me?"

"Yes," Dr. Schneider replied.

With her trademark gallows humor, she said, "I've left instructions with my children that if I die, the headline in the paper will be 'Nazi doctor kills last Holocaust survivor.'"

CHAPTER 42

The Philanderer

ONE OF THE THINGS I find hard to reconcile about my parents is that, despite their obvious and deep love, my father was a philanderer.

Sanyi and Ma's siblings knew he was a womanizer. They considered it "his nature," and they joked about it as one would speak of a naughty child's escapades. Still, they loved him and felt he was the glue holding the family together. Even when Miklós and Kati visited us in 2007 while my mother was hospitalized, they reminisced and laughed about it. They bantered that he chased women regardless of age, looks, nationality, or color.

I tried to make sense of my parents' relationship; over the years, starting when I was about fifty, I began to ask my aunts and uncles about it. They told me that Hungarian men were notorious for having affairs and that they selfishly thought they had a right to not use a condom. Abortions were legal and readily available in Hungary.

In 2003, when we were having one of our more intimate conversations, I asked Sanyi what his perception of my parents' marriage was. He replied, "Magdus was 100 percent devoted, 100 percent. Miki, not. You see, he didn't think it is—how shall I say it?—he didn't think there is anything wrong with having an affair with somebody else. It was normal human behavior." This helped me understand my parents' relationship a bit better, although I don't share my father's perspective that polyamory is acceptable if nonconsensual.[1]

I also thought of how unusually close my father was to his brother and how, in many ways, those two were opposites. Sanyi was pale, handsome, clean-cut, and studious. Miki was darker, happy-go-lucky and a charmer. Miklós described Miki as a "live wire" and used the expression "A jég hatan is meg él" (He can even live on the ice), explaining that "There is nothing on the ice, but he can flourish on the ice, making the most of anything, and survive."

Before the war, Miki and Magdus epitomized a romance between a small-town girl and a big-city boy. The young couple often took motorcycle trips through the countryside, traveling together for several days at a time. Given how devout Mór was and how protective of his daughters he was, I am surprised that he allowed these trips before my parents wed.

In many ways, Magdus was serious like Sanyi, though not as much of a perfectionist, and she was a diligent worker. She assumed a lot of responsibility, helping her father run the household after his wife died and working with him in the family's store and tavern. In Debrecen, she was a quick study at the orthopedics shop and took over running it when Miki was drafted.

While she was generally serious before the war, in rare photos of her from those dating years, I see a girlish, romantic side of her. In one from 1939, my father is wearing his army uniform and is perched on an end table, leaning intently toward my mother. She is lounging in a chair in the courtyard of her home in Sáránd, wearing a striped cotton blouse and a patterned knee-length skirt. Her right arm is draped behind her head, which is turned toward him, and her face is open and attentive.

In my favorite photo, also from that era, my mother is holding a letter from my father. She is wearing a feminine, floral-print dress and leaning out a window, looking girlish, her body coyly angled away. She said the note was X-rated and that Miki had explained that he had written his sergeant, offering him five liters of wine in exchange for getting the day and night off for a tryst with Magdus

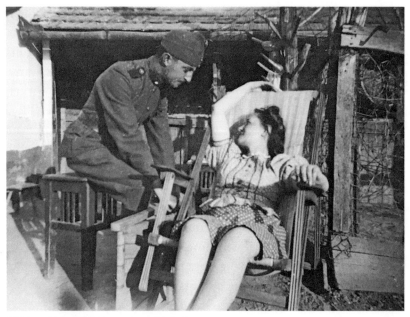

Miki and Magdus, circa 1939, Sáránd

near the site of their training exercise.

Magdus's quick reply: "I was only worth five liters?"

I FIND MY FATHER's having German mistresses while they were in Zennern particularly hard to understand. Was he attempting to feel more empowered and masculine again? Or was he simply seeking solace and glimpses of happiness wherever he could? Perhaps even more

Magdus, circa 1941

surprising was that my mother knew about the women and was still able to acknowledge that one of my father's mistresses likely saved my brother's life, although her acknowledgment was tinged with resentment.

My mother was pragmatic. She told me—at too early an age—that she could accept his affair if the woman was *különös* (extraordinary) in some way that she herself wasn't. She added that the woman had to be *különb*—better than her in some way.

Her candor gave me a distorted view of men that I believe was harmful as I began to form my own romantic relationships, and yet, despite my father's "renowned" reputation as a womanizer, my mother had his gravestone inscribed, "Together Forever."

I do, though, remember her bitterness when long after his death she inadvertently learned from a sibling about one of his affairs—with a woman who was not *különb*. She stopped going to the cemetery for a very long time.

I don't often go to the cemetery either. The quiet, parklike setting with red-winged blackbirds crying out from a marshy seep once was comforting, and around the time of the anniversary of my father's death, a mulberry tree would share its ripening fruit with me, bringing sweetness to an otherwise somber day. I was comforted, too, knowing that my uncle Sanyi had gifted me his plot next to my parents so I could one day rejoin them there and wouldn't be alone. But Mount Lebanon Cemetery, like the world, has changed and become less friendly and safe. The tiny pond has filled in and bird songs no longer fill the air, their singing replaced by noise from ever-increasing traffic nearby. Once I even encountered a drug deal happening near my parents' resting place. Visiting no longer brings me much solace.

I REMEMBER NOT SEEING my father as much as I would have liked and that he worked himself to death for his evil boss, whom we despised. But now I know that perhaps he was gone because he was out with his mistresses.

I share many traits with my father though—this I've come to recognize over the years. Wanting to make a better life for my family, I often worked too much, and I regret not being with my children more in their younger days, though my husband had infinitely more patience with them than I did. I also inherited my father's lipid pattern, if not his humor, and for many years, I assumed I, too, would die at age fifty. When I passed that milestone, I realized that part of me had always been waiting for the other shoe to drop.

When my children were little, I was so concerned about my own mortality that I spent some time crafting an ethical will, an old Jewish custom in which you impart the values that you wish to leave others. Thirty years later, reflecting on what I wrote, I can see that they are much the same values imparted by my family, with a focus on love, ethical behavior, social justice, and *tikkun olam*, leaving the world a better place.

Also, unlike my father's work, my solo medical practice allowed flexibility in scheduling, so I was able to work around my children's needs and the kids came out fine. Both are nice, caring people who want to make the world a better place. That gives me a sense of contentment.

My father died when I was young, and my mother ten years ago. Because I continue to ponder our complicated relationships, they remain with me in many ways. Occasionally I catch glimpses of my father and brother in my son. My daughter shares my mother's ability to charm anyone and to cook well without measuring, and this amuses me to no end, as I do not have that skill. And I know that my parents' values live on in my children and that their memories are a blessing.

CHAPTER 43

George's Babyhood

AFTER LOSING HER FIRST BABY in the ghetto, my poor mother had several frights with her second child, George, who was born in Germany in the fall of 1947, though she would have preferred otherwise.

In Zennern, my parents were not in a large DP camp like Pista, Klari, and Sanyi had been initially after liberation. Instead, they lived with a German family. Germans were required to share their homes with Jews who were displaced and were assigned families to house.

My mother had a wry sense of humor. She said the teenage daughter of the German family whose home they shared, Annaliese, said how beautiful George was when he was born. "I knew she was lying. He was ugly like the world war. He was small, dark, and hairy and already looked like a rabbi with his *payos*, or sidelocks. But he had beautiful eyes, intelligent eyes." A few months after birth, her baby was covered with ugly moles. They took the boy to a Catholic hospital and, for a carton of cigarettes, the doctor gave him an ointment that took care of the problem.

George almost died in Zennern. On Christmas, when he was but a few months old, my father's mistress asked to see his baby. When she went into the bedroom, the room was so filled with smoke from the faulty stove heating the house that she couldn't even see.

The baby had turned gray. My parents raced him to the refugee camp in Fritzlar, but a lot of other people there had carbon monoxide poisoning, and the camp didn't have oxygen. They then rushed him to a nearby town, Bad Wildungen, to seek help, with Magdus holding George out the car window so he would get fresh air. Magdus sent Imre, Klari's husband, to Kassel to fetch Dr. Rohr, who had cared for George before. The doctor came and cut under the baby's ear to let the "poison blood" out, his way of describing the carbon monoxide. While bloodletting for carbon monoxide poisoning is not the standard of care, the procedure was reportedly common in Europe for pneumonia and "toxic gas" exposure even in the 1940s. He then stayed to make sure the boy was all right, saying he would do anything for him because "his eyes were so smart."

AN ELDERLY GREAT UNCLE, Ignatz Lovenheim, provided a letter of support, enabling my parents' emigration from Germany. Again, their transition was anything but smooth.

My parents endured a very rocky ship passage, arriving in Boston in March 1949. Ella (Miklós's wife) met the ship and put them on the train for Little Falls, New York, to live with Ignatz's son Jerome, but a doctor ordered them to leave as Jerome's children had measles.

Fortunately, a Glattstein aunt and her husband offered to help them leave Little Falls, so Miki, Magdus, and George moved again and were placed in an apartment in New York City by the HIAS along with many other refugees from Germany. Two weeks later, George became ill with measles.

Magdus didn't speak English, except for the phrase "G-d damned DPs," commonly used by the GIs in the Zennern area, so she had no way of understanding why two men came and wordlessly took her sixteen-month-old child away. The incident rekindled her anguish over having lost her newborn son in the ghetto. Eventually, Aunt Etél found that the strangers took him to an infectious disease hospital ward, but it was some time before the family was allowed to visit. When they arrived, they found George looking very thin, rattling the bars of his cage, saying, "Allein, allein!" (Alone, alone). He was inconsolable and had refused to be fed or comforted. A few days later, Ma was allowed to take her son home.

CHAPTER 44

In Search of the American Dream

WHILE GEORGE WAS HOSPITALIZED with measles, my father found his first job—as a janitor in a corset factory—in July 1949.[1] He earned $14 per week, and the family moved into a tiny apartment on East Seventh Street. The crowdedness and filth of the Lower East Side, home to waves of immigrants, was overwhelming to the young woman from Sáránd, the village of two thousand. This first apartment was a fourth-floor walk-up, a difficult climb with a young child, and had a shared bathroom and no refrigerator. Its one room was furnished, so it commanded a $14 monthly rental. Sanyi joined them in that apartment after he arrived from Hungary and slept in the windowless, stifling pantry.[2]

After a few months, Miki was able to find a similar job in the Bronx through another transplant from Debrecen. My parents moved to a better apartment nearby on St. Ann's Avenue. Sanyi moved to Brooklyn but soon rejoined his brother and sister-in-law in their Bronx railroad apartment. Miki's boss raised his salary a bit but told him he would not increase it further. His boss was afraid Miki would then act like a New Yorker and go out on the weekends rather than work on Saturdays.

One day, Magdus took George to the park and was speaking to him in Hungarian. Attracted by the familiar language, a Hungarian man, Alex, approached them, and they chatted. By coincidence, this man's brother, Charlie, hailed from the same Debrecen school as

George (6) and Judy (2), 1954, Denver

Miki and was looking for an orthotist to join him in Washington, DC.

In 1950 or '51, my parents moved to DC, and once again, Sanyi followed them, having also received a job offer from the same shop, where he, too, became an orthotist. My family lived in a nice garden apartment on M Street NE, behind the National Arboretum, in a neighborhood with a mixed black and white population.

My mother was afraid to have another child, not being sure that they could afford a second one, but her American friends urged her on, and I was born in 1952. In contrast to my brother's dark, olive complexion, I was fair and blond. On hearing of my birth, George immediately asked, "Fekete vagy feher?" (is she black or white?) reflecting the makeup of their neighborhood. His two friends there, Gracie and Alice, were black and George was envious that, as he said, they didn't have to wash their hands since dirt wouldn't show.[3]

When my father took an examination for certification as an orthotist, he impressed Chester Haddan, the examiner. Hadden recruited my father to move to Denver, so off we went in 1952. This time, Sanyi stayed in DC because while working as an orthotist, he was studying for his master's degree in mathematics at night.

Haddan was a leading prosthetist and president of the Association of Limb Manufacturers, drawing patients from all over the Midwest.[4] Both Miki and Magdus worked at his company, Gaines Orthopedic Appliances, and later Bözsi joined my mother in making corsets there. As a young child, I remember Haddan playing cards with my father. I enjoyed hiding under the card table and knocking on Haddan's wooden leg as he was an amputee.

Stone family: George, Magdus, Miki, and Judy,1952, Denver (courtesy of *Denver Post*)

My earliest memories are glimpses from our life in Denver. We lived in a brick duplex home with both an arched entrance and an arch in the dining room; I thought that elegant, even as a young child. "Grandma Marshall" was my babysitter, and I remember sitting in her bright, fragrant kitchen and eating cinnamon toast. My aunt Bözsi lived in Denver as well, and we saw our cousins regularly. I learned to play tetherball and four square, and we went for trips high into the mountains. I recall it idyllically and still long for the Rockies.

But my father gave in to a Faustian bargain when Charlie enticed him back to DC with an offer of a partnership. Both my mother and Sanyi pleaded with him not to go back, as they hated Charlie. Sanyi said, "Don't do it; you will regret it. He'll chew you up and spit you out."[5]

Sanyi reflected back on this regretfully. "He didn't listen to me. But I was right."[6]

Ever in search of more money and the American Dream, my father, according to family lore, worked himself to death.

CHAPTER 45

Silver Spring Years

WHEN MY FATHER UPROOTED us from Denver and moved us back to the DC area in 1957, we lived in Silver Spring, Maryland, in a modest apartment complex called Northwest Park. Built in 1949, the apartments were utilitarian three-story rectangular brick boxes, each identical to the next. If you were drunk, you might not have easily recognized which building was yours. The saving grace was that the development had green space in the courtyards in front of the buildings and woods behind it. Our apartment faced a steep ravine that led into the forest. I was frightened of those woods. In fact, I still am scared of dark, shadowy woods like those, perhaps from getting lost there with my brother.

I remember only a few things about that time—mostly that I adored my first-grade teacher, Mrs. Griffing, and I learned how hard it was to churn butter from her. George had a wonderful teacher as well, Mrs. Brumberg. My mother was very fond of her, as were her students. She died tragically young, and a memorial fund for needy students at this school was made in her honor more than forty years later, as she had such an impact. Mrs. Brumberg made a point of introducing my mother to Marianne Shotland, a German Jewish woman, and they became lifelong friends. Marianne's son, Larry, also frequented our house and regarded my mom as a second mother, as did several other troubled teens. Everybody liked Ma. She was a good listener, confidant, and nurturer—to others, if not so much to me—and they shared their stories with her over milk and her homemade pastries. Larry continued to visit her until her death, as did another man who was once a lonely, ostracized boy. Sanyi's son felt his aunt offered him a unique, pointedly honest perspective, "dressed with a hard-edged wit and a wicked, wicked laugh that often came with a wink."[1]

After two years at Northwest Park, my parents continued their climb into the middle class, buying a home a few miles away. It was a good choice at the time, and they spent an extra few thousand dollars to get the one new house that was shaped a little differently from the others. It was a rancher at the end of a dead-end street, bordering Long Branch Park and a block from the playground.

Not many kids lived around our house, but I made a few friends at school. George was better than I was both socially and academically, particularly in math and sciences. It was very hard to follow in his footsteps, as teachers expected me to pick up difficult concepts as readily as he had done. I don't remember our parents ever saying anything explicitly, but it was clear that we were expected to excel in school.

My father continued to work long hours after he became Charlie's partner, driving to downtown Washington, DC, to their shop at 20th and K Streets, R&G Orthopedics. Some weekends he would take me with him. I liked many of the people there and think that's where I had my first interactions with African Americans. The smell of toluene and other solvents permeated the basement of the shop, where workers made the shiny prostheses with metal hooks for hands. Occasionally, I would accompany my father to see patients at their homes, as well as his office at the shop. Years later, I did something similar with my children. I wanted to both spend more time with my children and have them see "Dr. Mommy" in action. I enjoyed "parking" them in the rooms of older, lonely patients and having them absorb the value of helping others. That ritual was comforting and reminded me of my closeness with my father.

Elizabeth Kramm, one of his patients, became fast friends with my mother and often visited our home. "Elspie" couldn't walk without braces but taught me grit by example as she drove

Judy (about 3) and George (about 7), 1955, Denver

a specially fitted car, worked within her specialty of maternal childcare, and lived on her own. I suspect that was exceedingly unusual in that era, and it made a lasting impression on me.

I KNOW MY FATHER ADORED ME, and I him. I didn't recognize any favoritism toward me and remember his enjoying sports with my brother and allowing him to stay up late. My brother remembers life differently. He recounted that we were playing in the basement and I cried out at one point. Our father came downstairs and, without asking what happened, slapped George.

He recalls that I stubbed my toe, prompting my shriek, and added, "While at the time I was offended by the unfairness, in retrospect I deserved it for all the other crappy things I had done."[2]

I guess George had a certain reputation. He teased me, as older brothers commonly do, but I don't recall anything out of the ordinary—mostly.

One time, he told me to touch a catfish in a neighbor's aquarium. He egged me on, and I didn't believe him when he said that there were electric catfish. It was a shocking experience.

He would sometimes scare me with insects and garter snakes and tried to encourage an interest in biology instead of a fear of things that looked different. Sometimes, George just wanted to tease me as older siblings often do.

We each had hamsters and a series of other small pets. My hamster, Khandoshkin, was gentle and cuddly. George's,

Khatchatourian, bit. One day, he switched them out of their cages to see how long it would take me to figure out what he had done.

George and I grew up with the usual unspoken expectations. Boys—especially the first son—were valued more than were girls. I was to be sweet and look cute and girlish. At least our parents insisted on educated children—girl and boy—and my brother and I often read at mealtime to avoid squabbles.

My father protected me in several ways. When he introduced me to patients, it was to gentle old people whom I might cheer. I was spared the thalidomide babies for whom he fashioned prostheses and people with severe traumatic injuries.

When I was about ten, we had a school play that had seemingly endless rehearsals where we had to kneel on asphalt. I complained about the pain and abrasions from the rough surface, so Apu made me a pair of leather protective knee pads. While they helped and I appreciated his being so responsive, the teachers perceived me as a wimp.

Another time, we were working in the yard and I threw a rock, but instead of going straight, it curved and hit him in the mouth. How pained he looked. How mortified I was—and terrified of what Ma would do to me. He quickly promised not to tell her. This was one of our special little secrets.

Not all our secrets worked out so well. Apu taught me to ride a bicycle in the park next to our house. He helped push and steady the bike but then said he couldn't do that anymore. He didn't go into details but asked me not tell Ma. I had no idea then how ill he was.

Klari told me that once when they were together, Apu turned ashen and knew he was seriously ill. But he never said anything to Sanyi, and I don't think he told Ma. He always protected everybody and made light of problems.

MY PARENTS SEEMED CONTENT and were affectionate with each other. As the years passed, they became more secure financially and actually took a vacation to Florida without my brother or me.

They had decided, too, to get out of Charlie's clutches and for my father to go into business on his own after the one-year restrictive covenant imposed on him lapsed. Kati told me later that Miki expressed great remorse to my mother and tried to make up for his previous infidelities. Life was beautiful.

"Then," as the poet Lawrence Ferlinghetti wrote, "right in the middle of it comes the smiling mortician."[3]

CHAPTER 46

Cross-Country Trips

WITH THE EHRENFELD GIRLS scattered across the country, my father occasionally gathered us up to drive us across the country, stopping to visit each of the sisters.

First we drove to Klari's, arriving in Detroit after one long day on the road. Our first trip was likely in 1958. After only a couple of days in Detroit, we continued driving in the summer heat in a non-air-conditioned car to Bözsi's in Denver. I got motion sickness, so my parents drugged me with Dramamine and I dozed, sweating in my mother's lap as we crossed the interminable Great Plains.

We drove from there to Council Bluffs. Visiting Kati on the farm, I distinctly remember stepping into a cow pie and how humiliated I was—to say nothing of smelly. Drinking warm milk shot into my mouth straight from the cows was fun, and that experience made me a better infectious disease physician, as I consider possible zoonoses (infections from animals) and ask about unusual exposures to pathogens. But as a kid of six or seven, being on the farm and around so many animals was simply an exciting adventure. On that first trip, Kati's son Mike yelled at me for tying a silky green ribbon on their dog's neck because, he said, the dog could die if the fabric caught on something. His intensity scared me.

Our second trip was in 1963. I remember the year because Bob Dylan's "Blowin' in the Wind" frequently played on the radio, and Ma fell in love with that song. Another song I associate with that expedition is "500 Miles." We set out in my father's big black

235

Oldsmobile. I remember my mother hadn't wanted that car, but my father told her that Charlie expected his partner to drive a fancier car, one that was commensurate with his title.

KLARI'S HUSBAND, IMRE, had a gas station with a green Sinclair dinosaur in front. She would take his dinner to the station around six o'clock, and he would stay for several more hours. He always came home smelling of fuel, an odor that lingered even after he changed out of his greasy coveralls. He would go to bed immediately and around midnight, he would get up and forage for hearty foods like sandwiches or leftovers like stuffed cabbage or braised beef.

When I visited after my father died, Klari plied me with late evening snacks of fragrant corned beef sandwiches she steamed on the stove and with diós (walnut roll) and other pastries. Imre wouldn't let me learn to pump gas because "that wasn't for girls," and he didn't want me to smell bad. My cousins had an awesome train set in the basement. I think that is part of why I still love model trains. We ate and laughed, and life felt good.

Another early memory, likely from a different trip to Iowa, is of Kati redoing the floor in her tiny kitchen: she painted it white and then sprinkled colored, confetti-like chips onto the surface. I thought that was so cool how someone could magically transform a room.

Mostly I remember the boredom of the endless flat of the Plains and the thrill when we finally saw the Rocky Mountains in the distance as we approached Denver. Bözsi kept a constant supply of sweet minty tea. It was delicious, but I would never make it nor let my kids have it as it contained so much sugar, and after we drank it, we ran around, hyperactively energetic.

I was afraid of Jack because of his bushy white eyebrows, ruddy face, and quick temper. If we didn't like a meal, he would tell us to go eat grass with the moo cows. He had an inviting man cave in the basement with lots of mystery books; I first read Ellery Queen and Agatha Christie books there.

I particularly liked going up to the mountains, to Pike's Peak, or trout fishing with Bözsi, who loved fly-fishing. She made catching fish easier for me by letting me use salmon eggs as bait. I didn't know that was illegal, and I was thrilled when I caught rainbow trout. I loved watching her later at home, fixing fish for us fresh from the streams. I still intensely love and long for those mountains— breathing in the crisp, pine-scented air and hearing the rush of the water. I seem to have imprinted on those jagged mountains as a young child. I am always drawn to mountains and I feel a strong kinship with them.

After my father died, the families grew apart. It was hard to sustain closeness since the sisters were scattered across the country, each had so many responsibilities, and the expense of traveling was a burden then, especially for the two single parents, Kati and Magdus.

I think about how hard my father worked over the years to keep the sisters in touch. I never understood why he seemed more driven to unite the family than the sisters were. Was it because his mother was dysfunctional and his family fragmented after his father's death? When he thought that his wife had died in the war, he offered to marry any of the other sisters. Sanyi was the same, loving and wanting to marry Kati. Sanyi also tracked down relatives all over the world and kept in touch by calling or writing them annually. I tried to assume that role after he died and I inherited his files, and I even visited Glattsteins in Brussels and Paris and wrote many others. However, I was not able to sustain this connection as well as either Sanyi or Miki did.

I am sad that we have drifted apart and now have rare contact. The journey with this book reflects, in part, my desire to keep the family connected through their stories. But over the years, I've realized that I am not Sanyi, and my interests lie elsewhere now, focusing on trying to make the world better in small ways. I have come to think that it is time to focus on strengthening future relationships rather than on analyzing the past. Reaching this place has been a long journey.

Sputnik

When this book was just a dream, I joked with the editor of my first book that I was going to call it, "Sáránd to Sputnik," knowing that was a dreadful title. But that captured some of what I found remarkable about my mother. Here was this woman who grew up in a rural village in Hungary, Sáránd, with no electricity, indoor plumbing, or modern conveniences. She was the best-read woman I knew, and well-educated, despite leaving school when she was fourteen.

Anyu survived many losses, and yet each time she was able to pick herself up and start over. She learned to drive and nicknamed her first car in 1958, an old Pontiac, "Sputnik," after the remarkable changes she saw in her life through the beginnings of the space age. Sputnik was a tough teacher, with manual steering and brakes. Ma really had to crank the steering wheel to turn. A short woman, she had some trouble seeing over the steering wheel. Most memorable were the rusted-out floorboards through which bits of pavement were visible. And just as she wryly called her car Sputnik, Ma often liked to describe it, and other worn, broken things, as *kaput*. Yet she, like Sputnik, may have been creaky but was tough and kept going.

CHAPTER 47

The Aftermath

MY FATHER DIED while I was at Sunday school in June 1964. My brother came to pick me up on his bicycle and told me to climb on it with him. I was afraid to. He shrugged and said, "Okay. Then walk home." Black or white. No ambiguities. Our world was shattered.

After we arrived home, cousins drove us to George Washington Hospital, where my father had been taken. Charlie came down the hall and put his arm around my mother's shoulder as he escorted her to my father's room. There is no one I would have less wanted to see there. I felt that his presence desecrated my father's soul.

I didn't go into the hospital room at first; later, my cousin Florence made me, though I didn't want to see or touch death. Ma was weeping, holding my father's hand. George looked stricken.

Much of the rest of that time is indistinct except for bits and flashes.

Orthodox Jews have strict mourning rituals. Although our family wasn't Orthodox, we observed all the required customs. We covered the mirrors. We tore our clothes and wore black ribbons. We "sat shiva," the weeklong period where the family stays at home except for attending the funeral, a period of enforced mourning where we are forced to confront our loss. Restrictions loosen over time, but in the first year, we were not supposed to attend joyous events or listen to music since we were marking the death of a parent. After that period, mourners are encouraged to resume a normal life. My mother forgot that part.

For a long time, my mother was so depressed that she was barely functional. After Apu died, Anyu wanted to die as well. She mourned and waited but "no such luck," as she would say. After a few decades, she finally began to appreciate life again. She especially loved baking and growing flowers. When she hit ninety, she really began to enjoy some things—especially chocolate and her grandchildren.

A sense of normalcy and security was one of the most significant losses that came with my father's sudden death. After my father died, I craved routine. I had always enjoyed the reassuring rhythm of the holidays and rituals, but after he died, Ma didn't want us to celebrate Chanukah or any other holiday, although she allowed me to have my bat mitzvah the following year. I also lost sense of community and safety. I have since found myself always waiting for the other shoe to drop.

Whenever I am feeling the loss of my family more acutely, I am often drawn to and comforted by *The Two of Them*, a children's book by Aliki.[1] The grandfather in the story, who dies, is evocative both of Miklós and my grandfather Mór, and the rhythmic waxing and waning of the seasons provides me a sense of security.

Before Apu's death, we regularly attended services in Silver Spring, and I remember my father's index finger moving under the Hebrew words, pointing them out to me as he prayed and chanted the melodies.

Then, poof. Religion and ritual were gone. Although I occasionally missed them over the next two decades, I had little to do with formal Judaism until I was contemplating getting married. Then Jewish traditions again became important. I'm not entirely sure why, except that I desired to honor my parents' and families' suffering and losses. I suspect I felt that this would be a gift to them. And so, despite a meddlesome rabbi, I married Mark, a Jewish convert turned agnostic, under a chupah.

When we had children, I reintroduced some of the rituals— lighting candles and going to synagogue. I wanted to teach my children about their heritage and have them share the warmth and love that I had felt with my father at services. Although my husband strongly opposed my decision (or observance of any organized religion), it became critically important to me for my son to have his bar mitzvah, a gift to my mother and a public demonstration that the Nazis had not succeeded in eradicating our family. They had, rather, survived and gone forth to have children and resume rich, fulfilling lives. The bar mitzvah turned into a big family reunion and celebration.

After my father died, I spent long stretches of time visiting relatives, seeking to be part of a healthy family. I would go to the New York area and spend time with Uncle Miklós and then Jakus's daughter, Mari, whom I felt very close to. My parents and I had been close as well with Ancsi, my father's cousin who at age fifteen became the sole survivor in his family.

When I was fourteen or fifteen, I thought it only natural that family would take in a troubled teen, though Ancsi and Gloria had three young children of their own in suburban New Jersey. Later, especially after I had children and work to juggle, I marveled at their generosity. At Ancsi's, I became known as "Judy Pepper" because the kids found it funny that I put salt and pepper on cantaloupe.

Twenty years later, my husband and I began driving to Maine every summer, stopping for a night to visit Ancsi and Gloria in Lee, Massachusetts. Though they no longer are there, we still stop and reminisce about that close tie. I was touched that their daughter, Sharon, schlepped down from New Jersey for my mother's funeral, and her kindness rekindled our relationship.

I THINK THE WHOLE FAMILY felt it unjust that my mother lost her husband so unexpectedly, especially just as my parents' lives had become comfortable for the first time and also because everyone loved my father. He was great with all the cousins and knew how to cheer them up when they were having a rough time. Many baby boys in the family were named Michael—named after my father, I believed. This explains my surprise when I visited Kati in 2018 and she told me that her Michael was named after his grandmother's chauffeur who had taught Pete everything, and in gratitude, Pete named his first son for him. I haven't made further inquiries among the cousins; I know my resistance to asking is my desire not to be further disillusioned. Some things, I think, are better left as beliefs.

I don't know what helped my mother recover from her profound depression after my father died. Mostly, her gradual recovery reflected her strength and resilience. She was a survivor and had endured even worse adversity, and she knew she had two children to take care of.

Over the years I saw glimmers of renewal slowly emerging, and as she aged, she began to more fully embrace life, especially enjoying flowers and small outings, such as a trip to a local garden or a drive around lushly landscaped neighborhoods. Despite failing health, she seemed happier.

One of her greatest challenges had by then largely resolved. When she was just sixteen, Ma was afflicted by crippling arthritis, a fact that always seemed weird to me, and even when I became a physician, I could never understand the cause. For decades arthritis dogged her, especially before thunderstorms, when she would be bedridden with an excruciating inflammatory arthritis that primarily affected the right side of her body. Her joints, especially her wrist, became taut with swelling and redness. After two or three days, those symptoms would subside. In Hungary, when she was young, she was treated with bee stings. In the States, doctors tried strong anti-inflammatories. Whatever this plague, in her midseventies it gradually began to burn itself out and the acute episodes quieted.

Then, in her late seventies, Ma became legally blind from macular degeneration. Still, she lived alone, widowed for forty-five years, cooking and caring for herself almost until the end, spending her free time listening to the news discussions on *Washington Week in Review* and watching *Jeopardy!* In her later years, Larry Shotland, a friend of my brother's since childhood, often visited her. Larry understood her well, and he never failed to remind her of her strengths by saying, "You know, Mrs. Stone, you are a survivor. Every day you live, you cheat the Nazis again. Every day you live,

Heather, Michael, Anyu, and Judy, 2007, Silver Spring

another Nazi dies." Her whole face lit up as she contemplated that reward.

On her ninety-fourth birthday, after going out for lunch, her treat was being wheeled around the Giant grocery store by her grandchildren and me so that she could savor the vibrant colors, textures, and scents of the fresh produce.

She was thrilled when visitors came—old neighbors, an occasional cousin, or her friend Julia, who became a personal reader and confidant to her.

For a while after her husband's death, Ma continued to do piecework, sewing corsets in the basement for Charlie, but eventually (after perhaps five or six years), in her midfifties, she saw an announcement and enrolled in a program the county offered to teach people gardening and help train them to work at nurseries or in landscaping. She had always loved flowers and had a green thumb with her house plants. She loved the course, and caring for plants and being out in nature brought her back to life and became a passion. She filled our yard with azaleas, hydrangeas, peonies, and raspberry bushes. Violets brightened the kitchen and greenery enlivened the living room. I have no doubt that caring for her little green friends and watching them thrive helped her heal.

Ma also excelled at nurturing other people. My brother and his friends often played board games for hours in the living room.

I would wait on them, taking snack orders, and Ma would ply them with pies and cakes, as well as the occasional *dobos torte*—a waste on voracious teen boys who had no appreciation for either fine food or the amount of work involved in baking. Store-bought treats—such as Hostess cupcakes or Twinkies—would likely have suited as well and been far easier.

She often helped distraught young people too. While I was away at school, seven or eight years after Apu died, she took in two teens whose parents were friends. They had run away from home and then lived safely with her rather than being out on the streets. She quietly let their parents know they were safe, and they continued to believe they were being rebellious and independent. She gave them support and time to sort things out in a safe space.

WE MUDDLED ALONG. George soon went off to college, but I had several more years home alone with her before I, too, fledged. I made some inappropriate dating choices, but she—mostly—bit her tongue, not wanting to drive me further away. She allowed me to choose where I went to college, and I chose Washington University in St. Louis (WUSTL), halfway across the country from her. Staying closer would likely have been better for both of us, but she allowed me to make the decision.

My two top choices were WUSTL and Carleton College. My best friend chose Carleton. I ultimately decided I didn't want a school that was smaller than my high school and thought that I would likely get more depressed in the long Minnesota winters. That I had such insight then is surprising to me now. WUSTL had two other advantages. "Aunt Irén" (Irene) Abrams lived nearby, so it was comforting knowing that someone loving was around if I needed her. The deciding factor was that I thought I wanted to major in urban studies (this was soon after the urban riots and Martin Luther King Jr.'s assassination), and the school had a well-respected department in that field. Unfortunately, I so disliked the demanding professor I had my first semester and became overwhelmed by the unrealistically large reading load that I quickly changed majors.

What followed was a series of interests, the most long-lasting of which were counseling psychology and wildlife biology. I applied to graduate school in wildlife biology but was not accepted. However, I was accepted to medical school. I asked the University of Maryland (UMD) for a year's delay in starting as I was working in a research lab and supporting myself for the first time and wanted to continue that. Besides, I was ambivalent about medical school, but UMD said it was now or never, so I reluctantly moved to Baltimore.

When I made that decision, I had no idea that my mother had wanted to be a physician; I learned that fact long afterward. I tried to take the Trailways bus home for most weekends to visit my mother, and occasionally she drove up to visit me, a drive so stressful on the fast-paced, busy Baltimore-Washington Parkway that, she explained, she frequently had to stop and have a cigarette to calm her nerves. Both my parents smoked a couple of packs a day; for my mom, it was Pall Mall, then Carlton. I still often picture my mom sitting at her kitchen table, with a cigarette and a cup of coffee, reading the *Washington Post*.

When I graduated from medical school, Ma was immensely proud, and she gave me her mother's watch as a gift, causing a rift between the sisters. The pocket watch, visible in Anna's 1911 wedding photo, had been saved by friends of my mother's, initially squirreled away in the lining of a coat, then hidden under the thatches of a roof by their friend Bözske Losonczi. The other sisters received portions of the gold chain that held it. While Bözsi's daughter was the oldest granddaughter, the other siblings felt that the very observant Anna would not have wanted her watch to go to a Catholic grandchild.

For years, I wasn't aware that the sisters' not coming to my graduation caused a lifelong wound that festered in my mother. Perhaps this renewed Ma's hurt that her parents reneged on their promise to pay for her medical school education. I don't remember being bothered by my aunts' absence from the ceremony. It was a frenetic time for me, with studies and the transition to my new responsibilities of internship. Looking back, I wish I had been more attuned to my mother's upset.

Ma was vociferous in opposition when, after my fellowship, I chose to start a practice in a rural community in western Maryland. At that time, I was the only infectious disease physician between Morgantown, West Virginia, and the Baltimore-Washington area. I wanted to care for people in an underserved community and preferred small, quiet towns to crowded, fast-paced cities. Besides, Cumberland had the advantage of being partway between Morgantown, where my beau was, and my mother.

I met my future husband in Morgantown, where I went for my infectious disease fellowship training. By the time we met in 1983, I had sworn off men, having been burned by several. I was living happily with my old husky mix, whose owner had given him to me when she saw how attached we were. After about six months into my specialty training, a popular resident, Diane, who was doing a rotation with me, took me to Maxwell's, a coffeeshop and bar. It was the first time I'd gone to a bar. Mark casually knew Diane, and while we were there, he stopped by our table and asked me, "Are you a physician too?"

Early on I had learned that the quickest way to end a conversation with a date or a prospective date was to tell him that I was a physician. Mark was the first man I met who wasn't at all threatened by that news. In fact, he was incredibly supportive of me professionally, as well as personally, and it was he who helped me through the painful fellowship and my research. Even better, Mark had two Samoyeds, and his gentleness with my furry love, as well as with his own, quickly showed me what a kind soul he had.

My mother was not thrilled with my choice of partner because Mark was so different from me culturally. He is quiet and reserved and had a New England, Waspy upbringing. Before we met, he had converted to Judaism, but my mother would have preferred that I marry a traditionally (ancestrally) "nice Jewish boy" and that I have a suburban medical practice in an upscale area. I firmly told her none of that was going to happen and she needed to be

Left to right: Jack, Bözsi, Kati, Sanyi, Magdus, Imre, Klari, Ella, and Miklós, 1984, Cumberland

realistic. I knew—if only as a result of my parents' marriage—that no relationship is perfect. And I knew that in rural America, I was not going to find someone who met her specifications. I also knew that wasn't what I was looking for in a life partner.

And so, one year after I began practicing in Maryland, Mark and I had a lovely outdoor wedding on a farm on the outskirts of town. It was an idyllic setting in a beautiful valley, outside a historic farmhouse with beds of peonies. Most of my relatives, and all of Ma's siblings, came.

Ma charmingly told me that when I turned thirty, she had given up on my ever marrying. Once married, I rather foolishly hurried to get pregnant, in part to make up for all my mother's losses and traumas. She was the only widow among the sisters and the only one without grandchildren. I also was acutely aware that my biological clock was ticking. I was thirty-two and had wed a man seven years my elder. Mark and I spoke about the obstetrician's warning that I might be infertile. We agreed that we ought to try quickly to begin a family.

CHAPTER 48

Klari's Smile

GROWING UP, I DIDN'T SEE MY AUNTS very much except on our cross-country trips and now and then after my father died. They were all friendly to me, but Kati was working hard and stressed, and Bözsi always scared me. I've gotten close to Kati only in the past decade, and our relationship has blossomed over that time.

My favorite place to go was Klari's. Without our ever speaking about it, I knew she understood me and loved me unconditionally. Her mood and face were mercurial. One minute, she would appear brooding, with her thick dark brows knitted together. The next, she would have the broadest smile that would make her eyes crinkle closed.

I liked playing with Imre's and the boys' extensive train set. We had a train set as well, but it was simpler. My dad set it up on the Ping-Pong table. I'm still sad my mother made us give ours away after my father died.

Staying up late, eating corned beef or pastrami sandwiches and swapping stories around the kitchen table was a pleasant change from my more disciplined routine with my mother. I liked Klari's wry humor as well. For example, when I admired her menorah and asked how the family celebrated Chanukah in Sáránd, she told me they cut up a potato, put a hole in it, and filled it with oil and a wick for candlelight. I asked, "Did it last for a week?" and she quipped back, "We had more than one potato. These were homegrown."[1]

I spent longer times with Klari in my midteens, and she helped me learn to sew. She was a master seamstress and tailor. We made a variety of clothes for me from school dresses and woolen suits (using the fine fabric my father's cousin Ancsi gave me) to a prom dress. I learned the basics but lacked both the patience and the creativity to know how to adjust a pattern. She, in turn, was frustrated by my impatience and desire to take shortcuts. I so wish now that I had studied with her more diligently.

While I never learned to bake from her, Klari made the best diós of the sisters, and I was plied with that as well.

Late in her life I learned that she, too, was twelve when she lost a parent and that I was the daughter she longed for and never had. Of all the aunts, I always felt closest to her.

WHEN I HAD CHILDREN, Klari adored my daughter and found her endlessly entertaining. She visited a couple of times when my children were young. I came out to the kitchen one day to discover my daughter, then about four or five, sitting on the counter with her hands and legs covered in flour. Klari laughed as she told me that Heather put her feet in the mixing bowl to knead the dough, and then some peaches got in the way and joined the mix. I captured their expressions of delight with my camera, and it is one of my favorite pictures. My mother would never have stood for that

Heather
and Klari,
circa 1992,
Cumberland

kind of a mess. But Heather and Klari were joyful as they "baked" together—and for a moment, I wished that Klari had been my mother.

Klari's Death

I made one other long trip like the ones of my childhood, but this was to drive Ma out to see Klari before she died in 2001. It was a complicated production with Ma, George, and Heather along with a huge oxygen tank. Without my friends Polly-Jo and Steve, who had a medical supply company, we never could have gotten the oxygen set for Ma due to Medicare payment rules. They were the fixers who made the trip possible. Positioning the large tank was a problem, and if we had been in a major car accident, the van likely would have blown up. But we did it, and nobody complained during the trip because it was a sacred duty to fulfill.

Kati was already in Ann Arbor to be at her sister's side. She seemed to think that if Klari received more loving attention and was properly fed, she could be saved. I disabused her of that fantasy. My mother was realistic. She "knew the score" and showed little emotion. Each of us spent most of our time with Klari privately. Kati would sit by the bed, often holding her sister's hand, though none of the sisters liked public displays of affection. It was at that time, on her deathbed, that Klari reiterated to her younger sister that her mother hadn't liked her.

When it was my turn in the bedroom, we shared few words; Klari was too ill. I usually lay down on the bed beside her, cradling her. Unlike my mother and her sisters, I openly express my emotions and affection.

When he could, Klari's older son joined us, and we indulged in storytelling and laughter, especially about Imre's antics. Kati felt terrible that Klari was excluded from the fun—or perhaps guilty that we could be having fun while her sister was dying. But it was a relief to share joyful moments and still feel alive.

One treasured gift I have from Klari is the notebook with the measurements she learned to take to become a seamstress. I was shocked that she had allowed her son to draw in it when he was little. Most likely, he didn't know what it was and was only looking for scrap paper. The notebook is impressive, with detailed drawings of patterns that she kept with her from Sáránd and her apprenticeship in Debrecen to her stay with Bözsi in Budapest before the war. Studying it, I thought how amazing it was that it had survived the war and the trip to the States, only to be defaced by a kid's crayon. Still, I have it tucked away, one of the few mementos I haven't lost or misplaced.

CHAPTER 49

The Sisters' Grudges and Competition

RIFTS BETWEEN THE SISTERS widened and shrank over the years. This was unsurprising, given that they had such different personalities. Miklós was generally exempt from the spats; I'm not sure if it was because of his mellow nature or because he did not grow up with the girls, having been "exiled" to Hadház. He also looked and acted like their father, automatically earning him respect.

Much of the siblings' unhappiness with Bözsi reportedly related to her autocratic style. Kati never remembered Bözsi ever keeping house or cooking and Klari managed to get off by prioritizing her needlework over cleaning the kerosene lamps and dusting, her assigned tasks. They were both a bit aloof, and Bözsi was haughty. Neither Bözsi nor Klari could work in their father's store without alienating customers. In contrast, Kati described herself and my mother as "the *cseléd* [maid] type," ordinary and hardworking women, and they thrived on helping patrons. Bözsi's commanding, regal bearing stood her in good stead at Auschwitz when she fearlessly went from her barracks through the guarded areas to see Kati when she heard Kati was to be transported out.

They had their tender moments, such as when Bözsi went with Magdus to visit a palm reader when my mother was pregnant with her first child. And being ten years older than Kati, Bözsi took the role of her mother after the war. She consoled Kati when, after they were reunited, Kati finally realized that her father had been killed. Kati had been in denial until then, even saving her father's favorite foods for him after the war, dreaming of when they would be reunited.

I've seen beautiful portraits of Bözsi and Kati looking fondly at each other after liberation, and Bözsi was very kind to her younger sister then. But that was in sharp contrast to Bözsi's mocking Kati as a "little village goose," who Sanyi must have only felt sorry for, and influencing her to call off her engagement to Sanyi.

The sisters helped each other on occasion. Bözsi lived in New York with Miklós and then in Iowa with Kati when she first came to the United States, pregnant with her son. Kati and Pete sponsored Klari and Imre, enabling them to emigrate.

However, my mother never forgave Bözsi for refusing to sponsor their brother Pista, especially after she sponsored a German woman.

When Miki was alive, his joking and good nature often smoothed the sisters' ruffled feathers. After he died, however, there was no one to buffer their sometimes biting personalities.

When Bözsi had heart surgery in the mid-1990s she demanded that each sister come and care for her for a month and was stunned that they had other plans, though each visited her for a period of time. My mother was still stung because Bözsi had hardly stayed with her after my father died. And when Kati's son committed suicide, Bözsi told Kati, "You have to admit Mike was a bad boy and deserved to die."

What kind of woman says this, especially to her little sister? I've wondered how much of her attitude was due to growing up with a cold mother, who was similarly cruel to her daughter, and how much was due to the horrors she experienced in the concentration camp. When she was liberated, she was thirty years old, had been widowed, and had survived almost a full year in Auschwitz and a three-and-a-half month death march in the winter. The others had horrendous experiences as well, but Bözsi was turned into the most hardhearted of the sisters.

Kati, in contrast, was both the timidest and most forgiving. Despite all the heartache Bözsi had caused her, she summed up their relationship simply: "In spite of everything, she could be good."

My mother excelled at holding grudges. After my father died, Sanyi spent considerable time with us, as was to be expected in their culture. Sanyi's wife, however, resented the attention he gave us and decided to move to Los Angeles. Wanting to save his marriage, Sanyi soon left us and followed her, although he still called my mother regularly. Each time he called, my mother reminded him that he had abandoned us.

Cousin Linda, Miklós's daughter, organized two remarkably successful family reunions in 1992 and '93. But then another rift happened between Bözsi and Ma, and they didn't talk for about ten years. I understand that a similar decade-long feud occurred between Bözsi and Klari, who used to be very close when they were young, but I don't know the details.

I'm not sure what caused such deep hurt between sisters. With my mother, Kati believes the dispute was over something stupid, like which sister was going to pay the postage on the cartons of cigarettes Bözsi would ship my mother from Colorado because they were cheaper there.

Bözsi's son believed the rifts were over which of the sisters had suffered the most. He said, "Because my mother was queen, she would have a final 'Off with their heads' ceremony" and cut off people she was angry with.

Likely the problems were cumulative, going back to childhood. We'll never know, but it saddens me both that they wasted these years and that I learned to follow in their footsteps.

When Bözsi was on her deathbed in 2004, Kati raced out to Denver to be with her sister. Bözsi, who maintained her regal disposition till the very end, asked, "What took you so long? I thought you would never get here!"

Kati was desperate for Magdus and Bözsi to make up and called my mother. Ma reluctantly agreed to speak with Bözsi and as Kati and David held the phone to Bözsi's ear, Ma told her barely responsive sister, "Okay. You won. I called you first."

THE SISTERS HAD AN UNOFFICIAL RIVALRY in other realms as well. Their baking competitions were legendary, with ratings among the cousins (rather than directly among the sisters). Of course, we all had different assessments. I was partial to Klari's diós and pull-aparts, Ella's (honorary sister) *túrós béles*, Kati's buttery walnut cookies, and Magdus' gerbeaud, and *dobos*. Naturally, Bözsi's son ranked his mother's diós and *dobos* as his top choices and was partial to Kati's cinnamon rolls. I also remember Klari and my mother baking *rétes* (strudel), and it was heavenly, although an insane amount of work. While there was healthy competition among the sisters, baking also connected them, and they were always sharing recipes and tips. They all also enjoyed sharing their pastries with neighbors.

CHAPTER 50

The Brothers' Relationships

THE GLATTSTEIN BROTHERS were even more different in their temperaments than the sisters were.

Jenö, the eldest, was impaired from his bout with meningitis as a child. He wasn't able to hold a job and the other brothers weren't as patient with him as they would have liked. When Miki asked him to help in the shop, Jenö occasionally rebelled, and Miki would punish him. When Jenö was a teen, he was very good at shoplifting from the merchants at the quarterly street fairs. Sanyi felt that both of his brothers suffered from a "loose character" and that this was just their nature. Miki was also charismatic and witty; everybody loved him and his fun-loving nature. Sanyi, on the other hand, was inflexible, studious, and rule oriented. He also admired Miki and did almost anything to please his brother.

It was astonishing that Miki and Sanyi were together for almost the entire war, even both surviving Dachau. After liberation, Sanyi, a meticulous recordkeeper even then, set out to trace and reunite families, as well as serve as a liaison with the German mayor in Zennern. Miki's work in the black market supported Sanyi's efforts.

When everyone assumed that Magdus had died, Miki declared his desire to marry one of the other sisters. Sanyi also proposed to Kati; however, after a brief engagement, she cut that off and married a handsome American bomber pilot.

Miki decided to immigrate to America. Always following his brother's lead, Sanyi did the same—but he waited until the other siblings were all safely out of Germany before he immigrated.[1] First, the brothers lived in New York, near a Glattstein aunt and uncle. Chasing the American Dream of the almighty dollar and "opportunity," Miki uprooted his family again and moved to Washington, DC. While he would have liked to stay in New York, once again, Sanyi followed his brother.

Sanyi spent considerable time with us after my father died. That was to be expected, as he and his brother were close friends and had been almost inseparable throughout their lives. It was also part of the culture they grew up in for extended families to help take care of each other. Sanyi's wife, however, did not share those values and resented the attention he gave us, so she moved with their children all the way across the country, knowing that he would follow.

Sanyi had little choice but to leave us and move to Los Angeles as well. However, he still called my mother religiously every Saturday morning at eleven o'clock. Each week, she heaped abuse on him as he listened patiently, allowing her to vent. The conversation always went something like this:

Sanyi would ask, "Hogy vagy?" (How are you?)

My mother would respond, "Mit gondolsz? Hogy lennék?" (What do you think? How would I be [after what you've done to me]?)

Sanyi's son offered an interesting analysis of his father's motivations:

> Sanyi was ferociously devoted to the idea of love as sacrificial commitment—he only moved to DC for Miki in the first place; he changed his last name [from Glattstein to Stone] because Miki did. He moved to California because Zsuzsi demanded it [rightly having calculated that his reason for moving to DC was gone]. These were all huge, traumatic milestone events in his life that he did to appease the people he loved. Magdus would have to be collateral damage in the equation.[2]

Sanyi and my mother would do their passive-aggressive, "let's play guilt" dance for years, but eventually they, too, mellowed and spoke to each other kindly. I particularly enjoyed watching and listening to them trying to one-up each other in regard to their memory for poetry.

CHAPTER 51

Pesach

EREV PESACH, THE EVE OF THE SPRING HOLIDAY of Passover, is one of the two holidays that trigger intense sadness and a sense of loss for me. Pesach was the most important family holiday for Sanyi. In Hungary, more than in the United States, it meant an intense spring cleaning, ridding the house of any chametz, a grain product that has risen, as we are to eat only unleavened bread for eight days. A completely different set of dishes and cookware had to be used, too, dedicated to Pesach. Anna and Mór's dishes were colorful, with a floral pattern and gold edges. They were kept in the attic except for this one holiday. If duplicate cookware was not available, the pots and silverware had to be "kashered," or made kosher by either burning them in a fire or immersing them in boiling water.

In my mother's childhood home in Sáránd, the holiday meant repainting the kitchen ceiling, which required the girls to stand on a table to reach it. A chandelier over the dining table also had to be cleaned and polished and then covered with a liquid gold.

For Passover, a wagon would bring boxes of matzoh—at least thirty kilograms—to last for the week. The Ehrenfelds celebrated by indulging in eating more meat at this holiday, usually killing a calf at this time, in addition to geese. Ersatz gefilte fish was often made from chicken breast, ground and mixed with matzoh meal, carrots, and spices.

Other than the burden of preparing for the rituals, I never heard the sisters speak of this holiday. They did not have family get-togethers for Pesach in Hungary; I associate those Seder gatherings only with my father's family, both in Hungary and in the United States.

When I was a child, I knew whom to expect to see at these ritual dinners: family and a few Hungarian friends. Every year during our family's life in Silver Spring, while my father was alive, a long table was set in the basement recreation room at Sanyi's house, the only space large enough to accommodate everyone. The places were always set with the bright red-and-yellow-covered Haggadah, which walked us through the order of the Seder, the ritual meal recounting the story of Exodus and our deliverance from slavery in Egypt into freedom.

There were rituals with food items, such as dipping parsley into salt water to remember our tears. My favorite item, which I could devour, was *charoses*, a mixture of chopped walnuts, apples, and too-sweet wine, to remind us of the mortar the slaves used in setting bricks. Of course, every child liked chanting the four questions and hiding the broken piece of matzoh, the afikomen, to receive a reward for its safe return for the dessert. In many families, the adult hid the afikomen and the children would go on a treasure hunt. In ours, the children hid the piece and held it for ransom. I was mortified when, one year, I carefully wrapped it in a fine linen napkin and hid it in the oven, which had been set only on warm. The linen was nicely browned when I retrieved it, and dignified friends joining us at dinner bit their tongues about my thoughtlessness.

It's funny that I remember little about the food at the Seder, except for the *charoses* and horseradish, to remind us of bitterness, and the first course, *kocsonya*, carp with pieces of orange carrot to brighten the grayish, strongly scented chunks of fish surrounded by a salty gelatin. I'm sure we had chicken soup with matzoh balls, because what holiday meal doesn't start with that? Then there was roast chicken and veal. Since no leavened foods are allowed during the long holiday, desserts were a challenge. We might have had a sponge cake or apple cake made with flour from matzoh, along with coconut macaroons.

My birthday almost always fell during the holiday, and it was so hard to not have a cake like my friends did. Explaining my different bagged lunch was always awkward too. I didn't like being different from the other children.

What I liked the most about the Pesach dinner was the warmth and closeness of the family and how enthusiastic and happy Sanyi was when he led the Seder and the singing afterward. We sang the tongue twisting "Chad Gadya," a playful cumulative song about a goat, and "Dayenu," a song thanking G-d for abundant gifts, each of which "would have been enough." Our family felt more whole at the Seder, but this feeling evaporated when Sanyi and his family moved all the way across the country a couple of years after my father died.

Another, modern song comes to mind now at Pesach, although it is based on Genesis rather than Exodus, Debbie Friedman's "L'chi Lach," about setting out into the unknown.[1]

I'm not sure if I'm reminded of this because of Sanyi's leaving, now understanding and having forgiven his "going forth" as a necessity for him, or whether it reminds me of my own children's having fledged and needing to let go, happy that they are ready to do so successfully.

I did try to recreate the holiday celebrations when I had my own children, but the experience was very bittersweet and lacking.

Half a century after I last attended the family Seder, I asked Sanyi why the Seder was so important to him and why it was the one time of year he asked his sons to come home. Sanyi had grown up fatherless, with his uncles stepping up to help raise the three brothers. Rarely emotional, Sanyi teared up as he recalled that one uncle, normally focused on his own large family, always invited the boys and their mother to his Seder and that was one of his happiest childhood memories. Each year, he tried to reclaim that feeling for himself through leading his own Seder.

CHAPTER 52

Ambivalence.
Mixed Emotions—Muddled

MOTHER-DAUGHTER RELATIONSHIPS are often incredibly complicated, capable of generating either the most intense closeness and
deepest understanding or irrationally strong anger. My relationship
with my mother was no different.

My mother brought her many traumas—hidden from me at the
time—to the table, along with her baseline despondency. I brought
rampant adolescent hormones that caused wide mood swings.

My mom's doctor, Pat Kellogg, perhaps best summed up most
mother-daughter interactions, describing them as sometimes akin

Magdus (94), August 16, 2007, Silver Spring. These two photos illustrate Ma's
mercurial moods—funny and warm one moment and chiding the next.

to the United States military's scorched-earth policy during the Vietnam War. Pat shared this bit of wisdom after my mother woke up in the hospital following gallbladder surgery and her first words to me were, "Why are you trying to kill me?" I was devastated, and Pat helped console me with her sound perspective.

WHILE WE ALMOST NEVER SPOKE about it, I know that I hurt my mother deeply when I was in college. I was naive, away from home for the first time, and lonely, and I was seduced by a professor. Except for his name, I wouldn't have known that he was German, as he had no accent. I justified our affair, saying he was blameless in the treatment of Jews, not having been born before the war, but that didn't work with my mother, who hated anything German and did not even want German products in the house.

Ironically, my justifications at the time were similar to the ones Kati used about fifteen years later about her decision to return to Allendorf, and I was disappointed she would go.

I also asked Ma why her friend Marianne, who had a strong German accent, didn't raise her hackles. I was told that was different, as Marianne was Jewish.

While I was a poor judge of men, Ma was careful not to be too critical of my choices so as not to drive me away and into their arms. She would voice her concern and leave me alone to discover my mistakes. She understood human nature well. That lesson served me in good stead in my own parenting, and I've also learned how to develop a certain kind of fatalism.

Unsurprisingly, I came to my senses regarding the affair with the German professor after a while. We were studying *Les liaisons dangereuses* at the time, so as I look back, I realize I was remarkably slow to realize that he was reenacting part of that story and, in addition to me, was seducing other students.

When I first learned of his infidelity, it hurt, but I thought perhaps staying in the relationship was worth enduring that hurt. By that point, I had learned about my father's numerous affairs and knew also that he was otherwise a good guy who loved his wife. My mother had instilled in me the message that marriages are complicated and no one is perfect, that you muddle through as best you can, weighing the good and bad parts. However, the professor turned out to be a thorough scoundrel, unlike my father, and he and I parted ways.

Ma and I had another interesting dilemma in 1982, when I was doing my fellowship. The university had a visiting professor from East Berlin, Dr. Karl-Christian Bergmann, a brilliant researcher. My faculty supervisor, who was Jewish, decided I should visit Christian's lab in Germany for several months and that the university should establish a more formal collaboration and exchange program. This proposal required some careful negotiation with Ma. She agreed to allow it if the professor passed her inspection. Ultimately, Christian and I went to Silver Spring to visit her, and they hit it off. Her reservations melted and she gave me her blessing for that trip. Unfortunately, it never came to fruition.

I was surprised decades later when Sanyi's son gave his father a German car as a present. He explained he did not share the same aversion to anything German that Ma did and, in fact, had stronger feelings against American companies that were antisemitic, as Henry Ford's auto company was.

My ambivalence is something I struggle with to this day. While the guttural sounds of the German language cause a visceral reaction in me, I have great respect for postwar Germany and its efforts to teach about the Holocaust. I am particularly impressed by Angela Merkel's leadership in the refugee crisis and her humanitarian efforts. I joke with my daughter that we might need to seek asylum there given changes here. I would perhaps like to visit one day, but on her deathbed, my mother asked me to never set foot in Germany. My children and I even had to manage our trip to India in 2011 to avoid a transfer in Frankfurt.

So I'm muddled, a bundle of conflicted feelings that rise and fall like a staccato teetertotter. Hopefully, I've learned from my family and experiences about being more tolerant and focusing on individual rather than group behavior.

CHAPTER 53

Discovering András

A YOUNG MAN GREW UP in Derecske, the town one stop beyond Sáránd along the rail line south of Debrecen. He knew nothing about his origin beyond growing up with his mother and sister.

One day in 1977, as he ventured to the market in Debrecen, an old man he did not know accosted him. "I know who you are; you are an Ehrenfeld!"

The old man, Zsiga Kun explained to the young man that he looked exactly like the Ehrenfeld twins, whom he had not seen since the war.

Zsiga happened to have an address for Klari, and András (for that was the young man's name) sent her a photo and letter introducing himself. Klari, being rather cynical, thought it must be a scam. She wanted nothing to do with the matter but dutifully forwarded the material to her oldest sister, Magdus, to determine its fate.

My mother was stunned. When she opened the letter, there was a reincarnation of her brother Józsi, who had been killed in the war. They had been so close that she had awakened in terror on the night in 1942 when he was killed, having had a vision of him being blown up on the Eastern Front and lying there bleeding to death, a nightmare that was sadly soon confirmed by others.

Years later, she held a letter, written in a hand identical to her brother's. The handsome young man was the double of her brother. They even shared the same vocation. Ma wanted to meet him.

In May 1978, when I graduated from medical school, my mother and I set out for Hungary to meet András, stopping en route in England and Holland. The day before we embarked on our grand tour, I missed the step on a curb and badly sprained my ankle. I found a pair of crutches, determined to go on. Europe, I discovered, was more handicapped-inaccessible than the States. In the Netherlands, I was referred to as *een kreup*, a lame or crippled person. Although I didn't understand the language and didn't know why Ma looked disturbed, I later learned why: she had recognized the Dutch phrase as similar to the German *ein Krüppel*, which was a death sentence in the concentration camps.

First, we visited a friend of hers in a quaint old English village, Keeper's Cottage. After living in downtown Baltimore during my medical training, I felt culture shock in this bucolic village. I was charmed by the tiny white houses with thatched roofs and colorful cottage gardens. There was a remarkably slow pace there, as we went from the butcher shop to the bakery and to the produce market, patiently queuing up in each and chatting with our friend Linda's neighbors.

Then Ma and I went to Keukenhof Gardens near Amsterdam, as we both shared a love of spring flowers and gardening. It was also insurance for me: in case the rest of the trip soured, I wanted to have some pleasant memories tucked away.

I was terrified when we arrived in Budapest and were greeted everywhere by armed soldiers. At each town we visited, we had to immediately register with the police, who tracked our whereabouts.

My mother and I traveled by train from Budapest to Debrecen across the Hortobágy, the Great Hungarian Plains. We arrived in Debrecen at the site of the grand station where she had played hooky a half-century earlier before she quit school. The station had been heavily bombed during the war and then rebuilt, though not to its previous grandeur.

We anxiously scanned the platform, looking for a face that matched the image from the photo we had. There was no hesitation on Ma's part, and she quickly spotted András, dressed in his finest suit and standing nervously as we descended the stairs. They embraced and then eyed each other with disbelief before he shepherded us out.

András drove us to Sáránd, and Ma was devastated to find that their house and store had been razed. She had understood that it was still standing. Unexpectedly finding that her home was gone destroyed her emotionally for months and triggered a recurrent depression and ill health.

We stayed with András and his wife, Julianna, in Derecske, and they could not have been more loving. All the neighborhood yards in Derecske were surrounded by wooden fences. András's home was far more modern in style than I had expected, like a rancher, with beige stucco walls and a tile roof. The family had a small grape arbor, rows of vegetables, and several fruit trees. Many of the neighbors' yards had chickens or other small animals.

Inside, the walls were paneled and their kitchen painted white. The only thing unexpected was the *cserépkályha* (tiled stove) in the bathroom. I didn't realize what it was, and when I moved to lean on it, I almost got burned.

Julianna constantly asked if we were hungry and plied us with *kaja* (food). Many meals, even breakfasts, were mostly bread, salami, cheese, fresh peppers, and tomato. She also made hearty *pörkölt* (stew), and the paprika and *köménymag* (caraway seed) scented her home. We indulged in pastries and *barack pálinka* (apricot brandy) in the evening.

András and my mother had much history to catch up on as neither knew much detail about the other's life. We learned that his mother, Margit, was a classmate of Klari's and my mother had seen her occasionally in the town. Margit was apparently nineteen when she had her first child, a daughter, and this had been the talk of the small town.

My mother and I met Margit on that trip. My mother said that when she was young, Margit had been slim and beautiful "like a movie star." Margit told my mother that she and Józsi had planned to get married and take over a pub next to Mór's store in Sáránd.

Before any of that happened, Margit gave birth to András while his father, Józsi Ehrenfeld, was on the Eastern Front. There he was killed, never knowing he had a child.

Margit married and raised her children in Derecske, which was a bigger town with more economic opportunities. András knew nothing about his father's family in Sáránd. Ma believes that Margit hid the truth from her son to protect him from antisemitism, even long after the war. "Knowing his Jewish origin would have done no good," Ma explained when I asked.

Once he learned about his aunts, a recurrent, nagging question ate at András. He was convinced that the sisters had known about his birth and had abandoned him in Hungary, rather than taking him to America with them, and he wanted to know why. At that first meeting, my mother tried to help him understand that she had no idea about his existence, but he remained unconvinced, bitter about the fact that he believed he might have had an easier life. This theme of hurt and abandonment haunted him. Over the years, he brought it up repeatedly with the sisters and with me.

I have no doubt that my mother did not know about András's birth. She had adored her brother Józsi and would never have left his child all alone. After losing her brother, father, and child and barely surviving Auschwitz herself, I am sure she would have clung to the discovery of any close family. After the war, Magdus was unwell mentally as well as physically. She and Klari returned to Hungary for only a few months after liberation; Bözsi and Kati did not go back until the 1980s.

LAST YEAR—forty years after my visit with my mother to Sáránd and ten years since I was last there—I learned more details about both my grandfather and András's birth, and I discovered a kernel of truth in his belief.

In addition to the general store, Mór owned several small houses in town. One was the house on the far side of town where Anna's sister and brother had lived before dying of tuberculosis, which then became a general store for Pista. He also had two or three houses and one lot on the next block from his home. One was rented by a blacksmith, the other by an older woman and her daughter, Margit.

Kati did not remember knowing about András's birth until recently, but in 2018, the scene came back to her vividly. Margit, then about twenty years old, walked into Mór's general store in Sáránd and said, "Mr. Ehrenfeld, do you want to see your grandson?" Mór looked at Kati and told her to get out, and she promptly went into the next room. But Kati was nosy and eavesdropped all the time. She went down on her knees to listen with her ear pressed against the keyhole of the flimsy door. She heard Margit tell Mór that this baby was Józsi's. She assumes that Mór suspected that she was telling the truth because he gave her a pair of baby shoes from the store. Perhaps he gifted her because Margit was a neighbor and the daughter of his tenant, or perhaps it reflected his generous nature to be kind to this unwed mother. In the end, neither Mór nor Kati knew whether to believe Margit's claim. Or perhaps Mór didn't acknowledge his grandson as he was trying to protect the infant from the obvious growing antisemitism.

Kati stressed that none of the other sisters were home and none knew about this incident. After all, not that long after Margit came to their store, Kati and Mór were taken from Sáránd to concentration camps, and after liberation, Kati never wanted to set foot in Hungary again. I believe she never said a word about this to her sisters and this was after András got in touch with Ma.

The Tablecloth

While in Hungary, we were invited to dinner by my mother's old neighbors in Sáránd, Zsiga and Eszti Kun. They served chicken soup, and András laughed at me as I gasped when I saw a claw in the ladle approaching my bowl. The dinner soured when Eszti snatched the tablecloth off the table, exclaiming, "Oh, Magdus! This was yours." She offered to tell Ma which neighbors had each piece of the Ehrenfelds' furniture. Only years later did we learn how Zsiga himself had stolen so much from the family. In fact, Kati learned from a priest in Sáránd that Zsiga was afraid of dying because of all the bad things he had done to the Ehrenfelds. He worried about how G-d would punish him for these sins. But when we were visitors, we were deceived by his hospitality.

Ma accepted the tablecloth wordlessly, though she knew that it couldn't have been hers but was, rather, made by one of her sisters. She had ripped her trousseau tablecloth to make diapers for a stranger's baby after her own son had died.

After writing an early draft about my mother losing her first child, I awoke at four in the morning, thinking about how oblivious I had been to much of my mother's past. In the predawn darkness, I ruminated on how insensitive I was to have used that heirloom tablecloth ceremonially at my wedding, along with a brass Kiddush cup my father had stolen somewhere during their exodus, and I ached as I realized that seeing those items must have rekindled great sadness for her.

At that time, in 1984, six years after our trip to Sáránd, I had been trying to honor Ma and her family's heritage at my wedding. While I was not at all observant at that point, being married under a chupah with Jewish traditions had felt critical. I don't know how she happened to have a beautiful folkloric Matyó embroidered blouse, but I asked her about wearing it during our celebration. She asked me not to, as it represented the evil Hungarian nationalism that had betrayed their devotion to their country. But she didn't say anything about the tablecloth.

When I couldn't wear her blouse, I used that tablecloth for the challah and the wine and the blessings at my wedding, though we both knew it was not the one she had sewn. It was important to me to have ritual items my family had brought to this country with them as part of my wedding celebration, even though they brought up bittersweet memories.

Mark and I wed on Father's Day, twenty years after my father's death. The date was not intended as symbolism, but it turned out that way because of my on-call hospital schedule. My heart ached to not have my father at my wedding. At this joyous time, I felt my mother's piercing loss; it was so unjust that Ma had lost both her firstborn child and then her husband. I needed some heirloom from my family as part of my wedding, a sense of connection. That eyelet lace tablecloth, embroidered by one of the sisters for her hope chest, was as close as I could get.

"I Know Who You Are"

The day after meeting Zsiga and Eszti, Ma was too ill to go back to Sáránd to look for other old friends. I wanted to go out alone, but András wouldn't let me, and sent his son, the youngest incarnation of Józsi, with me. I walked down the dirt road, aware of looking odd. I was conspicuous, wearing my decidedly American trench coat and walking laboriously on crutches from an accident, with András's little boy, Tamás, by my side. An old peasant woman, bent over and dressed all in black, walked toward us, leaning on her cane. When she reached us, she cradled little Tamás's face in her wrinkled hands and said, "I know who you are. You are an Ehrenfeld." It was eerie, as she said she had not seen anyone from the family for almost forty years. I felt as though I had entered the Twilight Zone and thought how well she must have known my mother's brother Józsi and my family. I wondered if she had been friends with my uncle and grandfather or if she had been complicit in their misfortune and deportation.

CHAPTER 54

Finding Ma's Friends in Hungary

WHILE MEETING ANDRÁS and his family was the crown jewel of our 1978 trip to Hungary, other gratifying moments happened, primarily in helping my mother reunite with friends from her past.

I'm sorry that I did not know their stories and the depth of my mother's friendships at the time of our visit. She did not share that with me for at least another twenty-five years until she was ill. Had I known, I would have been far more attentive and tried to learn what it was like for them during the war. I would have asked about their own fears and how they mustered the courage to endanger themselves by helping my mother and Kati.

As I've learned more about the Holocaust, I've come to appreciate that these elderly and ordinary-looking individuals whom Ma had described casually as "friends" were also heroes. Each risked his or her life for my mother in quiet ways. Resistance took many forms.

Although born and raised in the United States, I speak passable "household" Hungarian, a challenging and obscure language related only to Finnish and Ugric language groups. My uncle Sanyi had bribed me with a bicycle to learn the language when I was five. People in Hungary tried to guess where I was from and couldn't place my accent. It was definitely not the refined dialect of Budapest, nor was it American. A few words gave me away as speaking the language of villagers.

My ability to read Hungarian is minimal, and I had some difficulty because the language and vocabulary of newspapers are different than in household Hungarian. Ordering food was more difficult because Hungarian restaurant menus didn't say something straightforward, like "chicken and dumplings" or "pork chop," but made up fancy, literary-sounding names for dishes having no bearing on the contents. I was stumped at one restaurant's menu, never having heard the word *özsike*. The waiter finally resorted to drawing a sketch of a deer, as I couldn't fathom what he was talking about. Other than such glitches and struggles on public transit, my ability to hold a conversation in Hungarian was a lifesaver. No one we encountered there in 1978 spoke English, and I would have felt lost and isolated for almost a month had I been unable to communicate.

Before going to Sáránd and Derecske, we went to southern Hungary to reunite Ma with her childhood friend Irén Szabo. They had grown up together in Sáránd, playing in the corn crib and around town. Later, after Irén had grown and moved to Debrecen, she had hidden Kati for a short time during the war.

Irén also unhesitatingly took Ma in when Ma first returned to Hungary and showed up on Irén's doorstep, skeleton-like and lice covered.

In Sáránd, by asking at different houses around town, little Tamás and I succeeded in finding Bandi Egri. Ma had known him since first grade and he tried to help her when she was in the ghetto. He offered to hide her in the woods if she wanted to escape, but she was afraid to try that with her new baby. When I found Bandi, I was excited and wanted to take him back to András's house immediately, but he demurred. He was unshaven and scruffy looking from having been working outside and didn't want to meet Ma looking like that. Instead, he came to Derecske to meet her the next day, clean-shaven and dressed in his Sunday finest.

My most gratifying success was tracking down Bözske Losonczi. She had been Miki and Magdus's apprentice in the corset shop. Then, as a young woman, Bözske had risked her life to help Kati by offering Kati her own identification card. Later, she and her father had brought Ma food when she was near starvation in the ghetto.

At the time of our visit, I only knew that Böske was a close friend who was very important to my mother. So I went knocking door-to-door in Debrecen in the neighborhood where she had lived thirty-five years earlier, desperately searching for her. By word of mouth and persistence, I was finally successful in finding her.

MA WAS EMOTIONALLY, as well as physically, devastated by our trip, her first return to Hungary after emigrating. The effect was cumulative, beginning the moment she saw the image of her brother Józsi reappear in his son's photo, looking identical to her last memory.

The next blow was finding that the family home had been razed. Discovering those good people again, all of whom had imperiled their lives for her and Kati, was likely bittersweet, triggering stronger memories of her traumas during the war. I worried about my mother when I saw how finding the empty lot rather than her home had so visibly shaken her.

Ma became ill with pneumonia on that trip. I suspect that the stress from the trip played a significant role in her falling ill soon after meeting Bandi. After all, the last time she had seen him was when he brought diapers and clothes for her newborn son in the ghetto—baby József, who developed pneumonia and died in her arms a few days later.

But at the time, I wasn't attuned to these connections; the trip was too frenetic, and I was trying to care for my mother. I was a newly minted doctor, and I was proud to make her diagnosis. I found her a physician and antibiotics as soon as we returned to Budapest, and we cut our trip short. We had planned on visiting Yugoslavia and Greece as well, as I was enthralled with the music and folk dancing of the Balkan peninsula, as well as photos of its beauty. I was tremendously disappointed in the change of plans, thinking I might never get to travel abroad again, given the expense and time constraints. I knew this was the one break I had in my training. It's good I didn't know how brutal the next years of residency and fellowship were going to be, or I would have been even more heartbroken. As it has turned out, I've never gotten to do the travel I longed for.

Ma never returned to Hungary after that, although her sisters and brother made subsequent trips to visit András and Auschwitz. She never again wanted to set foot in the country that had turned on her family so cruelly. I totally understand that and feel the same way. Were it not for wanting to see András and his family, whom I have grown to love, and wanting to conduct research for this book, I would never set foot there again. Hungary is a leader in the rise of nationalism and antisemitism in Europe, making my disgust and mistrust of the country almost palpable.

CHAPTER 55

Kati's Return to Allendorf

IN 1990, THE MAYOR OF ALLENDORF invited the thousand Hungarian Jewish women who had been prisoners working at the munitions factory to a reunion. Remarkably, only one woman had died during their stay. Two others, who were discovered to be pregnant, were sent back to Auschwitz to be murdered.

I was surprised that Kati decided to go, as my own mother adamantly opposed any of us setting foot on German soil. While I was upset initially, having assumed that everyone in the family shared this intense dislike of anything German, I learned through this and later conversations with Sanyi that my aunts' and uncles' feelings were more nuanced and spanned a wide spectrum. My mother was on the least forgiving end.

Kati learned that the invitation was prompted by the curiosity of the German children of wartime, now adults.

The town's children recalled that during the war, they heard the noise of the prisoners' wooden shoes echoing on the cobblestone streets as the women marched through town to and from the factory. Their parents denied ever hearing anything, but the children remained curious and troubled. As they grew into adulthood, still searching for answers, some of them visited Auschwitz and found a record listing the thousand Hungarian Jewish women who had been sent to labor in Allendorf. That's when they decided to locate them, and that led to the reunion.

Kati, being a more forgiving soul than her sisters, returned to Allendorf, along with a third of the survivors. She was awed at the response of a younger generation of Germans, who not only admitted to what had happened during the war but also were interested in meeting the people to whom it had actually happened, "to have us tell our stories and to find out," as she later said. The parents and grandparents had been in denial, but these young adults wanted to understand and make amends. Kati was touched to see tears in their eyes as they sought forgiveness for the sins of their elders.

CHAPTER 56

Suicide

I'm not sure when it started, but I remember suicide being a not uncommon topic of conversation around the dining table. I didn't find that particularly odd. Didn't every family chat so matter of factly about it?

Perhaps it started with the odd fashion trend when I was a teen of "poison rings" for jewelry, with a tiny compartment for cyanide or your drug of choice. Though the rings, a passing fashion statement, were easy to acquire, such drugs were not.

I remember my mother asking us to promise that if she were ever seriously ill or in agony that we would "take care of her" and help her die rather than suffer again as she had in the concentration camps.

No doubt suicide was an accepted part of the culture in Hungary and was in some cases portrayed as a heroic solution. In fact, Hungary used to have the highest rate of suicide in the world, and it is more than twice that of the United States.[1] There is even a song dedicated to it, "Gloomy Sunday"—the Hungarian "suicide anthem"—written by a Hungarian and popularized globally by Billie Holiday and Louis Armstrong, among others.

A friend gave me a copy of a memoir, *Piroska néni*, written about the matriarch of a family who had an estate not very far from Sáránd.[2] Ma's brother Pista had worked as a beekeeper on the estate that was Piroska's home, probably in the late 1930s. Piroska's descendant had shared his story with a mutual friend of ours, which is how I acquired it.

Ma read it avidly. In one scene, a woman dies agonizingly in the Debrecen ghetto from an attempted suicide. She was wealthy and Catholic, but her husband's family had some ancestral Jewish blood, causing her to be caught up in the transport. While awaiting deportation at the brick factory, she tried to kill herself. Not having obtained enough poison, she lay out on the road for days until someone gave her a second dose.

Although Ma witnessed this woman suffering from a failed suicide attempt, she still begged the doctors at the brick factory to poison her.

Ma had known this woman and wondered when and how she died. This scene haunted her until the end of her own life, seemingly more than many others.

MY BROTHER SPENT MORE THAN TEN YEARS of his life researching and writing a book about suicide.[3] While it was criticized as being a how-to manual, I always viewed the project as being about self-determination. His premise was that many people make a gesture for help, such as overdosing with Tylenol, mistakenly thinking it will be safe and not knowing that it can cause liver failure, and their botched call for help leaves them worse off than before.

Ma was very proud of the book and displayed it prominently on her coffee table. She was, I think, more gratified by George's becoming a published author than about anything else in our lives. At the time I likely felt a twinge of jealousy, but her reaction was no great surprise to me—I knew how much she valued books and also had by then long recognized my place as second in her affections. Besides, I was proud of my brother's important work on this topic.

SUICIDES HAPPENED IN OUR CIRCLE OF FRIENDS, and I wonder if this is so for most people. A high school friend of George's killed himself. Two young friends in my folk dance group in college took their own lives. We felt sad, of course, but I was also surprised, not having picked up at all that there was anything more serious than chronic low-level discontent in our group of social misfits. Their deaths were treated rather matter-of-factly.

After both her children had left home, my mother rented our basement apartment to a young woman from Sri Lanka. Ramya was petite and very soft spoken, with long black hair and very dark eyes. She was an isolated young woman in a strange and unwelcoming country; her few friends seemed to be from her church group. One day she overdosed but then managed to crawl out to the stairway. I still pause and think of Ramya whenever I descend those stairs at Ma's house. My mother often remarked that Ramya must have wanted to live so badly to have had the strength to drag herself to seek help at the end.

I also think of Ma's strength in dealing with cleaning up vomit and stool after Ramya died and clearing the apartment, as well as the ghosts on the descent into the dark basement.

DURING A PERIOD OF HER LIFE that she calls her second Holocaust, my aunt Kati found herself isolated on a farm in Iowa with an alcoholic, abusive husband. Three children later, her husband abandoned her when the youngest was two, and she struggled to support her family, working as a bank teller. She blames herself for expecting Mike, her eldest child, to help too much with the others. Not wanting to become like his father, he killed himself at age nineteen. Kati still holds herself responsible.

ONE CASE OF ATTEMPTED SUICIDE was never discussed. I learned of my own mother's attempted suicide during the war while working on this book, reviewing tapes and transcripts. Ma shared this story with her interviewer for the Shoah Foundation, telling how she was a forced laborer at the Argus Motorenwerke GmbH airplane factory in Reinickendorf, in the northwest part of Berlin.[4] She worked twelve-hour shifts on an assembly line, cutting holes as the metal moved by, in addition to standing for hours in *Zählappell* (roll call).

Magdus said her back was breaking from endless standing, having been left especially vulnerable by a savage beating in Auschwitz.

One day, she saw a woman hurt her hand and she was taken away. Ma recalled, "I figured, they are going to kill her. Great! I'll do the same." In a moment of despair, Ma cut her hand and washed it in the oily water where the motor heads were greased. Her hand became infected and excruciatingly painful, with pus collecting under her blackened skin, but she was not taken away. She had to keep living. If she had succeeded, there would have been no me and no one to share these stories.

As an infectious disease physician, I see people with cellulitis and abscesses all the time and am surprised she chose such a painful way to try to kill herself. She told the interviewer, "I didn't want to do another way to kill myself," having seen a woman shot for allegedly trying to escape. I would have thought that being shot would be much easier and less painful.

I was surprised not to have discovered this part of her story until after her death. I had watched part of the tape but must have stopped too early, as I was put off by how dispassionate she was during the taping. That she hadn't told me about the incident was not a surprise; she rarely said anything about her wartime traumas, except when she shared about losing her first baby. I was more surprised that she hadn't committed suicide after József's death. She likely considered it again after my father died but didn't follow through out of her sense of responsibility to her children.

CHAPTER 57

Family Reunions

AFTER MY FATHER DIED, visits with family became more infrequent. Part of the reason was due to the loss of my father's determination to sustain a close bond between the two families. In addition, the cousins grew up, scattered, went away to college, and started their own families, further fracturing the nucleus. They rarely got together, but one family reunion was especially memorable for its warmth.

Brookdale

Miklós's daughter, Linda, arranged a get-together in 1992 at the Brookdale Resort, near the scenic Delaware Water Gap, in northeastern Pennsylvania in the Pocono Mountains. The resort offered activities to entertain the three generations that gathered. Linda even designed clever T-shirts with a map showing Ehrenfeld hot spots, and the title gently teased my mother, declaring, "Jaj, Istenem!" (Oh my G-d), one of my mother's favorite exclamations. During the day, the kids played softball and soccer, roller-skated, or raced on little boats in the pond, cheered on by the older generations.

In the evening, the sisters, Miklós, and Sanyi held court before their audience, reliving adventures from their childhood and their sibling rivalries.

Left to right: Kati, Magdus, Miklós, Klari, and Bözsi, 1992, Brookdale Resort

When Bözsi started telling the grandchildren about how she was unappreciated, being the *cigány*, Klari and Magdus laughingly groaned, "Not again!"

Kati bemoaned that she had to do more than her fair share of the work around the house and, in particular, that Klari would sit at the window reading or doing embroidery while Kati toiled.

Klari recounted the time that sweet little Kati was ironing and asked her older sister to read to her. When Klari refused, Kati held the hot iron to her sister's face. Despite the burn, Klari admitted it was perhaps well-earned for all the teasing Kati had put up with from being the youngest.

In another famous incident, Kati went to visit her older sister Bözsi, who by then had moved to Budapest. Kati said Bözsi would often lie in the backyard, sunning herself. Kati's job was to stand and shoo the flies away from her with a small, leafy branch.

One day, Miklós added, "Queen Elisabeth" (as Bözsi was known) asked for a raspberry soda. Magdus had coincidentally cut her finger, so she took a glass of water and soaked her finger in it, and served the pink water to the queen.

BESIDES TEASING EACH OTHER and recalling their rivalries, the siblings offered other glimpses from their youth.

Miklós shared how proud he was that as a teen he had taken wrestling lessons from Károly Kárpáti, a Jew who won a silver medal in wrestling in the 1932 Olympics as well as a gold medal in Berlin's 1936 Nazi Olympics.

Bözsi joked about how Magdus, usually the more responsible daughter, would skip school. After the fourth grade, the girls had to take the train to Debrecen. Some days, Magdus might give the train conductor a bottle of wine, and then he would conveniently run late, handy when she was not prepared for her first class. She also had a friend who taught her how to hide under the bridge near the Debrecen train station and play there until the train's return to Sáránd. Magdus wrote her own excuse slips, as she boasted how she could write just like her father and was never caught. "'My daughter was sick, and she couldn't go to school'—little things," she said, shrugging her shoulders and laughing.

While Bözsi said she was scared to skip school with Magdus, she also told the children that she was a tomboy and enjoyed riding the family's horses bareback across the wheat fields of the plains.

Linda's Wedding

Most of the family managed to gather for weddings of the cousins, but these reunions were briefer, and of course, the focus was on the younger generation. Cousin Linda's wedding in 1982 stood out because it brought together Mari and András, the children of the twin brothers, Pista and Józsi, who had never met. Pista's daughter, Mari, came from Israel to meet András, Józsi's son, who traveled from Hungary for the occasion. Mari, too, immediately noticed the striking resemblance both in appearance and mannerisms between András and her own father, who had died fifteen years earlier.

I was again happy that I speak Hungarian—I was the only cousin who could speak fluently with András and Mari. They have stayed in touch since then, as have I.

Miklós's Seventy-Fifth Birthday

The next family get-together after Linda's wedding—to celebrate Miklós's seventy-fifth birthday—was on a much more modest scale. Only one thing stands out in my memory—how bizarre it was that Miklós and most of the guests decided to go to the Holocaust Museum. I found that incomprehensible—and still do.

It also made me angry that our family often seems incapable of just having fun and doing something celebratory, so their decision to visit the museum was a special letdown after the joyous Brookdale reunion.

CHAPTER 58

Obsession with the Holocaust

ONE OF THE THINGS that I found mystifying was that my mother read and watched everything she could on the Holocaust. This ranged from books on the United States' complicity, which she wanted me to be fully aware of, to its representation in theater. I, on the other hand, could not stand any imagery and avoided anything related to that time—until conducting research for this book. I already had frequent nightmares about both my family's experiences and the possibility that such horrors could happen again and didn't want to provide them further sustenance.

As I've gotten to know Kati better, I've seen the same pattern in her as in my mother. Why not read about the Holocaust? It's always with her and permeates every cell of her being. Kati wants to compare her experiences to those of others.

I read and then sent Kati two Holocaust memoirs that I thought she would "like" to kindle discussion and memories for this book. The first was Rabbi Laszlo Berkowits's *The Boy Who Lost His Birthday*.[1] This was because his family was from Derecske, only five miles from Sáránd, so I thought they likely had some shared experiences. Little did I know that Kati and Mór had been deported with the Derecske Jews to the ghetto in Nagyvárad and then taken to Auschwitz on the same transport from the Mezey lumberyard. Perhaps they had even met the Berkowits family in the ghetto.

The second book I shared was *Fragments of Isabella*, by Isabella Leitner.[2] The writing is spare and stunning.

I was eager to discuss both books with Kati and surprised when she said that she is reading only a little bit of the books at a time, "savoring" each portion as it rekindles memories for her.

At night, for many in my family, the images of horror recurred, and they often cried out. Sanyi would seem so sane and rational by day, but when I visited, I could hear him scream at night. His wife shrugged nonchalantly. That was their normal.

I'm understanding this obsession with the Holocaust more viscerally now. As I've worked on this memoir day after day for months, I've become relatively desensitized. I have had to read more about the Holocaust and turned to both historical references and memoirs to better educate myself. I've read accounts I couldn't have touched a few years ago. Some images still give me nightmares, but I've felt a numbing that I find a bit disturbing. Sadly, this distancing has been fueled by the too frequent mass shootings and the barbarism of the current United States regime and others globally. Perhaps that is part of their plan: normalization of what was previously unthinkable. Family separation, kids in cages—all part of nationalism heightened by fanning fears and hatred of "others."

Seeing the worsening cruelties, speaking with Kati frequently, and writing have begun to make me less sensitive to this grim topic, at least in written form. They have even inexplicably managed to make my horror and grief over the 2018 Pittsburgh Tree of Life synagogue shooting more bearable and given me a sense of resignation about the future.

Kati is similarly perturbed by her transformation. On an early job application, she was asked what her father died from and ran out of the room crying. Now she speaks about Tóth bácsi saving her from being raped and her father's murder very matter of factly, telling their stories to hundreds of people without hesitation.

CHAPTER 59

Independence

MY MOTHER WAS THE TOUGHEST WOMAN I've ever met. She was fiercely independent until the end, living alone until she was ninety-two, cooking and baking. She couldn't do two things because of severe macular degeneration—drive and read—but she finally accepted help with both.

One small legacy of my parents' privations was the fear of going hungry again. The first things they did when they bought a house were to line a wall in the basement with shelves for canned goods and get a large freezer. Kati has done the same. I, too, have a too small doomsday stash of nonperishable food, and like my mother before me, I eat food that is spoiling rather than letting it go to waste. "Builds immunity!" I tell my family when they look askance.

Also, whenever we went anywhere, we took a sweater and a small amount of food and water. My mother usually had a little bit of chocolate, as well as Coffee Nips hard candy to suck on.

While she got rattled if any misfortune befell her family, Ma was unfazed by threats to herself. In one big storm, an old tulip poplar came crashing down through the roof and into my brother's old bedroom, across the hall from where she was sleeping. Ma refused to leave her home, so neighbors climbed up onto the roof and put a tarp over the hole to try to keep the rain out.

Similarly, she boasted that after a fall in the kitchen, she was able to crawl out and get into her recliner without activating her emergency alert system.

UNFORTUNATELY, MA HAD BECOME ADDICTED to cigarettes offered to her by the American soldiers. She was able to go cold turkey and stop smoking when her emphysema worsened, and she needed almost continuous oxygen. It was good that Ma could detach the tubing at times, given that oxygen poses a fire risk and she caught her sleeve on fire while cooking twice when I visited. She just shrugged off these accidents.

Even when she was in her nineties, I was impressed at how hard Ma worked with small dumbbells and ankle weights, even from her recliner next to the television, wanting to maintain her strength and independence. Sanyi was the same, doing stretching exercises and walking on a treadmill every day. They were both more disciplined than I.

Kati, too, at ninety-four, attends water exercise and tai chi classes at the community center, drives all over Omaha, and frequently spends days baking and cooking for guests. This is when she isn't off to speak to schools or community groups for Holocaust education.

Klari, Bözsi, Miklós, and Sanyi all lived full and long lives and remained independent until their last years, when the latter three needed help with activities of daily living from home health aides.

I can only dream of being as strong and determined as my elders were.

CHAPTER 60

Speaking Out

ONE NOTABLE DIFFERENCE among my family members was the degree to which they hid their past and responded to antisemitism. Their responses ran across the spectrum from hiding their identities after immigration to being very actively involved in Holocaust education.

My own reaction has run the gamut as well. I grew up in suburban Maryland where there was a significant Jewish community. Cumberland was the first place I've lived where I felt conspicuously aware of being Jewish. At first, I neither hid nor advertised my identity. Since I didn't "look Jewish," people regularly shared their antisemitic views with me.

We were always one of two Jewish families with children in the public schools, and it was a constant, losing battle to try to get the schools to acknowledge—let alone teach about—other cultures and religions and not to have holiday concerts filled with "little baby Jesus" songs. Each year, I reminded the schools and community groups that our children are of many faiths and that they should embrace the opportunity to educate them about the larger world. (We have fair-sized Muslim and Hindu communities here.)

When my son was preparing for his bar mitzvah, our community was torn apart by a proposal to merge the secular community hospital with the Catholic one, which would have put all health care in Western Maryland—a seventy-five mile radius—under the control of the Catholic Church and its Ethical and Religious Directives for

Catholic Health Care Services.[1] This would have meant, for example, that women would not be able to have a tubal ligation at the time of a Caesarean section and that autonomy in end-of-life decision making was at risk, among other impacts. (The directives state that living wills and other advance directives will not be honored if "contrary to Catholic moral teaching.")[2]

I felt a moral responsibility to oppose this plan, especially where distance, poverty, and geography, being surrounded by mountain passes, made seeking alternative care impossible for many. I also felt driven to set an example for my children of standing up for what was right. That naive decision exacted a steep personal and financial toll, as the health system promptly retaliated by putting a stranglehold on my practice.

In high school, both of my children had excellent units on history that included obtaining oral histories and contributing to a book compiling them. The projects included the Vietnam War and World War II. My daughter's teacher interviewed my mother and had Heather talk to each of his classes about her grandmother's experiences in the war and being a survivor. Afterward, he asked each student to write a brief essay answering, "What can we do to prevent a Holocaust from happening again?" One of the students wrote, "There is nothing wrong with killing Jews or Gypsies." Shocked, we and the teacher spoke with the principal, who did nothing about it. We were even unsupported by the Jewish community here. The rabbi refused to intervene—marking the last time we attended services during his long tenure. Another congregational leader chastised me for calling attention to us and the synagogue, fearing vandalism or worse.

CHAPTER 61

Grandchildren

AFTER MARRYING LATE, I hurried to have a baby so my mother would have a grandchild and something to live for. My husband thought that a reasonable plan since we were both older and assumed it would take a while.

When my son was a toddler, I told my mother that I was dismayed by the infrequency of her visits. After considerable discussion, Mark and I had elected to name our son Michael, after my father. So I was even more stunned that she remained distant and said, "It won't hurt them so much when I die if they don't know me." I believe I told her that was nuts.

Ma did eventually allow herself to grow close to her grandchildren. For some time, she showed clear favoritism toward my son, being more attentive and generous with praise. Whether that was because boys were more valued in Jewish culture, as in many others, or because of the loss of her firstborn son, I don't know. I found her partiality painful to witness, as it rekindled unpleasant memories of a lifetime of her favoritism toward my brother. Eventually, I called her out on her behavior. To her credit, she reflected on her actions and changed her ways and in her later years developed a deep bond and closeness with her granddaughter, Heather. We, as parents, paid special attention to trying to avoid comparing our children to each other and encourage and support each in finding his or her own interests and paths.

While Ma had carefully avoided talking to me about the Holocaust until I was an adult, as the years passed, and especially with her grandchildren, she became considerably more open.

That day in 1994 when she spoke to Michael's class about her experiences, she was open and responsive to every question posed. I kept my eyes on the children, worried how her story would affect them. Some seemed bored, others uncomfortable, but most were brimming with innocent curiosity. I was especially stunned, though, when one young girl asked her what the most valuable thing she had lost was, and Ma didn't hesitate to respond, "My baby."

When I asked her what had prompted her deep honesty (after all, she had not told me this story until I was much older than these children), she said she was so taken by the young girl's keen interest and her perceptiveness, she wanted to be honest with her.

Later that year, my mother also spoke to students from my secretary's elementary school. This talk did not go as smoothly as the previous one, in part because the students weren't as mature and in part because their teacher wasn't as knowledgeable or sensitive to the topic as Michael's teacher, Valeria Arch, had been.

Telling her story became more and more part of Ma's experience, and in 1996, she sat for an interview for the Shoah Foundation, which was collecting oral histories of survivors.

As the years passed, Ma visited our family more often, especially when my daughter was in musical theater productions, beginning with *The Music Man*. Klari came to that first production, too, and as I ironed Heather's dress for the show every night, I joked that she would never see me iron again. We reminisced about Ma's teaching me to iron when I was young, beginning with pillowcases; progressing to sheets, collars, and cuffs; and graduating to my father's shirts. It's funny how, at the time, that became a source of pride.

One of the first songs Heather's singing teacher had her learn was "Röeslein Rose," a German folk song. My mother was shocked and furious, chiding me to never again expose her to someone in her family enjoying German. I had slipped up one more time. I knew she recoiled at anything German but hadn't given that more than a passing thought when Heather sang for her grandmother. I should have been more sensitive to what would trigger Ma.

When my mother came to watch Heather playing the role of Louisa Von Trapp in the local 2001 production of *The Sound of Music*, I felt guilty for again not having adequate foresight. I had seen bits of rehearsals but not the entire show. The show concluded unexpectedly with the dropping of a huge Nazi flag, covering the stage. I sat stunned, shocked, and remorseful that I had subjected my mother to this rekindling of the horrors of the Holocaust.

My mother, although half-blind, could not mistake what was happening. She was shaking from the suddenly triggered memories. Afterward, I paused to speak with the director and chide him for not having warned me, as he knew my mom was a Holocaust survivor. He replied that he had done his job well if the play was that evocative.

The director knew that we were Jewish. Heather had been in his production of *Fiddler on the Roof* in 1999, and we had coached him on some Jewish mannerisms and customs, such as mezuzahs on doorposts and praying not with your hands clasped in front but, if anything, with open hands, palms facing upward, as in imploring G-d for help or receiving something.[1]

I WAS TOUCHED to see my fifteen-year-old boy sitting with his arm wrapped around his grandma's shoulder as they watched his sister chant from the Torah on her bat mitzvah. Ma had fallen that morning and was in pain, and he was so gentle as he helped her and sat there stroking her hand, as she had done for all of us whenever we were hurt. Later, he wrote an essay I still cherish called "Blessed Warmth," in which he recounts the warm, golden light in our natural cherry kitchen, the spiciness of csirkepaprikás and the tantalizing scents of his grandmother's gerbeaud baking, a mix of chocolate, walnuts, and apricot and raspberry jam in a layered pastry. Michael concluded, "As my family rises to join me,

I reflect once more on how lucky I am, blessed with such warmth, my world, my home, and my family."

These words bring me great joy and comfort in the way Mark and I raised our children.

BY THE TIME MY DAUGHTER had her bat mitzvah in 2001, Klari had been diagnosed with lung cancer and others were in declining health. I wrote a letter to the sisters saying, "I have been especially saddened by two things—one is that, instead of drawing closer together through these family difficulties, and comforting each other, the sisters have grown further apart." The other was how private my mother-in-law had been and when she had died, we found a scrapbook with wonderful newspaper clippings and a photo of her in a flapper dress. It saddened me that she never took the opportunity to share these stories with us or her grandchildren. My letter continued,

> I have tried to learn from these, and previous losses, to try to celebrate life more fully, and focus on the important things. I ask that you all help make this a memorably joyous occasion. I have planted thousands of bulbs to welcome family with their cheer and sense of rootedness, stability, and continuity that they provide. I hope you will come, and bring your blessings for the younger generation, making this a true celebration as well as rite of passage.

The photos and video clips of Miklós and the sisters taken then are among my favorites. The Ehrenfelds all stood out with their distinctive snow-white hair and smooth complexions.

One of my friends, a psychiatrist who was interested in gathering oral histories, expressed surprise at how dignified they appeared and how little alcohol was touched compared to celebrations of other (non-Jewish) families he had attended. I was pleasantly surprised. Not being much of a partygoer, I hadn't realized that this was out of the ordinary. "Dignified" was not a description I would have immediately chosen, but I was glad he had.

It was a beautiful, cool, crisp spring day, warm enough that we were able to set tables outside and eat inside a windowed white tent that provided some protection from the breeze. I chose to spend most of the luncheon reception with my aunts and uncle Miklós at one end of the deck. Sanyi and some Glattstein relatives I was only peripherally acquainted with had their own reunion at another table. I don't remember where the rest of my family members were—off socializing with the cousins, who spoke in English, while much of our conversation was mixed with Hungarian.

The videos capture the essence of the siblings' relationships. As we sat down to chat and I started the recorder, Miklós joked, "We're going to send a copy of this to Bözsi (who had not come), so be careful what you say." My mom, Nagy Száju (Big Mouth), replied predictably, "I don't care." They continued, making thinly veiled allusions that Bözsi had learned more than one trade in Debrecen from the woman she studied under, who they claimed was promiscuous. Kati tried to calm the situation, saying, "I tell you. It's not easy for Bözsike to be good."

After the laughter quieted down, I asked them to tell me about fun stories from their childhood. While I had heard most of the stories before, this time I heard about Ma producing musical plays for the neighborhood children, including writing the songs. She charged an admission fee, which included a trip to her lemonade stand. One of the young actors was Irén Szabo, who later hid Kati in her apartment.

They continued to reminisce and tease each other about their sibling rivalries and childhood adventures, with tears of laughter streaming down their faces.

Having grown up with an often depressed mother, this family reunion was more than a celebration of my daughter's rite of passage—it was a good lesson for me to see that despite the poverty of their childhood and all the terrible things they had endured, they still had such capacity for joy. As I watched them telling funny stories, shooting the breeze, and poking fun at each other I, too, felt a rare lightness as we rejoiced in our being together for a happy occasion.

A Hebrew prayer perfectly captures my feeling of gratitude, both then and now, each time I see the image of the family happily together.

> Baruch atah, Adonai Eloheinu, Melech haolam, shehecheyanu, v'kiy'manu, v'higiyanu laz'man hazeh.

> Blessed are You, Adonai our G-d, Sovereign of all, who has kept us alive, sustained us, and brought us to this season.

That joyous gathering was bittersweet. I knew we would not all be together again; by then the siblings were all in their late seventies to late eighties and in declining health. As the weekend drew to a close, I was impressed by the fortitude with which they said their goodbyes. Knowing that some would not see each other again, I was surprised at how nonchalant they appeared. I was breaking up inside, but I managed to hide my distress, mirroring their self-control. A casual hug, kiss on the cheek, walk down the path, and they were gone.

MA WAS PROUD of her grandson's academic abilities and of the fact that he read voraciously. He also excelled at mathematics, as did many in our families. To Ma's dismay, I was the notable exception. "Where did I get you from?" she would ask as I struggled with multiplication.

Although always frugal, Ma surprised me when we were deciding about colleges. Michael and I were visiting an Ohio college where he had been offered a full scholarship and special promises of mentoring when we received a call that he had been accepted to Swarthmore, a revered school in our family and his dream school. I called my mother, asking her to help us weigh the full scholarship at one college versus no financial help from the dream school. Knowing the importance of being able to follow one's dreams, she unhesitatingly said, "Forget the scholarship. It's Swarthmore." We

Heather (24) and Magdus (94), 2006, Silver Spring

were both taken aback at her unexpected advice. I knew she was right, though I was momentarily hesitant because of the financial implications of the decision. But my wavering was fleeting, as we all sensed that Swarthmore was by far the best school for Michael and have had no regrets.

MY DAUGHTER WAS TALENTED in many ways beyond academics, including singing and theater. With grudging pride after a performance in which Heather starred, even my mother was forced to acknowledge, "Abba minden benne van" (She has everything in her). To our dismay, Heather was also interested in beauty pageants. I found a way to reluctantly support her.

Carol Clulee, one of my patients, couldn't walk and was in a wheelchair yet still was able to coach the girls on poise and bearing. She made the pageant experience become about learning interviewing skills, public speaking, and supporting area charities rather than just primping, which is why I let my daughter participate. One year, Heather gained a teen title. The following year at the pageant, the young women gave short speeches as they crowned the new winners. As Heather gave up her crown, she named Ma her "woman of distinction." "Grandma," she said, "you are the woman that I strive to be. Intelligent, far beyond what one learns in school, wise, nurturing, and with such a sense of independence."

Reflecting about the experience, Ma said, "While I didn't think I would like it, I really did!" Heather also sang "For Good," from *Wicked*, lyrically expressing how Heather felt knowing her grandmother had helped her become a better person.[2]

Two years later, Heather sang the same song at her grand-mother's funeral, tears streaming down her face. She told me recently that she always felt it encapsulated her relationship with Ma, and to this day, she sings it when she is alone and misses her.

CHAPTER 62

Ma's Death

THE LAST YEAR OR TWO OF MY MOTHER'S LIFE were a blur of hospitalizations and remarkable rallies before the next sudden crisis. It was challenging to be both Ma's daughter and a physician, torn between leaving my husband and practice to be with her and needing to be ever vigilant because I felt so strongly that her care was often mediocre and fragmented.

During this time, Mark was a saint, providing Ma and me with tireless support. His love of old people and loyalty to family were among the first things that drew me to him, and at this time, those qualities came to mean the world to me. Despite Ma's prickliness, he welcomed her to live with us and showed infinite patience with her—far more patience than I had. He put up with my mood swings and frequent outbursts of anger. She stayed with us for more than six months and then was able to return to her home. Having seen so many patients abandoned by uncaring children, I felt even more grateful to Mark for his generosity and love.

The first night of Ma's hospitalization, she asked me to stay with her in the ICU, afraid she was going to be killed. She was remarkably astute and always a good judge of character, so I stayed, and along the way, I learned a great deal.

The ICU was poorly designed, with a layout that precluded the nurses from seeing patients without making a concerted effort to do so. On almost every shift, someone would suggest that Ma was old and should be made a "no code" status (also known as a "do not resuscitate"). I would refuse, reminding the staff that was not what she wanted. Having been a physician for so many years, I knew that "no code" meant "no care" in many hospitals and that staff would drag their feet in responding to problems.

Ma recovered and went to a "rehabilitation" center. I met with the center's gerontologist and reviewed her care and detailed advance directives. There she also encountered problems: aides forgetting to put her back on oxygen and running out of her inhalers. When I thought she was stable, I returned home and went on to visit Heather, who was a freshman at college. When Ma became so ill, I bought my first cell phone—a decision that turned out to be lifesaving.

One day while visiting Heather in Northampton, I unexpectedly got a call from an emergency room physician at Sibley Hospital telling me that this was a "courtesy call" to let me know that my mother was in respiratory failure and was dying since she was listed as "no code." I discovered that after I left, the gerontologist had changed Ma's status—against my explicit orders. When I told the ER physician that she was to have full care, she was put on a ventilator and the doctors aggressively treated her acute problem.

That night was the only time I have ever lied to my daughter, hiding that her grandmother was critically ill. I could not bring myself to distract her from the conference she had worked so hard to organize. After the close of her meeting, I relayed the news to Heather and other family, and we all flew to Washington, despite delays due to a blizzard.

I regret not filing an ethics complaint about the gerontologist. I spoke with him, the facility's administrator, and a patient care ombudsman, but by then I had no energy to go to the board of medicine.

Ma got good care at Sibley and was then transferred back to the rehab center. This cycle repeated two more times, and with each admission, I found out about medication errors and adverse outcomes. I learned from a nurse, for example, that Holocaust survivors need to be in a bed next to a window or they become extremely agitated. This happened with Ma and she greatly improved when she could look outside. Another nurse shared that many survivors are terrified of German shepherds. Others have different triggers from their past experiences.

Ma had a series of hospitalist physicians—doctors who do shift work, usually for one week at a time. Generally, these physicians know next to nothing about the patients, unlike a person's family physician, and often they are too busy to care. The focus is on a fast discharge, and communication during transfers between shifts and between specialists is often lacking.

Many doctors order antibiotics according to standard guidelines or ease of administration rather than thinking about an individual patient's needs and history. From my experience in clinical research, I long ago learned that quinolone types of antibiotics (e.g., Levaquin, Cipro, and Avelox) can cause confusion, dizziness, and even hallucinations, especially in the elderly. While these are a favorite broad-spectrum choice of ER docs and hospitalists, I rarely prescribe them. But in this facility, doctors kept trying to prescribe these for Ma, and I kept refusing to let them give these drugs to her. I tried to behave nicely, but I did have a few tense showdowns with young doctors or physician's assistants who saw me as a busybody daughter rather than, as I tried to tell them, an infectious disease physician with many more years' training and experience than they had.

At a different hospital, we did have a notable breakthrough in Ma's care when the risk manager (whom I was by then regularly calling on to run interference) arranged a meeting between me; Dr. Sabyasachi Kar, the head of the hospitalists; and Dr. Alfred Munzer, Ma's pulmonary specialist. I began by calmly explaining that they needed to know that Ma was a Holocaust survivor and as a result had special needs. When I was done speaking, Dr. Munzer told me that he had been a hidden child in the Netherlands during the Holocaust, and my sense of relief at having someone who understood and I trusted to be an ally was palpable. Both of these physicians were wonderfully kind to Ma and to me, and they helped ease some of the pain of others' treatment and behavior—like one cruel nurse who refused to let Ma have a sip of water or swabs, though she was crying out for these and becoming increasingly agitated and short of breath. The nurse said she was afraid Ma would aspirate the water.

I tried to explain that Ma was a Holocaust survivor and agonizing thirst rekindled memories of the deprivation and tortures of Auschwitz. I was determined to relieve her parched anguish, no matter the outcome. The nurse told me she was Jewish but refused Ma liquids, and that day, frustrated beyond control, I spat out that she had just helped me understand what a Kapo was.

Soon after that incident, Dr. Munzer had a word with the nurse, and Ma was given a sponge stick to suck on. We dipped it in coffee, which she had been longing for.

Throughout Ma's final illness, I came to see vividly that Auschwitz was still there inside her, and I stayed with her to try to shield her from pain as best as I could.

One day, for the first time, Ma complained of being tired. She didn't want to eat. And then, unexpectedly, she sat up and out of the blue said, "I love you."

I thought that would be the end. Once again, she surprised me.

AFTER HER PACEMAKER was put in and I brought her home, she thanked me for enabling her to return home again. "You don't know how grateful I am," she said and then paused and added, as she typically did, "but not completely."

I smiled wryly and thought, "The Lord giveth and the Lord taketh away."

At one point before she returned home, one of the friendlier ICU doctors challenged her. If she wanted to get out of the ICU and go home, he told her, she would have to show she could walk, and despite having been bedridden for days, she mustered her strength and walked across her room. I stared in disbelief and soon brought her home.

The week before her final illness, we had a spat. She had gone downstairs to the freezer so she could cook dinner for me. I reminded her that she had promised to stay off the stairs. "Sometimes I have to lie to you," she said matter-of-factly.

On my next visit to her home in Silver Spring, I found her sitting and watching her beloved *Jeopardy!* I was in the kitchen and didn't notice that she was rapidly becoming short of breath, but when I did, I called an ambulance that took her back to the nearest hospital. We figured out that she had been going into flash pulmonary edema—a rapid buildup of fluid in her lungs—and later Ma told me the drowning sensation was worse than anything she had experienced at Auschwitz.

Once again, she received compassionate care from the cardiologist, Dr. David Brill, and from one of the intensivists, though another doctor was unspeakably cruel and again I had no energy to file a complaint beyond the hospital administrators.

Finally, Ma decided she was ready to die, but sadly, she was so strong it took two more days for her to do so. Even ten years later, I continue to have occasional nightmares about her being tortured. These nightmares are usually triggered by a patient I am caring for.

Despite the occasional pain inflicted by Ma's sharp tongue, caring for her in those days offered many invaluable lessons. At times I felt like a lemming, driven by instinct to be by her side to protect her from her "caregivers" and support her desire to live the way she wanted to as much as possible. In some way, I wanted to shelter her and care for her to make up for all the bad things that had happened to her. I wanted to envelop her with love and make her passing easier and gentler than her life had been.

In 2013 I was interviewed by journalist Judith Graham for her *New York Times* article about PTSD, "For Some Caregivers, the Trauma Lingers."[1] To Graham I confided, "I've never been able to overcome the feeling that I failed her—I let her down. It wasn't her dying that was so upsetting, it was how she died and the unnecessary suffering at the end."

Unfortunately, in my practice I often see critically ill patients and am appalled time and again at what we do to people. Without a strong advocate, someone named in a medical power of attorney document, no one is allowed to die in peace. In many hospitals, a living will isn't worth the paper on which it is written. Still, I think and hope I was able to give my mother some comfort in her last days.

CHAPTER 63

Tchotchkes

I AM A HOARDER. I keep many things "just in case." And my house is way too cluttered since I've always wanted to keep items in sight so I know where they are. This has been a major source of stress for me and the family. All of us would like the house to be more orderly, neater, and more calming. Instead we have belongings from three generations crammed into our living space, and the sheer number can be paralyzing.

In 2017, Heather came home for Christmas and agreed to go through her belongings that I had stored in the basement since her college days and choose what to take or give away. Suddenly, I felt an overpowering need to see the little yellow ceramic house that had always sat on my mother's dresser and that I had loved playing with when I was younger. Heather and I started looking through the boxes of Ma's things that we had packed hastily but carefully almost ten years earlier, and I began to ponder with amazement that it had been almost a decade since her death.

Some days the pain and longing are still raw and feel so immediate, and that was one of those days. Heather and I searched the two likeliest boxes labeled "chotchkas" because who knows Yiddish or can spell it? The yellow ceramic house wasn't there.

Later, after Heather had gone, I remained obsessed with finding the house. I was kicking myself for having misplaced it. We have a family joke that the more important something is to me, the more carefully I tuck it away for safekeeping and then can't remember where. This fact stands in such stark contrast to the way I so obsessively cared for my patients that my inability sometimes to find things I've lost is all the more striking and frustrating for everyone in our family.

All that week I was teary and irrationally depressed about not being able to find the house; for me it stood as evidence of my failure as a daughter and disloyalty to Ma's memory. I decided to immerse myself in the basement, despite the fact that basements have always frightened me.

My husband hauled over boxes from the huge pile and I obsessively went through each one, this time more carefully labeling and cataloging the contents than I had when we hurriedly packed up Ma's house. After days of excavating, I finally found the ceramic house. I still haven't turned up her Israeli wall plaques and another trinket container or the two small square glass dishes with light silver gray tops and the tray they sat on, which I also had loved to play with as a child. But I do know that the more upset I get, the less likely I am to find a missing item, even one that is right in front of me. I suspect I simply missed seeing those other childhood treasures.

I did find several "items of historic interest," as my brother and I called them. I stayed up most of the night, wondering again about their stories and what they had meant to my mother—especially the neat black, low-heeled shoes that laced up above the ankle, clearly "vintage," made in Germany, and likely what Ma wore in 1949 when she came to this country. I wonder what they meant to her—obviously they were important since she kept them through several moves across the country. I had never before seen them. Later I asked Kati about the shoes.

"Oh, I have these lovely leather boots I had made after the war too!" she said. She also has kept shoes from Germany for seventy years.

We found a couple of pieces of heavy, dark gray silverware like others that we still use and that I know were also brought from Germany. "Did the small warped soup pot travel the seas?" I wondered. If I were packing to leave my country and head into the unknown, what would I choose to take? How would I know what to take and what to leave behind? These were the questions I pondered as I rifled through those boxes, and I thought, too, about the bugout bag we'd made years earlier when we thought we might have to evacuate our home because of a fire. Our bag held mostly photos and irreplaceable sentimental objects.

I also found a taxi medallion. I hadn't known that my dad drove a cab when they lived in DC, though that was a common occupation among immigrants. In fact, Ma's brother Miklós was a New York cabbie for his entire life here in America.

I also found two white porcelain vases painted with beautiful flowers and gold trim and odd, rather creepy coiled snake handles. I remembered the couple who gave them to her—an elegant, cultured couple from Budapest who lived in DC, Dezső and Bözsi Korn. "How had they known each other and become good friends," I wondered, "given that they came from such different social classes?" I remember tiny Korn néni, who I was told was my godmother.

I wish Ma had been more open and I more observant and inquisitive. When I was younger, these questions hadn't seemed important, and we were all too busy struggling through work, childrearing, and complicated relationships. But now sometimes, in the quiet of the night, I wonder what else I missed.

CHAPTER 64

The Second Aftermath

DESPITE THE TRAUMA of my mother's illness and cruel death, which still sometimes haunts me, I learned some important and positive lessons on this journey.

I saw many people whose lives my mother touched. In this age of transience, I heard from people who had grown up with Ma as a neighbor and, despite having moved away decades ago, still came back to see her. She opened her home to young people and reached out to them, accepting them, baking and cooking for them, and providing a source of constancy and security. She similarly provided a rootedness for the neighbors, as she lived in the same home for fifty years.

While I wish to be better in all these areas, I have learned that I am, at times, tougher than I ever dreamed I could be.

I have learned to be much more patient.

I have learned about stubbornness and resilience, spitefulness and kindness, charm and charisma, and the power of words to wound or to heal (though I still need to learn to bite my tongue).

I learned to be a better doctor, mother, and friend. I became much closer to a few friends and more appreciative of them.

I learned from Ma's reader, Julia, that Ma never forgot a kindness and loved funny stories.

I got to know and love one of George's friends. Virginia Singer generously provided us evening sanity breaks where she fed us and surrounded us with warmth and humor in her comforting home.

I am so grateful Ma's illness brought Virginia into my life and that she still takes care of us with food and much laughter.

I've grown much closer to Kati. Her ability to be so active, reinvent herself in her eighties, and still reach out to young people in her nineties, trying to make the world a better place (*tikkun olam*), gives me something to aspire to. So does her ability to forgive, an attribute I didn't often see in the other sisters. It makes her life happier and richer. I wonder if that ability can be learned.

One of the best aftereffects has been my growing appreciation and understanding of both my husband and my brother.

My brother and I have developed great respect for each other. I'm no longer just his kid sister, an adulating pest. Only once before did I feel the kind of respect he now shows me—and that was all the way back in 1966, on my first day of high school.

That afternoon, George took my mother and me canoeing at Great Falls. He had been on the river the day before and wanted to share its beauty with the two of us. The water apparently had risen overnight. I wasn't a strong paddler, and our canoe swung sideways, catching perpendicular to the water on two rocks. We waited for some time, considering our limited options. Ma was growing increasingly agitated, verging on hysterical, so George opted to risk leaving us to swim to shore to get help. I was successfully able to calm her, speaking gently and reassuringly to her. Eventually, emergency personnel rescued us and George thanked me for not flipping out. The respect and love he showed me that day was what I have experienced more and more as we have grown older, and most of all in those days in the hospital as our mother was dying, and since then in the aftermath of becoming orphaned.

I became an emotional wreck facing my mother's steeply declining health, but I had the professional skills and experience to deal with the medical system better than George did, and because of that ability, I once again earned his respect as I had that day so long ago.

In the aftermath, we worked well together. I had matured, too, watching a close friend go through this process just a couple of years earlier and learned from her wisdom. Her experience confirmed for me that nothing was more important than our relationships.

At one point, while going through the "items of historic interest" that had the most emotional draw for us, I looked at my mother's wedding ring, which I had placed on my finger for safekeeping when her hands had become too swollen to keep it on, and asked him if he would like it. He looked up at me from his seat at her desk and asked, "Aren't we supposed to be fighting over this?" I felt closer to him than ever. I still do, and that experience has been an unexpected gift from Ma's death. I am thankful for these lessons.

CHAPTER 65

My Return to Hungary

I RETURNED TO DERECSKE IN 2008, after Ma died, wanting to visit András and understand more about the family's life in the nearby little village of Sáránd.

As I wandered around, I thought about my mother's life there. I walked the same streets, past the same church and train station— except that now there is a memorial plaque on the church with the names of those killed in the war, including my family's names. I felt melancholy. I could not understand living in such a small place where everybody knew everybody and reconcile that with what had happened to my family there.

I spoke with Irén Bakó, who lived across the street from the sisters and had been Kati's childhood friend. Irén's father had been tasked by Mór with meeting seven-year-old Kati at the train and breaking the news to her that her mother and younger sister had died. Within a few years, however, Irén also became afraid of the consequences of speaking to or being friends with a Jew. Knowing she was going to be deported, Kati asked Irén to keep her good clothes for her until she was allowed to return. She took them over to Irén's house, but the next day, Kati found the clothes hanging on the gate to her family's yard. Irén or her parents had reconsidered and felt that even having the clothes for safekeeping was too risky.

When I visited in 2008, Irén was friendly. She remembered the Ehrenfeld home well and drew me a sketch of the layout. She also showed me her house and what the construction of my grandfather's place had been like. The walls were built from thick brick, made from mud and straw by the Gypsies, and covered with a whitewashed stucco. Because of the thickness of the walls, the homes were well insulated. Most of the houses now had tile roofs, rather than thatch, and the storks far preferred to nest on telephone poles rather than on the rooftops as they had in the old days.

I MADE ONE OTHER ODD DISCOVERY on this trip. A stranger welcomed me to town, knowing I was going to look for information about the Ehrenfelds. (News ricochets quickly around a small village.) She directed me to Böske Petö, now elderly and living alone in Debrecen. András's son drove me to meet her. She was like a frail little bird with a high-pitched voice, animated as she told us about her romance with Miklós. She shared a grainy photo of him as a young man, sitting on a haystack, and said she had saved his letters. Although she had other suitors, she claimed only to have ever loved him. When I, in turn, showed her photos of Miklós with his snow-white hair, she was dismayed, exclaiming, "How can this be? He's gotten so old!"

I brought Miklós photos of his old girlfriend and a recorded message from her. I shouldn't have encouraged him to call her; he later told me he regretted having done so, though he did not offer details.

THE ONLY STRONG RESISTANCE I encountered was from a cousin in Hungary who admitted to having many photos of the older Ehrenfelds but no desire to share them, saying, "Let the dead lie in peace." This cousin's wife was anxious as they spoke with me, visibly fearful that our voices would be carried along the pipes and be heard by their upstairs neighbors. She was right to be worried, given the steady rise of antisemitism and fascist governments, especially in Hungary.

Yet on this same visit, I met other cousins (the descendants of our great-grandfather Herman from his second wife). Although not raised Jewish, they could not have been friendlier or more gracious, even driving me out to Jákó, the village in northeastern Hungary where my grandmother Anna had been raised, and the family farm that Mór had helped her siblings buy.

A FEW DOORS UP FROM THE EHRENFELD HOME, I met an older man. András asked if we could see his yard because, except for being run-down, it looked like it would have in the 1930–40s, when my family lived nearby. We entered through a rusty metal gate, skewed on its hinge. The adobe walls were crumbling in places, revealing the underlying vertical wooden slats, but I could get a closeup of the original bricks of clay and straw and the low ceilings of some rooms.

This slovenly dressed man, with his bulbous nose and beer-belly paunch, proceeded to tell me that he remembered my grandfather, who had been nice and at times gave the children candy from his store. To my dismay, he then actually boasted how, when he was a teen, he had helped deport my grandfather from town on a wagon. He was nonchalant as he spoke, as if this deportation were the most normal thing in the world. I turned to András and his wife and asked if I had understood correctly. They nodded yes, and we left wordlessly.

I caught similar snatches of antisemitism and nationalism on that trip. Statements that ranged from how maybe they shouldn't have killed the Jews but the Gypsies were a problem in Sáránd to the full-blown "we should get rid of the Jews" again, heard as I walked near a synagogue in the bigger city.

These antisemitic statements were but a mild preview of what is happening in Hungary today with its rapidly growing xenophobic and increasingly fascist government. My cousin in Budapest is justified in his worry.

CHAPTER 66

My Reconciliation with Kati

EHRENFELDS, I HAVE LEARNED OVER THE YEARS, excel at holding grudges—a trait I am working to overcome. Alas, I learned many years ago how much I am my mother's daughter. After my daughter's bat mitzvah, as Kati stood in my drive preparing to leave, she burst into tears. "Only a doctor could afford a place like this," she wept.

I couldn't believe what I was hearing. Our home is understated and tucked unobtrusively into the woods. Mark and I designed every square inch, even incorporating the locust trees we had to cut down to clear the site into our flooring.

I was so hurt and angry, then and there I swore I wouldn't speak to Kati again, and for the next fifteen years, I had little to do with her. This is something I now regret.

Unsurprisingly, when Kati and I at long last—some years later—spoke about this incident, I learned we each remember that incident quite differently. She felt I unjustly accused her of being jealous—not a trait that anyone would ascribe to her, and we both have long-lasting scars from that rare altercation.

I share this vignette as it illustrates again the power of words. Whether the hurt was intended or not, the words could not be unsaid. I know I could have better controlled my temper and my mother's grudge-holding genes. We wasted so many years needlessly.

I had never really understood how two Auschwitz survivor sisters could be so angry with each other so as not to speak for ten years. And here, I had regretfully followed in my mother's footsteps.

Hopefully, I am learning to avoid the same pitfalls, and am glad that Kati and I got over that episode. Over this last decade, as I've come to know Kati well, my love and respect for her have only grown.

OVER THE NEXT TEN YEARS, I saw how devoted Kati was to Klari, who died in 2001, and then Bözsi, who died in 2004. In 2007, my mother's health rapidly deteriorated, and she was in and out of the hospital. Her two remaining siblings came to visit. I was stunned when, on New Year's Eve, the normally reticent Miklós asked me to take him back to our house so I could tape his story and Kati asked, "Can I come too? I've never heard your story."

"How could that be?" I wondered. Then Kati reminded me of how poor they were and how they struggled for years after immigrating, unable to afford telephone calls, let alone visits. This fueled my determination to tell their story, though it has been a longer process than intended. The 2008 Holocaust conference cemented my resolve.

I very much appreciated the support Kati gave during that nightmare period, both to my mother and to me, and ever since I have felt more close to her. We've had several visits, and each time, she has helped fill in bits about the family history. Each tidbit is a little piece of the puzzle—not just about the Holocaust, but about how the siblings grew up in that small village, something that I have been fascinated by since elementary school. Each story gives me a fuller understanding and makes me feel closer to my family and not miss them as intensely.

FOR FORTY YEARS AFTER MOVING TO IOWA, Kati largely hid that she was Jewish. I wasn't surprised. She had learned in Auschwitz that a key to survival was never to call attention to yourself. I also live in a rural community with few Jews. I understand wanting to stay under the radar, and the fact that I understand also makes me sad for Kati. I feel for those who think they have to hide who they are. I have always relished embracing cultural diversity and learning about others and know that doing so enriches our souls, whereas secret keeping kills a bit of us inside.

Kati began sharing her story and educating others about the Holocaust only in 2008, after the *Omaha World-Herald* wrote a story honoring liberators and World War II vets and interviewed her as well.[1] Leo Adam Biga wrote an extensive profile of Kati later that year.[2] After that, her teaching through the Institute for Holocaust Education in Omaha took off, and she has passionately worked to educate students about genocide, speaking as far away as Minden, Nebraska, and Grand Junction, Colorado. As I speak with her frequently now on the phone, I am increasingly impressed by her evolution and the fact that in her eighties, she was able to reinvent herself as an impassioned Holocaust educator.

IN 2012, KATI AND I ATTENDED the Holocaust Conference in Cleveland,[3] again gaining more insights. Kati expressed mixed feelings, especially of having the sense of being an outsider because she didn't have an upbringing in a Jewish community nor familiarity with traditional prayers or songs. When some in the group sang "Hatikvah," Kati's memories of Allendorf were triggered, as the women had sung Jewish songs while marching to work during the night, despite the presence of SS guards. Recalling those songs was bittersweet, reminding her of the close bonds the women made at Allendorf and how that helped them survive. She looked sad, so I put my arm on hers; neither she, Klari, nor my mother ever liked hugging or public displays of affection.

After an evening of listening to and watching music and dancing, Kati commented, with a twinge of envy, about the Israelis who were "full of life," that being their heritage. She reflected that her own upbringing lacked joy, especially after her mother died, and that "everything was so dreary." Kati never felt like she belonged anywhere. However, as she has done more teaching, I can see how that has changed.

Kati (90), in Holocaust Survivors' Gallery, 2014, Omaha

KATI BECAME ILL after her trip to Colorado, and I went out to be with her in the hospital and run interference in her care, as I had for my mother (and, to a lesser extent, for Miklós), and I've continued in that role of protector and patient advocate. While the task can be frustrating, I am happy to do it and find it gratifying to have been able to help them have a longer and better quality of life. Taking care of people is what I most like to do. It is who I am.

I've enjoyed watching Kati blossom as a Holocaust educator and am awed by her stamina and persistence—traits she shared with my mother, the toughest woman I've known. I'm also determined to help educate others as I have felt a renewed sense of dread particularly since 2016. It is clear to anyone who pays attention that we are headed back to the 1930s Germany mentality, with the increasing "othering" and rising nationalism and fascism. Indeed, this has been a driving impetus for me to finish this book as part of my contribution to Holocaust education, a longing to try to prevent such atrocities from ever happening again.

Now ninety-four and widowed, Kati still lives independently, cooking and baking and driving herself all over the Omaha area. She continues to suffer from imposter syndrome and survivor's guilt, feeling that she is unworthy of attention as her suffering was not as great as that of some others. But Kati thrives on the questions from students and their seeing the importance, now more than ever, of standing up to hate, and she appreciates the impact her stories have on the kids.

After explaining to students how "othering" and bullying were the precursors to the Holocaust, Kati tries to impart the need for simple kindnesses and caring to the students she speaks to. Kati reminds me—and her young audiences—what a significant impact the protectiveness and support women at both Auschwitz and Allendorf showed each other and how that helped them survive.

These lessons cross generations. Kati was moved and buoyed by the attentive, concerned response she received on a panel called "Stories of Survival: Three Generations of Surviving Genocide" in November 2018.[4] The other panelists included women who had survived the Cambodian killing fields and the Yazidi genocide, and the moderator was a genocide and political science scholar at the University of Nebraska–Omaha, Dr. Lana Obradovic.

Prescient author Sarah Kendzior, who has a doctorate in anthropology, studying autocracies, said in one of her earlier articles, "If you cannot be brave—and it is often hard to be brave—be kind."[5] She offers more sage advice about writing down your own values, dreams, and memories to later remind yourself of what you hold dear. When I read Sarah's lines, I was reminded of the women in the camps sharing their food or helping nurture their friends, both physically and emotionally, and how meaningful even seemingly small gestures of kindness were in sustaining them. Kindness was critical to their survival.

Although speaking at schools is exhausting to Kati, I have no doubt that it is also what keeps her alive.

Since Kati "came out" in 2008, she has spoken to thousands of students; that number is growing each year as the number of survivors is dwindling. The Institute for Holocaust Education in Nebraska does a phenomenal job in outreach and education. Three of their staff, in particular, have supported Kati over the years, Beth Seldin Dotan, Liz Feldstein, and Donna Walter.

Kati saves all the letters she receives after her speeches. Here is a sample of some of the comments:

- "You wanted to change one person's life, and you did. Mine!"

- "I cannot believe how strong, smart, and optimistic you were."

- "I hope the tragedy of the Holocaust will not always be a burden but a memory that shows how strong you are."

- "You are a great inspiration."

The students applauded her being able to start a life from scratch, speak courageously, and give them hope that things can get better.

In each of her talks to students, Kati tries to address bullying in general: "Speak up. Do whatever you can do in your power. Don't be a bystander. Be brave enough that if you see injustice or discrimination, speak up."

Kati stressed to me that when she speaks, she very much wants her audience, especially students, to know that good people exist. She defines success, in part, as showing them that there is hope and goodness left in the world, emphasizing that this is what sustained her through the Holocaust.

The two hardest questions she faces are about religion and politics. People ask if she still believes in G-d. Kati told me,

> It's very hard to answer. I tell them that I do. I can't tell them that I don't. I tell them I have some doubts now. I know that I'm in a part of the country where they have a religious upbringing, and I don't want to disillusion them.
>
> I always emphasize that there is one race, the human race. I even say we are all G-d's children because that appeals in this part of the country.

She is also asked about the forty-fifth president. She explains,

> That's how it started. I emphasize our freedom of speech. Hitler started the same way, with suppressing the press

320

... and the racial hatred. Jews are different, almost like not human.

Kids are our future. When they come around me, they have questions about what's going on in this country, the discrimination. The black kids, Hispanic ones, really get it. The young people understand more about racism. When I see their interactions, the black kids, and Hispanic, and white, they seem to get along better than the whole nation. The kids are more tolerant. I can see it.

CHAPTER 67

Records from the USHMM

OVER THE YEARS—first in 2011—I had sent inquiries to the International Tracing Service in Bad Arolsen, Yad Vashem, and the USHMM. I received no helpful leads and did not pursue the matter further until early 2018, as I was writing this book, when I submitted detailed requests to the USHMM. Months later, I received a treasure trove of digital copies of records.

I began to feel dazed when I received photos of WWII era information cards the Nazis kept on their prisoners; the Holocaust Museum sent me those they found on Kati late in the process of writing this book. They didn't appear to contain too much information, but I was stunned—actually shocked—to see her *Häftling* (prisoner) records.

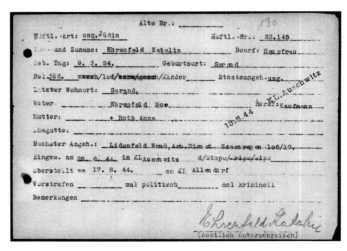

Kati's prisoner record from Auschwitz, 1944[1]

The Germans were meticulous, even noting on one card that she had seven documents associated with her. By that time I had spent years trying to find when my grandfather was murdered, among the millions with no one to say Kaddish for them. I had long wondered when people said Kaddish for those whose death date is unknown; I suppose it is just at Yizkor, a memorial service on specific holidays.

I've long found it curious how different people and cultures acknowledge grief anniversaries. My husband, raised Christian, commemorates his mother's birthday, not the date of her passing, while in the Jewish tradition, we observe the Yahrzeit, or anniversary of someone's death rather than the person's birthday. We say a traditional prayer, the Mourner's Kaddish and light a twenty-four-hour candle. The Kaddish prayer says nothing about death but extols G-d and concludes with a prayer for peace.

LOOKING AT THE CARDS, I was able to tell what some of the fields were by context, but for some parts I could find no translations online and I worked hard to find someone to translate. For example, I don't know why Ernö Lindenfeld was listed on Kati's cards, or where the Germans got the information to list him as next of kin, with a number that is likely a labor battalion, in Szászrégen, in Transylvania. Kati didn't know where he was, and she would have listed a sister as next of kin, not her cousin Ernö.

I was sorry I couldn't be with Kati when she first saw the images I forwarded to her. When I told her about them, she said she felt as if a hand were reaching out from the grave. She was obviously shocked, and I would have worried about causing her nightmares, but I knew these war images are always with her.

Kati told me she thought she had solved the mystery of what date she and her father arrived at Auschwitz from reading Rabbi Berkowits's memoir. They were with the Derecske *csoport* and likely even with Berkowits's mother. I emailed Berkowits requesting information about his sources since even Bad Arolsen had reported that it had no records about some of the specific transports from Nagyvárad.

As I looked for someone to help translate the records I received, I ran into a Swiss woman I had seen on occasion. She has a noticeable German accent—an accent that often causes me to recoil—so I asked if she might help with a translation but gave her no details. She hesitated but agreed to set aside some time. I thought she was old enough to have been a child during the war.

WHILE I WAS STILL AWAITING THE TRANSLATIONS, I found myself staring at the records for long stretches, wondering about the Nazis' obsessiveness and the detailed organization of their slave labor and killing machines.

One of the cards has a mysterious entry, labeled "Buchenwald," and dated October 20, 1944. I hadn't realized before then that Allendorf was a subcamp of Buchenwald. Kati hypothesized that she was to have been transferred there on that date to be killed, having likely outlived her usefulness. In fact, she was never in Buchenwald and stayed in Allendorf from August 1944 until April 1, 1945, the date of her liberation, and also her father's birthday.

Kati also told me that Bözsi was listed on one card as being from Košice, not Sáránd, and has an incorrect date of birth. Apparently, after her liberation, when bureaucrats were compiling lists of survivors and displaced persons, someone made an error in recording Bözsi's information. She was too afraid to correct it—we "were all afraid of everything," Kati explained. Bözsi's fear snowballed when she met Jack, as she was afraid he would ask, "What else did you lie about?" and not accept that "the lie" was a clerical error. That small mistake followed her for the rest of her life, and she hid the error from everyone until she was dying, when she wanted her family to better know her story. It reminded me of the line I recently read about practicing lies until they became a part of you.[2]

A WEEK OR TWO LATER, I met the Swiss woman for lunch, feeling that breaking bread together would help us overcome barriers. Elizabeth was gracious, charming, and helpful. Most importantly, she shared stories about being a young child in Germany during the war and the hardships she and her family endured. When she had finished telling me about her life, I asked if I could give her a hug.

IN REVIEWING THE CARDS AGAIN, I was surprised to pick up one date I had overlooked previously: "28.6.44" (June 28, 1944). It gave me chills, as I recognized that the Nazis had recorded the day Kati arrived in Auschwitz and thus the date her father, my grandfather Mór, was murdered. Seeing that date, I felt profound sadness, some anger, and surprising relief that I had discovered this missing piece, allowing me on that date to rise and join others in reciting Kaddish in remembrance of my grandfather.

I will still rise and join others in reciting Kaddish for those with no family or no known death date, in respect and remembrance of our ancestors.

CHAPTER 68

Except for Kati

THINKING OF KATI DYING has always felt threatening. She's the last tenuous link to her generation. My dear friend Larry told me that when he was leaving his parents' home after seeing his mom for what he knew would be the last time, he felt daunted, particularly as he is the eldest child and the repository of all his family's history. While I am not the eldest, I feel the weight of having promised my mother and Sanyi that I would assume their burden; remembering feels like a sacred duty except that few in the family seem to care now. I often think back to the plaintive epigraph at Yad Vashem, "I should like someone to remember that there once lived a person named David Berger."[1]

Although Kati is the eldest now, she was the "baby" for most of her life and has never viewed herself as the family matriarch. The cousins have drifted apart; we are so scattered that nothing will likely bring us together again or recapture the closeness we once felt. Some in our family neither ask questions about the past nor offer contributions to the family history. I was shocked to learn that some had thrown out their family members' personal items, when I can barely part with a scrap of paper with my parents' writing or a sentimental item of clothing. I'm fascinated by how differently different people value similar things.

As I struggle now to capture the family lore, viewing myself as an anthropologist describing a tribe and culture that are facing extinction I wonder if perhaps I belong in another time.

I try to focus on enjoying my relationship with Kati, even as I work to capture all I can from her, the only living witness to our family's travails. I know that inevitably she will be gone, and I can't shake an underlying sense of impending doom, another sign, perhaps, that I am my mother's daughter, that I perhaps absorbed too much of her almost telepathic terror. The overwhelming feeling I often have is akin to staring into an abyss, being tiny. I feel like a lost child, orphaned and inconsolably crying. I'm terrified of the dark, of being alone.

I want to spend more time with Kati, but she keeps saying she is too busy—and in fact, she is. Yet if I didn't ask to see her, I know she would be hurt. I want to enjoy her laughter and energy and her baking and learn everything I didn't learn from my own mother.

I wonder what will be lost when the older generation is gone: the sounds of laughter on those rare occasions when they were together, the gesturing and animation while they spoke. I loved watching my clan sitting around the table, gossiping, and I cherish still Ma's and Klari's rapier wit. They considered sarcasm a fine art, and they engaged in competitive stiletto stabbings, intended to be so subtle that the victim barely noticed being pierced. Their sarcasm was both admired and feared, and when I was the recipient, I found it extraordinarily painful. And yet I can't imagine the world without it.

Conclusion

I BEGAN THIS PROJECT curious about life in the "olden days" of nineteenth- and twentieth-century Hungary, and the story has taken unexpected turns. It next evolved into making a record of the family history, initially just for the relatives, as Sanyi had done. But as I learned more about my family and the Holocaust, I realized that our family's story is unique in its complexity and the intertwined relationships—as well as the fortune of having so many survive.

I started more seriously trying to put together the family's story. I had no intention of serving as more than a reporter, but as I learned about family members and the impact their experiences had on my second- and third-generation cousins, it became clear that I had to share my journey with this project as well and our complicated relationships.

As I completed this book, I was struck by our family's successes. The members of the older generation came from poverty and homes broken by death through the Holocaust. Yet after immigrating to a distant country with unfamiliar customs and a very different language, they all built good, accomplished lives, supporting themselves and their families. They also raised successful children, emphasizing the need for a strong education. Most went into math and computer science or into the helping professions—medicine, nursing, legal aid, and teaching.

In her talks at a women's prison and at schools, Kati shares how our family's story inspires listeners that they, too, can overcome obstacles in their lives. That is her legacy.

As one cousin aptly observed, "The one hundred years between 1900 and 2000 as framed by our family is the story of the Western world. It pivots from thatch-roofed shacks with dirt floors to satellites and websites."

I learned so much about human nature and the lasting impact of words. We all need to use them more carefully and be mindful of their power.

I want people to study history and to wake up to the parallels between what is happening here—and globally—to what happened in the 1930s with the rise of nationalism. I hope we can hold back the tide of divisiveness and autocracy. But this requires people to learn from the past and to care about others and the greater good and not just themselves. Studies of the Holocaust and other genocides should be a part of every curriculum as well as religious education for all faiths.

My mother was like a phoenix rising from the ashes of grief. In her spirit of persistence, survival, and resilience, with a nod to our family's legacy, we concluded her funeral singing the refrain to "We Are Lights"—as our family has become the lights of memory.[1]

Epilogue

NOT ALL WAS GLOOM, especially after a few years following Apu's death.

My mother enjoyed having the company of some neighbors as well as my brother's friends with their ravenous appetites.

We liked watching *Jeopardy!* and *Washington Week in Review* together. *Jeopardy!* was a sacred time and heaven help anyone who called and interrupted her show.

Ma's other favorite show was *Hogan's Heroes*.[1] It was a comedy about a German POW camp in World War II that ran from 1965 to 1971 (and then longer via reruns and syndication). The prisoners ran a resistance operation under the direction of Colonel Hogan (Bob Crane). Werner Klemperer, a German Jew (and son of the famous symphony conductor Otto Klemperer) played the commandant, Colonel Klink, a bumbling fool, and John Banner, also a Jew, played Sergeant Schultz, Klink's incompetent right-hand man. Several of the other major actors were Jewish (which I didn't know at the time) and had escaped but lost family in the camps. Robert Clary, who played Corporal LeBeau, had been in concentration camps for three years.

Some people were surprised that Ma watched *Hogan's Heroes*, let alone loved it, but she always had a fine appreciation for satire and gallows humor.

Occasionally now, if I have an unexpectedly bitter swig of my first morning coffee, I also get a strong sensation and taste of cigarette smoke in my mouth. It reminds me of my mother, who, until her later years, often perched at the red-and-white enamel kitchen table with a cigarette and a cup of coffee when she wasn't cooking or cleaning. That was her relaxation, sitting at the table, wearing her worn apron, her uniform, with her mug and smoke.

OTHER TIMES, when I try to picture my mother, I see only her back as she stands at the sink washing dishes or at the stove cooking foods, usually heavy with garlic and grease. She is always wearing a thin 1960s cotton housedress—sleeveless, pullover, and floral—with a mismatched worn bib apron tied at the waist.

How I wished that she was paying attention to me and that I remembered more than her back.

MY DAUGHTER STILL LIVES in my mother's home and has transformed it into her own, except for the 1950s kitchen. Grandma's enamel table is still there by the sunny bow window filled with potted plants. The table was the item with the greatest sentimental value for all of us. While visiting one evening, I found myself looking in the medicine cabinet, hoping that my father's Old Spice was still there. I remember his scents, lingering on his clothes long after he died, and my just wanting to bury my nose in them. It's funny how powerful scents are in rekindling memories, perhaps more than anything else.

The only scents I associate with my mother are her cooking and fresh laundry. But those aprons! I still have them somewhere, the piping frayed and the patterned material thin and faded. The cotton was so soft from wear, I always loved to touch it.

I saved many of her clothes to make a quilt and consulted an experienced local quilter, but trying to design it has been daunting, and the quilter said the fabric I have isn't suitable. A lot of Ma's clothes are too thin to work with if they are cotton and unsuitable polyester otherwise. Perhaps just fusing the cotton scraps to interfacing and making a small collage might work. I even bought a program to design this project with and scanned some of the fabrics from her clothes. Perhaps now that the book is complete, I might return to that project. More likely, I'll continue to focus on trying, in some small way, to make the world a better, more peaceful, and just place.

Glossary

afikomen. Broken pieces of matzoh.

Anyu. Mother, my mother.

Apu, Apuka. Father.

"Arbeit macht frei." Work Makes You Free.

asztalos. Furniture maker.

Aufseherin. Female officer.

bácsi. Uncle. Also used as a title of respect for an older man, like Mr.

barack pálinka. Apricot brandy.

Bris. Circumcision.

bundás kenyér. A dish similar to French toast.

büntetés század. A unit of men who were to receive extra punishment.

chametz. A grain product that has risen, forbidden during Passover.

charoses. A mixture of chopped walnuts, apples, and too-sweet wine.

cheder. Religious elementary school forcx Jewish children, with secular and religious education.

cholent **(Yiddish),** *sólet* **(Hungarian).** Sabbath dish of baked beans, barley, potato and sometimes meat. It was prepared on Friday and baked in the oven overnight for the Sabbath meal.

chupah. Wedding canopy.

cigány. Gypsy.

csajka. Tin cup, canteen cup.

cseléd. Maid.

cserépkályha. Tiled stove.

csibész. Mischievous rascal.

csirkepaprikás. Paprika chicken.

csoport. Group.

csúnya. Ugly.

cukrászda. Sweets shop.

diós. Walnut rolls.

dobos torte. A seven-layer chocolate cake, traditionally topped with a burnt sugar icing.

édesanyám. Mother, my mother.

elteste. Head of the barracks.

fa kutya. Wooden dog.

fasírt. Fried meatballs.

félmesztelen. Half-naked.

fémipari. Technical school to study machinery and tools.

fleischig. Meat, or a dish containing meat.

foghagymás bab leves. Bean soup with garlic.

gahal. Enlistees from overseas in Israel's War for Independence in Palestine, used (sometimes derogatorily) to describe Holocaust survivors, recruited from abroad.

gerbeaud. Pastry with layers of jam and walnuts.

góré. Corn crib.

gumi labda. Rubber ball.

Häftlings. Inmates.

Haganah. Jewish underground military, before and during the War for Independence. Predecessor of the Israeli Defense Forces.

Halachah. Collected totality of Jewish law.

hegedű. Violin.

húsos. Meat-containing meal.

kaja. Food.

kancsi. Cross-eyed.

kamara. Pantry or storage chamber.

Kapos. Prisoners who held privileged positions.

kashrut. Dietary laws regulating keeping foods kosher.

kemence. Wood-fired oven.

keréskedelmi. Trade.

kocsis. Teamster.

kocsonya. Carp and carrots within gelatin.

köménymag. Caraway seed.

kötény. Apron.

középpont. Center, hub.

Krankenrevier. Sick bay, infirmary.

különb. Better or special in some way.

különös. Extraordinary.

Lager. Camp (concentration, transit, labor, or death camp).

lavor. Basin.

ma'apalim. Illegal Jewish immigrants to Palestine during the British mandate, until 1948.

mahal. Volunteers from abroad. Enlistees from overseas in Israel's War for Independence in Palestine but who were from English-speaking countries.

mákos. Poppy seed.

mákos tészta. Egg noodles with ground poppy seeds and sugar.

megye. County.

milchig. Containing dairy.

mohel. Person trained to perform the ritual circumcision of male Jewish newborns.

Munkaszolgálat(os). Forced labor units; forced laborers.

nagyszájú. Big mouth.

néni. Aunt. Also used as a title of respect for an older woman, like Mrs.

nokedli. Egg dumplings.

nyilasok. Arrow Cross, or Hungarian Nazis.

nyomortona. A world of poverty and misery.

olim. Immigrants making Aliyah, returning to Israel, which they considered the Jewish homeland.

orlah. The prohibition of eating or using the fruit of a tree for the first three years after planting.

özsike. Deer.

pálinka. Brandy.

Palmach. Strike force of the Haganah.

paraszt. Peasants.

payos. Sidelocks.

pengő. Hungarian currency between 1927 and 1946, when the forint replaced it; 5,000 pengő equaled $1,000 in 1944.

piac. Market.

pidyon ha ben. A Jewish ritual for the redemption of the first newborn male.

pogács. Biscuits.

polgári. Middle school, or junior high.

pörkölt. Stew.

payos. Sidelocks.

rétes. Strudel.

Revier. Short for *Krankenrevier,* or infirmary.

shochet. Ritual slaughterer.

Sonderkommando. Prisoners who worked in the crematoria.

spájz. Pantry.

SS, or *Schutzstaffel*. Shield squadron. The part of the Nazi party responsible for security and racial policies. They also controlled the police department and the concentration camps.

szellem. Ghost.

szikrázot. Sparked.

szoknyavadászok. Skirt hunters.

szomorú. Sad.

tejes. Dairy-containing products.

tér. Place.

teknő. Trough.

tepertő. Cracklings.

tikkun olam. Repair of the world (making the world a better place).

töltött káposzta. Stuffed cabbage.

túrós béles. Pastry like a cheese Danish.

uborkasaláta. Cucumber salad.

utca. Street.

vén troger. Decrepit old good-for-nothing.

vidék. Countryside.

Wehrmacht. Nazi armed forces.

Yahrzeit. Jewish anniversary of death.

Zählappell. Roll call.

Notes

Preface

1. "Magda Stone," interview 11980, Visual History Archive, USC Shoah Foundation, February 11, 1996, http://vhaonline.usc.edu/viewingPage?testimonyID =11604&returnIndex=0.

2. Rabbi Jack Paskoff, "Shabbat Service," December 21, 2018, Congregation Shaarai Shomayim, Lancaster, PA, Facebook video, 1:15:30, https://www.facebook .com/ShaaraiShomayim/videos/ 316930162245878/.

Introduction

1. "2008 Washington DC: 20th Annual International Conference of Child Survivors and Families, 2G & 3G: 'Remembrance and Continuity,'" World Federation of Jewish Child Survivors of the Holocaust & Descendants, accessed December 29, 2018, https://www.holocaustchild.org/past-conferences/2008/12/2008 -washington-dc.

2. Hearing that almost no one (the figure I recall is 10 percent) from rural Hungary survived the Holocaust has stuck in my head since 2008 and was a major premise motivating this book. I have been looking for some time for specific numbers.

Fact checking in 2018 made the answer less straightforward. Wikipedia says, "A Jew living in the Hungarian countryside in March 1944 had a less than 10% chance of surviving the following 12 months. In Budapest, a Jew's chance of survival of the same 12 months was about 50%." Wikipedia, s.v. "History of the Jews in Hungary," last modified January 31, 2019, https://en.wikipedia.org/wiki/History_of_the_Jews _in_Hungary.

I reached out to Agnes Vertes, a Hungarian whom I met at the conference, but she said she did not know who told me that statistic. Agnes Vertes, personal communication, December 18, 2018. I then came across an interview with Vertes that discussed her documentary *One Out of Ten*, though the title refers to children. Vivien Orbach-Smith, "Never Forget, Never Again: Agnes Vertes," Federation for Jewish Philanthropy, accessed December 14, 2018, https://www .jewishphilanthropyct.org/agnesvertes. Perhaps I had misremembered.

I then consulted with Dr. Peter Hayes for clarification on a passage from his book, *Why? Explaining the Holocaust*. He graciously responded that Randolph Braham's figures in *The Politics of Genocide* "suggest a survival rate of 18 percent." Peter Hayes, personal communication, December 16, 2018. The numbers vary, however, depending on what provinces from the interwar period are being included in the counts. Of course, the Nazis also did not keep an accurate count of all their victims. My grandfather, among so many others, does not appear in their records.

Chapter 1

1. "Lénártóv: Charakteristika obce," Lénártóv: oficinále stránky obce, last modified January 27, 2014, http://www.Lenartov.sk/obec-Lenartov/charakteristika -obce/.

2. "Hungary—the Jewish Community," International Jewish Cemetery Project, last modified February 2009, http://www.iajgsjewishcemeteryproject.org/hungary /index/Page-2.html; and "Prewar Jewish Life in Budapest," Yad Vashem, accessed December 17, 2018, https://www.yadvashem.org/articles/general/prewar-jewish-life -in-budapest.html.

3. "Prewar Jewish Life in Budapest."

4. "Tiszaeszlár Blood Libel," *YIVO* Encyclopedia of Jews in Eastern Europe, accessed December 30, 2018, http://www.yivoencyclopedia.org/article.aspx /Tiszaeszlar_Blood_Libel.

5. "Hungary—the Jewish Community."

6. "Magda Stone," interview 11980, Visual History Archive, USC Shoah Foundation, February 11, 1996, http://vhaonline.usc.edu/viewingPage?testimonyID =11604&returnIndex=0.

7. Katherine Williams, interview with author, November 16, 2014.

8. "Orlah," Chabad.org, accessed December 30, 2018, https://www.chabad.org /search/keyword_cdo/kid/1427/jewish/Orlah.htm.

9. *Magyarország kereskedelmi, ipari és mezőgazdasági címtára*, (Budapest: Rudolf Mosse, 1924), Hungaricana, accessed December 30, 2018, https://library .hungaricana.hu/en/view/FszekCimNevTarak_27_024/?pg=0&layout=s.

Chapter 2

1. "'Sena'—Encyclopaedia of Jewish Communities, Slovakia," JewishGen, updated May 19, 2013, https://www.jewishgen.org/yizkor/pinkas_slovakia/slo392 .html, from Yehoshua Robert Buchler and Ruth Shachak, eds., *Pinkas Hakehillot Slovakia (Encyclopedia of Jewish Communities, Slovakia)*, trans. Madeleine Isenberg (Jerusalem: Yad Vashem, 2003).

2. Alexander G. Stone, interview with author, 1994 and 2006.

3. "Timeline of the Second World War," Holocaust and the United Nations Outreach Programme, accessed December 30, 2018, http://www.un.org/en /holocaustremembrance/PDF/Timeline%20WWII.pdf; "World War II Key Dates," United States Holocaust Memorial Museum, accessed December 30, 2018, https://encyclopedia.ushmm.org/content/en/article/world-war-ii-key-dates; and "Nazi Occupation—Hungary," The Holocaust Explained, accessed December 30, 2018, https://www.theholocaustexplained.org/life-in-nazi-occupied-europe/jews-in -occupied-countries/hungary/.

Chapter 3

1. *A Taste of the Past* by András Koerner gave me valuable insight and guided my interviewing questions to my mother and Kati regarding cooking and housekeeping. András Koerner, *A Taste of the Past: The Daily Life and Cooking of a Nineteenth-Century Hungarian-Jewish Homemaker* (Lebanon, NH: University Press of New England, 2004).

2. Katherine Williams and Magda Stone, interview with author, December 6, 2006.

3. Reuven Hammer, "Kapparot, Swinging a Chicken over One's Head," My Jewish Learning, accessed December 24, 2018, https://www.myjewishlearning.com /article/kaparot/.

4. Clara Gray, personal communication with author, 2001.

Chapter 9

1. Peter Hayes, *Why? Explaining the Holocaust* (New York: W. W. Norton, 2017); and Yuri Slezkine, *The Jewish Century* (Princeton, NJ: Princeton University Press, 2004), 48.

2. Tim Cole, "Hungary, the Holocaust, and Hungarians: Remembering Whose History?" in "Hungary and the Holocaust: Confrontation with the Past" (symposium proceedings, Center for Advanced Holocaust Studies, United States Holocaust Memorial Museum, Washington, DC, January 2001), accessed December 19, 2018, https://www.ushmm.org/m/pdfs/Publication_OP_2001-01.pdf.

3. "Holocaust Chronology," Illinois Holocaust Museum and Education Center, accessed December 30, 2018,https://www.ilholocaustmuseum.org /pages/learn/holocaust-history/holocaust-chronology/.

4. "Anschluss," United States Holocaust Memorial Museum, accessed December 30, 2018, https://www.ushmm.org/collections/bibliography/anschluss.

5. "Holocaust Chronology."

6. Katherine Williams, interview with author, December 2018.

7. Katherine Williams, interview with author, November 16, 2014.

Chapter 12

1. Katherine Williams (lecture, Holocaust Awareness Week, Colorado Mesa University, April 9, 2015); and Robert Rozett, "Conscripted Slaves: Hungarian Jewish Forced Laborers on the Eastern Front during World War II," Yad Vashem, accessed April 2, 2019, https://www.yadvashem.org/articles/general/conscripted-slaves -hungarian-jewish-forced-laborers.html.

2. "Census for Cumberland, Maryland 2010," American Fact Finder, https://factfinder.census.gov/faces/nav/jsf/pages/community_facts.xhtml?src=bkmk.

3. Peter Hayes, *Why? Explaining the Holocaust* (New York: W. W. Norton, 2017).

4. Hayes, *Why? Explaining the Holocaust.*

5. Hayes, *Why? Explaining the Holocaust,* 185

Chapter 13

1. Bill Demain, "This Song's a Killer: The Strange Tale of 'Gloomy Sunday,'" Mental Floss, August 16, 2011, http://mentalfloss.com/article/28525/songs-killer -strange-tale-gloomy-sunday.

Chapter 14

1. "Berettyóújfalu, Hungary," Encyclopedia Judaica, Jewish Virtual Library, accessed March 5, 2019, https://www.jewishvirtuallibrary.org/berettyjfalu.

Chapter 16

1. Randolph L. Braham, *The Politics of Genocide: The Holocaust in Hungary,* cond. ed. (Detroit: Wayne State University Press, 2000).

2. Katherine Williams, interview with author, July 17, 2018.

Chapter 17

1. "Auschwitz Revolt," United States Holocaust Memorial Museum, accessed March 6, 2019, https://www.ushmm.org/research/the-center-for-advanced -holocaust-studies/miles-lerman-center-for-the-study-of-jewish-resistance/medals -of-resistance-award/auschwitz-revolt.

2. "Elisabeth Kasik," interview 4666, Visual History Archive, USC Shoah Foundation, August 18, 1995, http://vhaonline.usc.edu/viewingPage?testimonyID =5165&returnIndex=0.

3. "Death March from Auschwitz," United States Holocaust Memorial Museum, accessed March 6, 2019, www.ushmm.org/learn/timeline-of-events/1942-1945/death -march-from-auschwitz.

4. Steven Vitto (USHMM researcher), personal communication, March 7, 2019. Mohlhof is not referenced on current maps, but Vitto found three other survivors whose paths matched the information and other details given by Bözsi.

5. Elisabeth Kasik, interview, Visual History Archive; and "German Civilians, Soldiers and Released Allied Prisoners Cross Mulde River Bridge," Critical Past, YouTube, April 9, 2014, https://www.youtube.com/watch?v=5OPop5joa-M.

Chapter 19

1. Katherine Williams (lecture, Holocaust Awareness Week, Colorado Mesa University, April 9, 2015); and "2013 Wahoo High School Holocaust Assembly #1— Kitty Williams," Wahoo Public Schools, SchoolTube, https://app.schooltube .com/video/c03a881858f948a4a452/2013_Wahoo_High_School_Holocaust _Assembly_%231_-_Kitty_Williams.

2. Manya Friedman, "A Headstone in the Air," Echoes of Memory, United States Holocaust Memorial Museum, September 17, 2006, https://www.ushmm.org /remember/holocaust-reflections-testimonies/echoes-of-memory/a-headstone-in -the-air.

3. "Death Trains in 1944: The Kassa List," Deportáltakat Gondozó Országos Bizottság, accessed January 3, 2019, http://degob.org/tables/kassa.html.

Chapter 20

1. There is a curious discrepancy about where exactly my family arrived in Auschwitz. Magdus and Kati clearly recalled seeing the famous sign at the entrance gate to Auschwitz, "Arbeit Macht Frei," immediately upon their arrival. "Surprising Beginnings," Auschwitz: Inside the Nazi State, PBS, accessed January 1, 2019, https://www.pbs.org/auschwitz/40-45/beginnings/. The gate was at Auschwitz I, the administrative area of the camp. Haroon Siddique, "Arbeit Macht Frei Sign Stolen from Auschwitz," Guardian, December 18, 2009, https://www.theguardian.com /world/2009/dec/18/sign-stolen-auschwitz-death-camp.

But the Auschwitz-Birkenau State Museum's website says that an unloading ramp was built inside Birkenau—also known as Auschwitz II—to accommodate the arrival of Hungarian Jews in May 1944. "The Unloading Ramps and Selections," Auschwitz-Birkenau Memorial and Museum, accessed January 7, 2019, http://auschwitz.org/en/history/auschwitz-and-shoah/the-unloading-ramps-and -selections.

Kati believes that they arrived at the gate in Auschwitz I and then were marched to Birkenau, two miles away.

2. James A. Grymes, Violins of Hope: Violins of the Holocaust—Instruments of Hope and Liberation in Mankind's Darkest Hour (New York: Harper Perennial, 2014), 137–140, quoted in "The Birkenau Women's Camp Orchestra," Facing History and Ourselves, https://www.facinghistory.org/music-memory-and-resistance -during-holocaust/birkenau-womens-camp-orchestra.

3. "Birkenau," Music and the Holocaust, World ORT, accessed December 28, 2018, http://holocaustmusic.ort.org/places/camps/death-camps/birkenau/. Regarding musicians in Auschwitz, orchestras were formed initially with Aryans; subsequently

Jewish musicians were allowed to join in Birkenau, which had separate men's and women's groups. The prisoner musicians were given better food, clothing, and work assignments, and even were spared from the gas chambers. In addition to playing lively military or folk music to speed the prisoners on, they sometimes had to entertain the Nazis with light music and their requests. The orchestra's story was portrayed in the movie *Playing for Time*.

4. "Basic Information on Auschwitz," Auschwitz-Birkenau Memorial and Museum, accessed December 30, 2018, http://auschwitz.org/en/press/basic-information-on-auschwitz/.

Chapter 23
1. Katherine Williams, interview with author, March 10, 2019.

Chapter 25
1. "Stadtallendorf Documentation and Information Center, in Detail," Holocaust Memorials, accessed January 4, 2019, https://www.gedenkstaetten-uebersicht.de/en/europe/cl/deutschland/inst/dokumentations-und-informatio/.

Chapter 26
1. Nicholas Field, interview with author, December 31, 2007.
2. Field, interview, December 31, 2007.
3. János M. Rainer, "Stalin and Rákosi, Stalin and Hungary, 1949–1953," 1956 Institute: Oral History Archive, National Széchényi Library, October 4, 1997, http://www.rev.hu/ords/f?p=600:2:::::P2_PAGE_URI:tanulmanyok/1945_56/rmj5.

Chapter 27
1. Randolph L. Braham, *The Politics of Genocide: The Holocaust in Hungary*, abr. ed. (Detroit: Wayne State University Press, 2000), 113–114.
2. Peter Hayes, *Why? Explaining the Holocaust* (New York: W. W. Norton, 2017), 232.

Chapter 28
1. Rabbi Jack Paskoff, "Shabbat Service," December 21, 2018, Congregation Shaarai Shomayim, Lancaster, PA, Facebook video, 1:15:30, https://www.facebook.com/ShaaraiShomayim/videos/316930162245878/.

Chapter 29
1. Arthur Allen, personal communication, October 20, 2014; and Arthur Allen, *The Fantastic Laboratory of Dr. Weigl: How Two Brave Scientists Battled Typhus and Sabotaged the Nazis* (New York: W. W. Norton, 2015).

Chapter 31
1. Alison Owings, *Frauen: German Women Recall the Third Reich* (New Brunswick, NJ: Rutgers University Press, 2005), 325.

Chapter 32
1. City Population, "Zennern in Schwalm-Eder-Kreis (Hesse)," accessed March 30, 2019, http://www.citypopulation.de/php/germany-settlements-hessen.php?cityid=06634025_oBK5.

Chapter 33
1. Hans Peter Föhrding and Heinz Verfürth, trans. Jefferson Chase, *When the Jews Fled to Germany: A Forgotten Chapter of Postwar History* (Cologne:

Kiepenheuer and Witsch, 2017), chap. 1, https://www.kiwi-verlag.de/files /foehrdingverfuerth_alsdiejuden_englishsample.pdf.

2. Clara Gray, interview with author, 2001.

3. Föhrding and Verfürth, *When the Jews Fled*, chap. 1.

4. Peter Gray, *Hungary to America* (blog), http://goldsteinehrenfeld.blogspot .com/, adapted with permission; and Peter Gray, email messages to author, October 19–29, 2018.

5. Katherine Williams, personal communication with author, September 8, 2018.

6. Esther Allweiss Ingber, "Memories of Sol & Zygie's and Other Jewish Gas Stations," *Michigan Jewish History* 53 (Fall 2013): 10, https://www.michjewishhistory .org/assets/docs/Journals/Michigan_Jewish_History_2013_09.pdf.

7. Gray, email, October 29, 2018.

Chapter 34

1. Linda Elkin, personal communication with author, October 2018.

2. Nicholas Field, interview with author, December 8, 2003.

Chapter 36

1. Magdus Stone, interview with author, September 2003.

2. Katherine Williams, interview with author, October 2016.

3. Katherine Williams, personal communication, February 6, 2018.

4. Magdus Stone, personal communication at family reunion in Brookdale, 1992.

5. "Jozsef Ehrenfeld," Holocaust Survivors and Victims Database, United States Holocaust Memorial Museum, accessed March 28, 2019, https://www.ushmm.org /online/hsv/person_view.php?PersonId=3420040.

6. Katherine Williams, interview with author, February 6, 2018.

7. Gordon Williamson, *German Special Forces of World War II* (Oxford: Osprey Publishing, 2012), 17.

8. Admont Displaced Persons' Camp, accessed December 30, 2018, http://www .dpcamps.org/admont.html.

9. Beth Rowen, "Immigration Legislation: A Detailed Look at Immigration Legislation from the Colonial Period to the Present," Infoplease.com, accessed December 30, 2018, https://www.infoplease.com/us/immigration-legislation.

10. Mari Deutsch, interview with author, October 5, 2017.

Chapter 37

1. Marianna Gersch, interview with author, December 26, 2018; and Shoah Resource Center, "Debrecen," https://www.yadvashem.org/odot_pdf/microsoft%20 word%20-%20185.pdf.

2. Gersch, interview, December 26, 2018.

3. Avi Baumol, *The Poetry of Prayer: Tehillim in Tefillah* (Jerusalem: Geffen Publishing, 2009), 283.

4. Record for Marianna Grünberger, 1949, "New York, New York Passenger and Crew Lists, 1909, 1925-1957," database with images, *FamilySearch*, https://familysearch.org/ark:/61903/1:1:24RK-LKT, last updated March 16, 2018.

5. Judy Abrams and Evi Blaikie, eds., *Remember Us: A Collection of Memories from Hungarian Hidden Children of the Holocaust* (Bloomington, IN: AuthorHouse, 2009); and *Remember Us: The Hungarian Hidden Children*, directed by Rudy Vegliante (Bethlehem, PA: Green Leaf Productions, 2017).

Chapter 38

1. Andor Glattstein, interview with Heather Stone and author, August 2000.

2. "Auschwitz," Holocaust Encyclopedia, United States Holocaust Memorial Museum, accessed March 23, 2019, https://encyclopedia.ushmm.org/content/en/article/auschwitz.

3. Hedvig Turai, "Waldsee 1944 Postcard Exhibition: A 'Woodland Lake' in Auschwitz," *Judaism: A Quarterly Journal of Jewish Life and Thought* 55 no. 3–4 (Fall–Winter 2006), https://www.questia.com/magazine/1G1-171034151/waldsee-1944-postcard-exhibition-a-woodland-lake.

4. "Concentration Camp: Unknown Part of Petržalka History," *Slovak Spectator*, June 1, 2015, https://spectator.sme.sk/c/20057720/exhibition-shows-unknown-part-of-petrzalka-history.html.

5. Maroš Borský et al., eds., *Engerau: The Forgotten Story of Petržalka*, Jewish Heritage Foundation (Bratislava: Synagoga Bratislava/Forschungsstelle Nachkriegsjustiz, 2015).

6. Hisham M. Mehanna, Jamil Moledina, and Jane Travis, "Refeeding Syndrome: What It Is, and How to Prevent and Treat It," *BMJ* 336 (June 28, 2008): 1495–1498, https://doi.org/10.1136/bmj.a301.

7. Aviva Halamish, *The Exodus Affair: Holocaust Survivors and the Struggle for Palestine* (Syracuse, NY: Syracuse University Press, 1998), 68.

8. Andor Glattstein, "Voyage of Hope," circa 1955, unpublished essay.

9. Uri Goren, *On Both Sides of the Crypto*, trans. Aryeh Malkin (CreateSpace, 2010).

10. Glattstein, "Voyage of Hope."

11. Glattstein, "Voyage of Hope."

12. Yossi Melman, "Inside Intel: Survivors, Forgotten but Now Remembered," *Haaretz*, August 16, 2007, https://www.haaretz.com/1.4962824; and Martin Gilbert, *Israel: A History*, (London: Black Swan), 2008.

13. Benny Morris, *The Birth of the Palestinian Refugee Problem, 1947–1949* (Cambridge: Cambridge University Press, 1987), 115.

14. D. Thomas Lancaster, "The Burma Road," First Fruits of Zion, December 20, 2016, https://ffoz.org/discover/israel-history/the-burma-road.html.

15. Mitch Ginsburg, "Left for Dead in 1948: The Battle That Shaped Arik Sharon," *Times of Israel*, January 12, 2014, https://www.timesofisrael.com/left-for-dead-in-1948-the-battle-that-shaped-arik-sharon/.

16. Andor Glattstein, personal communication, April 29, 2010.

17. Ginsburg, "Left for Dead"; and Aaron Hecht, "The Fight for Latrun," *Jerusalem Post*, May 3, 2007, https://www.jpost.com/Local-Israel/In-Jerusalem/The-fight-for-Latrun.

18. Sharon Singer, eulogy for Andor Glattstein, June 15, 2015.

Chapter 42

1. Susan Dominus, "Is an Open Marriage a Happier Marriage?" *New York Times*, May 11, 2017, https://www.nytimes.com/2017/05/11/magazine/is-an-open-marriage-a-happier-marriage.html.

Chapter 44

1. "Magda Stone," Visual History Archive, USC Shoah Foundation, February 11, 1996, http://vhaonline.usc.edu/viewingPage?testimonyID=11604&returnIndex=0.

2. Alexander G. Stone, interview with author, October 2003.

3. George Stone, personal communication, December 29, 2018.

4. Bess Furman, "Progress in Prosthetics: A Summary under Sponsorship of the Prosthetics Research Board of the National Academy of Sciences," National Research Council, US Department of Health, Education, and Welfare, Office of Vocational Rehabilitation (Washington, DC: National Academies, 1962), http://www.oandplibrary.org/assets/pdf/ProgressInProsthetics.pdf.

5. Stone, interview, October 2003.

6. "MacArthur II Dies at 88," *Washington Post*, November 16, 1997, https://www.washingtonpost.com/archive/local/1997/11/16/macarthur-ii-dies-at-88/1e85cedc-bfe5-46c7-a83b-342ad4c82e2f/?utm_term=.e3bdb2f603c2.

Chapter 45

1. Victor Stone, personal communication, February 3, 2008.

2. George Stone, personal communication, December 29, 2018.

3. Lawrence Ferlinghetti, "The World Is a Beautiful Place," in *A Coney Island of the Mind* (New York: New Directions, 1958).

Chapter 47

1. Aliki, *The Two of Them* (New York: Harper Collins, 1987).

Chapter 48

1. Clara Gray, interview, September 10, 2001.

Chapter 50

1. Victor Stone, personal communication, October 22, 2018.

2. Stone, personal communication, October 22, 2018.

Chapter 51

1. "L'chi Lach," track 6 on Debbie Friedman, *And You Shall Be a Blessing*, Sounds Write Productions, 1997.

Chapter 56

1. Zoltan Rihmer, Xenia Gonda, Balazs Kapitany, and Peter Dome, "Suicide in Hungary—Epidemiological and Clinical Perspectives," *Annals of General Psychiatry* 12, no.21 (June 26, 2013), https://www.ncbi.nlm.nih.gov/pmc/articles/PMC3698008/; and Freakonomics, "The Suicide Paradox (Ep. 40)," June 21, 2011, http://freakonomics.com/2011/06/21/the-suicide-paradox-full-transcript/.

2. Michael J. Baum, *Piroska néni* (Bloomington, IN: A. Leonard, 1987).

3. Geo Stone, *Suicide and Attempted Suicide: Methods and Consequences* (New York: Carroll and Graf, 1999).

4. "Magda Stone," interview 11980, Visual History Archive, USC Shoah Foundation, February 11, 1996, http://vhaonline.usc.edu/viewingPage?testimonyID=11604&returnIndex=0.

Chapter 58

1. Laszlo Berkowits, *The Boy Who Lost His Birthday: A Memoir of Loss, Survival, and Triumph* (Lanham, MD: Hamilton Books, 2008).

2. Isabella Leitner, *Fragments of Isabella* in *Isabella: From Auschwitz to Freedom* (New York: Anchor Books, 1994).

Chapter 60

1. National Council of Catholic Bishops/US Conference of Catholic Bishops, *Ethical and Religious Directives for Catholic Health Care Services*, 2003.

2. National Council of Catholic Bishops/US Conference of Catholic Bishops.

Chapter 61

1. Lorne Rozovsky, "Hand Signs of the Jews," Chabad.org, accessed January 7, 2019, https://www.chabad.org/library/article_cdo/aid/407512/jewish/Hand-Signs-of -the-Jew.htm.

2. "For Good," written by Stephen Schwartz, track 18 on *Wicked*, Verve, 2003.

Chapter 62

1. Judith Graham, "For Some Caregivers, the Trauma Lingers," New Old Age (blog), *New York Times*, January 30, 2013, https://newoldage.blogs.nytimes .com/2013/01/30/for-some-caregivers-the-trauma-lingers/.

Chapter 66

1. Erin Grace, "Happy Ending," *Omaha World-Herald*, May 24, 2009.

2. Leo Adam Biga, "Kitty Williams Finally Tells Her Holocaust Survivor Tale," Leo Adam Biga's My Inside Stories (blog), May 4, 2010, https://leoadambiga .com/2010/05/04/104/.

3. "2012 Cleveland Conference," World Federation of Jewish Child Survivors of the Holocaust & Descendants, accessed December 29, 2018, https://www .holocaustchild.org/2013/02/2012/-cleveland-conference.

4. "Stories of Survival: Three Generations of Surviving Genocide," panel discussion, University of Nebraska–Lincoln, Lutheran Family Services, https://www .lfsneb.org/2018/11/08/stories-of-survival-three-generations-of-surviving-genocide -discussion-panel/.

5. Sarah Kendzior, "We're Heading into Dark Times. This Is How to Be Your Own Light in the Age of Trump," *Correspondent*, November 18, 2016, https://thecorrespondent.com/5696/were-heading-into-dark-times-this-is-how-to -be-your-own-light-in-the-age-of-trump/1611114266432-e23ea1a6.

Chapter 67

1. "EhrenfeldKatherine89821742_0_1" record, ITS Digital Archive, United States Holocaust Memorial Museum, accessed August 29, 2018.

2. Kate Quinn, *The Alice Network* (New York: William Morrow, 2017).

Chapter 68

1. "The Search for the Six Million: Uncovering Their Names, Recovering Their Identities," Yad Vashem (blog), January 26, 2014, https://www.yadvashem.org/blog /uncovering-their-names-recovering-their-identities.html.

Conclusion

1. "We Are Lights (The Chanukah Song)," composed by Stephen Schwartz, written by Steve Young, Hal Leonard Corporation, 2006, https://www.jwpepper .com/10010366.item#/.

Epilogue

1. Wikipedia, s.v. "Hogan's Heroes," last modified February 26, 2019, https://en.wikipedia.org/wiki/Hogan%27s_Heroes.

Index

Note: The author's family members and their acquaintances are indexed by their first names. Historical figures are indexed by their last names. Page numbers in italics refer to images and photographs.

New York City (*continued*)
Magdus and Miki in, 226–228
Miklós and Ella in, 132, 179–182
nyilasok. *See* Arrow Cross

obedience, 83–85, 87, 101
Obradovic, Lana, 319
Ocean Vigor (destroyer), 203
Operation Yoram, 205
Oranienburg, Germany, 125
orthotics, 58–61, 216–217, 221, 227–229, 231
othering, 44, 318–319
Ottoman Empire, 8
Ottomanyi néni, 48
outhouses, 13

Palestine. *See* Israel
Palmach, 203–204
palm reader, 69
Pál Weisz, 68
Parenting
Anna, 10–19, 47–50
Bözsi, 217
Herman Róth, 12
Kati, 213–214
Klari, 178
Judy, 224, 232, 263, 292
Magdus, 41, 68–69, 232–233, 240, 242, 292
Paskoff, Rabbi Jack, xix–xx, 106, 152
Passover. *See* Pesach
Pat Kellogg (doctor), 262–263
Paul Porter, 175–177
Paulus, Friedrich von, 139
Pesach, 29, 75, 259–261
Pesl (Pepi) Czuker, 21
Pete (Clarence) Peters, 174–175, 209–216, *210*, 241–242
Peter Gray (Klari and Imre's son), 174, *176*
Philadelphia, Pennsylvania, 205
Piroska neni (memoir), 278–279
Pista (Istvan) Ehrenfeld, *90*, 189–190, *190*, 253
Anna's treatment of, 10, 13
birth of, 6, 187
and mother's death, 53–54
and Piroska, 278

Pista (Istvan) Ehrenfeld (*continued*)
return to Pest after liberation, 150
in Sáránd after liberation, 166, 172
poverty, 26, 33–34, 48, 54–55, 140–141, 316
prosthetics. *See* orthotics
psychology/attitudes
denial, 45, 79, 83, 101, 277; and Kati's belief that father was still alive, 87–88,105, 129–130, 253
depression: Ancsi and, 200; Kati and, 213–214; Magdus and, 55, 169–170, 240, 242, 267, 296
finding meaning, 69, 224, 310
guilt, 34, 84, 258, 318–319
humor, 219, 225, 248, 330
obedience, 83–85, 87, 101
survivor's guilt, 318–319

Ra'anana, Israel, 190
Rabin, Yitzhak, 204
Rachel Leah Horowitz Glattstein, 21, 198, *198*
Rákosi, Mátyás, 138, 139
Ramya (Sri Lankan woman), 280
Rausch family, 168
Ravensbrück, Germany, 121–122
Rebus néni (Regina) Horowitz-Margareten, 198
Red Terror, 62
Református (Calvinist) church, Debrecen, 4
Regina Simsovits, 95
Reinickendorf (borough of Berlin), 122
reparations, 218
reuniting family
Kati's reunion with Miklós, 140–141
Klari's reunion with Magdus after liberation, 153–154
Klari's reunion with Pista, 150
Magdus's reunion with Klari after liberation, 153–154
Magdus's reunion with Miki after liberation, 162
R&G Orthopedics, 231
"Röeslein Rose" (German folk song), 293–294
Rohr, Dr., 226

About the Author

JUDY STONE, MD, is the daughter of Hungarian Holocaust survivors and has a longstanding interest in genealogy and oral history. This interest, as well as changes in global politics, prompted the writing of her survivor family's memoir, *Resilience: One Family's Story of Hope and Triumph over Evil.*

Stone is an infectious disease physician experienced in conducting clinical research. She is the author of *Conducting Clinical Research: A Practical Guide for Physicians, Nurses, Study Coordinators, and Investigators*, which has been adopted as a text throughout the country.

Stone spent twenty-five years in solo practice in rural Cumberland, Maryland, and now cares for patients part-time as a locum tenens (substitute) physician. She is a graduate of Washington University in St. Louis, Missouri. She completed medical school at the University of Maryland, residency at Rochester General Hospital in New York, and fellowship at West Virginia University.

Stone is a *Forbes* Pharma and Healthcare contributor and previously wrote the Molecules to Medicine column for *Scientific American*. She especially loves writing about ethical issues and tilting at windmills as she advocates for social justice. She is particularly interested in neglected tropical diseases. She hopes to teach overseas and has a growing interest in Holocaust education and teaching tolerance. She also enjoys photography, gardening, and woodworking.

You can reach Judy Stone at
Website: www.drjudystone.com
Twitter: https://twitter.com/drjudystone
Facebook: https://www.facebook.com/drjudystoneauthor